COLONIAL
CONNECTICUT

A HISTORY

A HISTORY OF THE AMERICAN COLONIES
IN THIRTEEN VOLUMES

GENERAL EDITORS:
MILTON M. KLEIN & JACOB E. COOKE

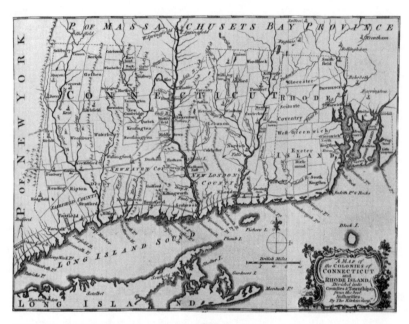

MAP OF CONNECTICUT AND RHODE ISLAND, 1758. Drawn by Thomas Kitchin, this earliest extant printed map featuring Connecticut appeared in the *London Magazine* for April 1758. Although most towns are reasonably well located, the colony is drawn too narrow in longitude by about one-sixth of a degree on both the east and west sides. It can be observed that town lines are not fully defined for a number of towns, and only three counties are named at a time when there were six. The dip in the northern boundary of the colony, centering on the Connecticut River, leaves out Suffield, Enfield, and Somers, all decreed by the Crown in 1755 to be part of Connecticut rather than Massachusetts—this despite Kitchin's inclusion in Connecticut of Woodstock, which passed to Connecticut in 1755 along with the other three towns. Obviously the mapmaker was relying upon old information. *Courtesy of the Massachusetts Historical Society.*

ROBERT J. TAYLOR

COLONIAL CONNECTICUT

A HISTORY

kto press

A U.S. DIVISION OF KRAUS-THOMSON ORGANIZATION LIMITED
MILLWOOD, NEW YORK

First printing 1979

Printed in the United States of America

Library of Congress Cataloging in Publication Data

Taylor, Robert Joseph, 1917–
  Colonial Connecticut: a history.

  (A History of the American colonies)
  Bibliography: p.
  Includes index.
  1. Connecticut—History—Colonial period, ca. 1600–
1775. I. Title. II. Series.
F97.T25   974.6′02   79-1099
ISBN 0-527-18710-0

To the memory of my parents

JOSEPH TAYLOR
1881–1939

H. JANE TAYLOR
1884–1957

Born in England, but lovers of this country.

CONTENTS

ILLUSTRATIONS

EDITORS'
INTRODUCTION

The American colonies have not lacked their Boswells. Almost from the time of their founding, the English settlements in the New World became the subjects of historical narratives by promoters, politicians, and clergymen. Some, like John Smith's *General History of Virginia*, sought to stir interest in New World colonization. Others, such as Cotton Mather's *Magnalia Christi Americana*, used New England's past as an object lesson to guide its next generation. And others still, like William Smith's *History of the Province of New-York*, aimed at enhancing the colony's reputation in England by explaining its failures and emphasizing its accomplishments. All of these early chroniclers had their shortcomings but no more so than every generation of historians which essayed the same task thereafter. For it is both the strength and the challenge of the historical guild that in each age its practitioners should readdress themselves to the same subjects of inquiry as their predecessors. If the past is prologue, it must be constantly reenacted. The human drama is unchanging, but the audience is always new: its expectations of the past are different, its mood uniquely its own.

The tercentenary of John Smith's history is almost coterminous with the bicentenary of the end of the American colonial era. It is more than appropriate that the two occasions should be observed by a fresh retelling of the story of the colonization of English America not, as in the case of the earliest histories, in self-justification, national exaltation, or moral purgation but as a plain effort to reexamine the past through the lenses of the present.

Apart from the national observance of the bicentennial of American independence, there is ample justification in the era of the 1970s for a modern history of each of the original thirteen colonies. For many of them, there exists no single-volume narrative published in the present century and, for some, none written since those undertaken by contemporaries in the eighteenth century. The standard multivolume histories of the colonial period—those of Herbert L. Osgood, Charles M. Andrews, and Lawrence H. Gipson—are too comprehensive to provide adequate treatment of individual colonies, too political and institutional in emphasis to deal adequately with social, economic, and cultural developments, and too intercolonial and Anglo-American in focus to permit intensive examination of a single colony's distinctive evolution. The most recent of these comprehensive accounts, that of Gipson, was begun as far back as 1936; since then a considerable body of new scholarship has been produced.

The present series, *A History of the American Colonies*, of which *Colonial Connecticut* is part, seeks to synthesize the new research, to treat social, economic, and cultural as well as political developments, and to delineate the broad outlines of each colony's history during the years before independence. No uniformity of organization has been imposed on the authors, although each volume attempts to give some attention to every aspect of the colony's historical development. Each author is a specialist in his own field and has shaped his material to the configuration of the colony about which he writes. While the Revolutionary Era is the terminal point of each volume, the authors have not read the history of the colony backward, as mere preludes to the inevitable movement toward independence and statehood.

Despite their local orientation, the individual volumes, taken together, will provide a collective account that should help us understand the broad foundation on which the future history of the colonies in the new nation was to rest and, at the same time, help clarify that still not completely explained melodrama of 1776 which saw, in John Adams's words, thirteen clocks somewhat amazingly strike as one. In larger perspective, *A History of the American Colonies* seeks to remind today's generation of Americans of its earliest heritage as a contribution to an understanding of its contemporary purpose. The link between past and present is as certain as it is at times indiscernible, for as Michael Kammen has so aptly observed: "The historian is the memory of civilization. A civilization without history ceases to be civilized. A civilization without history ceases to have identity. Without identity there is no purpose; without purpose civilization will wither."*

Of the New England colonies, Connecticut seemed always the most inconspicuous. Smaller by far than Massachusetts, less controversial than Rhode Island, and without New Hampshire's economic resources, this offshoot of the Bay Colony nevertheless developed in ways that made it unique among its neighbors. Charles M. Andrews consigned it to obscurity with the condescending remark that its colonial history was "almost without colorful incidents." But it was precisely Connecticut's extraordinary ability to transform itself from a Puritan to a Yankee commonwealth without dramatic internal convulsions that gives the colony its special place in our early history.

Begun as a Puritan settlement, Connecticut persisted in its visionary goal of establishing a New Zion in the wilderness much longer than its parent and closest neighbor. While Massachusetts was becoming more commercial, less homogeneous, and increasingly intertwined with the empire, Connecticut resisted all these changes successfully, partly because of its isolation and relative unimportance in the imperial scheme of things but, more, because of the conservatism of its leaders. Despite a liberal franchise and an expansive political system, Connecticut adhered to the concept of rule by the fittest. Buttressed by the principles of religious piety and social deference, the colony's "standing order" held a tight rein on local governments and churches alike, leading to the province's sobriquet as the "land of steady habits."

Earlier chroniclers tended to attribute the steadiness of habits to the influence of Puritanism, but Robert J. Taylor, in this new—and first—comprehensive history of the colony, demonstrates that the explanation is more political than religious. Under its remarkably liberal charter of 1662, Connecticut was virtually self-governing: it was not compelled to transmit its laws to England for royal assent, nor were its judicial decisions appealable to the Privy Council. Whenever internal dissension threatened to upset the standing order, the fear of crown intervention and the possible abrogation of the charter were sufficient to persuade Connecticut's inhabitants to resolve their differences within the framework of the traditional social system. The eighteenth century brought alterations

* Michael Kammen, *People of Paradox* (New York, 1972), p. 13.

in Connecticut society, and Professor Taylor delineates them fully: demographic changes leading to a high density of population, sectarian divisions and the expansion of religious liberty, social stratification, and a modest efflorescence of education, science, and literature. But none of these changes shook the foundations of the social fabric. Contentiousness which in other colonies led to bitter strife produced much less turbulence in Connecticut; its inhabitants continued to accept the leadership of a relatively small number of men, who ruled responsibly and were rarely challenged.

What, then, led the colony to sacrifice its benign relationship to the empire for the stormy path of protest, resistance, and rebellion? Professor Taylor suggests that it was less the new economic measures that were imposed after 1763—which affected the colony only mildly—than the political implications of internal taxes like the stamp duties. The latter portended encroachments on Connecticut's charter privileges. Drawn rather than propelled into revolution, the colony's prudent behavior was demonstrated by its alacrity in dispatching minutemen to the aid of embattled Massachusetts in 1775 but its hesitation in approving the Declaration of Independence until October 1776. Connecticut fought, then, in the end to protect its traditional framework of constitutionalism, which was so little modified by the Revolution that the state was able to live comfortably under its old charter until 1818. The American Revolution was no simple affair, nor was Connecticut's role in that event exactly like that of any of its sister provinces. The colonial history of Connecticut, viewed in conjunction with the histories of the other twelve colonies, thus helps clarify the meaning of a revolution whose inception, however fortuitous, produced consequences so momentous that they live with us still.

MILTON M. KLEIN
JACOB E. COOKE

PREFACE

Compared to Massachusetts, early Connecticut until recently has had little attention from historians. Too often the assumption has been that a book about the Bay Colony could be called a book about New England. More than one such work has used the region in its title only to make the barest mention of Connecticut or even to ignore it entirely, devoting its analysis solely to Massachusetts. Yet those living in the seventeenth and eighteenth centuries were well aware that despite similarities there were fundamental differences between the two colonies in government and religion, to name only two characteristics. During the early stages of the American Revolution, John Adams more than once called attention to Connecticut's governmental institutions as models that all the colonies might emulate, especially his own province. His contemporaries were quite familiar with the greater Presbyterianism of the Connecticut churches and their role in maintaining the Standing Order, that is, the leadership that gave the colony political and social stability. Church and other leaders were the more effective because of the homogeneity and relative freedom from outside interference that Connecticut enjoyed.

The past decade has seen a quickening of scholarship devoted to Connecticut as colony and state. The change has been encouraged by the activities of the Association for the Study of Connecticut History, which sponsors semiannual meetings, hears papers, and issues a publication that has grown from a few mimeographed sheets to a respectable booklet of articles and reviews. We are on the threshold of a much fuller understanding of early Connecticut, which was so overshadowed by its more populous and affluent neighbor.

The present volume attempts to synthesize some recent scholarship as well as work done earlier and, when opportunity permits in so general a survey, to pursue certain themes somewhat beyond existing studies. My debt to scholars is acknowledged in detail in the bibliography. More general thanks are owed to Edmund S. Morgan, who not only read the manuscript at an early stage but offered needed encouragement, and to Christopher Collier, who made a detailed and useful critique. I must also express my appreciation to editors Milton M. Klein and Jacob E. Cooke for their suggestions and their persistence on the long road to publication. The author is responsible for any shortcomings that may remain.

My wife, Alice Jo, did the things that scholars' wives always do and seldom receive full credit for. But beyond offering practical assistance, she was patient, understanding, and loving through it all. No man could ask for more.

ROBERT J. TAYLOR

COLONIAL
CONNECTICUT

A HISTORY

1

THE BEGINNINGS

Connecticut is one of the several daughters of Massachusetts, none of them in their infancy gracefully acknowledged by their mother. Like most of the Bay Colony's offspring, Connecticut was Puritan in character, but its relative insulation from the stimulus of overseas commerce and the influx of foreign peoples allowed it to evolve a society that was politically and religiously unique and that changed only slowly under the pressure of events.

As is well known, the nucleus of the Connecticut colony was the towns of Wethersfield, Windsor, and Hartford, founded on the Connecticut River between 1634 and 1635. The men and women who built the first houses and faced the rigors of the severe winter of 1635–36 had come to the river from Watertown, Dorchester, and Newtown (Cambridge) in Massachusetts Bay; and before that, they had emigrated from southeastern and southwestern England, from the counties of Essex, Devon, Dorset, and Somerset. Many quailed before the icy blasts of their first winter in the Connecticut wilds and made their way down river to a relief boat sent from the Bay to resupply them with food. When they freed the boat from the ice that had gripped it, they escaped back to the Bay; but they returned in a few months, and, joined by many others, they remained.

The families that came to the Connecticut country had first heard about its advantages from the explorations in 1632 of Edward Winslow of Plymouth Colony; he and William Bradford, also from that colony, tried unsuccessfully to persuade Massachusetts Bay to join with Plymouth in exploiting the opportunities for Indian trade in the region. But John Oldham, an Indian trader then living in Watertown, and three others went overland to the river to see for themselves. They brought back accounts of plenteous beaver, wild hemp, and graphite. Meanwhile, the Dutch had built a small fort on the Hartford River to promote trade with the Indians. It was Oldham and his associates who built the first houses at Pyquag (Wethersfield) in the fall of 1634, about one year after Plymouth had erected a trading post just south of the Farmington River on the west side of the Connecticut. That they built houses rather than just a trading post suggests that they recognized the agricultural possibilities the valley afforded.

Families were attracted to the Connecticut River country because of the rich meadows strung out along its banks. Open land along navigable streams was at a premium in the heavily forested New World. The earliest settlers in the English colonies had been happy to buy from the Indians lands that the natives had already cleared, for the task of taking down trees and preparing the soil for planting was slow and hard, given the simple agricultural tools the colonists possessed. The early towns in Massachusetts Bay had been laid out close together so that the steady influx of new settlers each year, fleeing from religious persecution in England, had quickly used up readily available land. Shortage of land was particularly acute for those who raised cattle as well as crops, as did the people of Newtown.

A number of times Newtown people complained to the General Court, or legislature, about the overcrowding and asked for additional tracts. When land at Ipswich and at Merrimack offered by the General Court proved unsatisfactory, they talked of going to the Connecticut River. Massachusetts Bay leaders, however, did not like to see them move so far away. From the beginning the Puritans had envisioned a city where those likely to be saved would live in close contact, an instructive example to the world of the right way in religion and in day-to-day living on this earth, fraught with peril for the immortal soul. The establishment of a number of towns rather than one had not been part of the plan, but at least they were in close proximity. A move to the river, however, threatened the unity of the holy experiment and the defenses of the colony, to say nothing of the hazards the migrants would face from the Dutch and the Indians. For these reasons in September 1634 the General Court, in a vote that pitted the deputies, or town representatives, against the magistrates, denied permission to Newtown people to migrate.

Governor John Winthrop felt that the departure of Newtown people with their pastor, Thomas Hooker, would be a serious loss indeed, for many would want to follow him, and many would never come to Massachusetts Bay at all when they learned Hooker had departed. Hooker, who had been in exile in Holland for several years after being driven from his pulpit in Chelmsford, Essex, by the activities of Archbishop Laud, was a minister of considerable renown, associated for a time in exile with the leading divines Hugh Peter and William Ames. He arrived in the Bay at the same time as the Reverend John Cotton, but while Cotton stayed in Boston and associated with Winthrop and other magistrates, Hooker went to Newtown. There may have been some rivalry between the two men; certainly they had some doctrinal differences, although these were confined to private correspondence in 1635 and 1636 and did not become public enough to align their congregations against each other.

Cotton, in contrast to most of the Bay ministers, insisted upon man's complete passivity in receiving grace and upon the total absence of any steps leading to conversion. Hooker mentioned certain means to this end, although God was the one who brought means and end together and only for the elect, that is, for the few destined by God for salvation. Such subtleties of reasoning perhaps caused some misunderstanding; Hooker may have thought that Cotton was imputing to him an emphasis on preparation for grace that he did not hold and that suggested a doctrine of works, a belief that man through his own merit might help to bring about his salvation—a heretical idea in the eyes of all Puritans.

Hooker, in addition, was more lenient than some in his attitude toward admission to church membership. By 1636, just a few months before Hooker left the Bay for Connecticut, a number of Massachusetts ministers had concluded that saving faith indicated by a narrative of one's conversion was necessary for membership in a church, a test that would limit members to the elect; but Hooker, who was behind no one in extolling saving faith, believed that a person who lived an exemplary life and could "give a reason of his hope towards God" should be admitted.

Because the Bay had voted to limit freemanship—meaning the right to vote and hold office—to church members, strict tests for membership would have political as well as religious significance. Although Hooker left little in his writings to suggest his political beliefs, hints in notes for several sermons and a passage in a letter to John Winthrop justify the conclusion that Hooker disapproved of the political system in Massachusetts Bay, particularly as conceived by Winthrop. Hooker would apparently have given the people greater power in setting limitations on the authority of their magistrates than the Bay leaders contemplated. For Winthrop, the magistrates, called to their office by God through the votes of the people, ought truly to exercise their calling by using wide discretion in decision making; that is partly why Winthrop opposed codification of Massachusetts laws. He wanted judges, as well as legislators, left free to employ their talents. Hooker would have given the people a larger voice in their government than Winthrop intended and a greater check upon their rulers. Hooker spoke out forthrightly: "In matters of greater consequence, which concern the common good, a general counsel, chosen by all, to transact business which concern all, I conceive, under favour, most suitable to rule and most safe for relief of the whole." Yet since Hooker expressed these sentiments in 1638, some two years after his migration to Connecticut, and in connection with voting procedures in a proposed confederation of colonies, we can only guess whether they were important in Hooker's thinking in 1635 and 1636.

Apparently Hooker was not alone in his dissatisfaction, although in the case of others, like John Haynes and Roger Ludlow, we are left with hardly more than a surmise. Haynes, who was governor of Massachusetts Bay in 1635–36 and a member of Hooker's church, took Winthrop to task for too great leniency in dispensing justice. Ludlow, who as a magistrate had opposed Newtown's bid in 1634 to migrate to the Connecticut country, himself led a migration from Dorchester in 1635, having failed meanwhile to be reelected to the magistracy. Hooker, Haynes, and Ludlow may rightly be regarded as the founding fathers of the Connecticut colony, although Haynes did not migrate until a year after the Hooker-led exodus. The dissatisfactions of these leaders were, however, only contributing causes for emigration from the Bay. In all probability the feelings of the leaders were not widely known. Overcrowding and the beckoning opportunities of the river valley swayed ordinary people, who found ready leaders in strong men looking to a new country where they could order affairs after a different fashion than was possible in Massachusetts Bay.

By 1635, despite the General Court's recently expressed opposition to large-scale migration, people in Watertown, Dorchester, and Roxbury, as well as in Newtown, spoke of their desire to leave. In the spring of 1635, the General Court changed its mind and specifically allowed the inhabitants of Watertown, Roxbury, and Dorchester to depart "provided they continue still under this government." The records make no mention of Newtown, but presumably the same permission was given to its inhabitants, for a year later that town is mentioned with the others as one from which people were to migrate.

Thus in the summer of 1635 the exodus began. Roger Ludlow led a group from Dorchester, perhaps joined by some from Newtown and Watertown, which established a settlement just north of the Farmington River on the west side of the Connecticut—the nucleus of the town of Windsor. In so settling, the Dorchester people ignored the rights of Plymouth settlers who had established themselves just south of the Farmington River in 1633 and had purchased from the Indians the lands they settled on as well as the lands claimed by Dorchester. Not until 1637 did Plymouth get proper recompense for this rather high-handed appropriation of vacant land. Ultimately the Plymouth settlement became part of the town of Windsor. In the fall of 1635, a group of about fifty migrated overland from Newtown to start a settlement just north of the Dutch fort on the opposite side of the Hartford River, the nucleus of the town of Hartford. Many of these people in the newly established river towns struggled back to the Bay, driven by the severity of the winter of 1635–36, but their departure was only temporary. The Connecticut Valley was where they wanted to be.

Meanwhile, a challenge to the newcomers arose from an unsuspected quarter. John Winthrop, Jr., had arrived in Boston in October 1635, armed with a commission as governor to lay out lands and build houses at the mouth of the Connecticut River on behalf of a group of peers and gentlemen who had presumably obtained a patent to land running from the Narragansett River west and southwest along the seashore for 40 leagues or 120 miles and thence to the South Sea. (Only a copy of this patent exists in the Connecticut Archives, and real doubt has been cast on whether an original ever existed.) The patent was granted to Lord Saye and Sele, Lord Brook, and others named by the Earl of Warwick, a member of the Council for New England, which had secured title to New England from the king in 1620. Thus those who had already built houses at sites later to become Wethersfield, Hartford, and Windsor were called upon to defend their right to settle where they had. John Winthrop, Jr., joined by agents Hugh Peter and Henry Vane, Jr., issued the challenge, probably in January 1636. Here was an embarrassing impasse, for the men that Winthrop represented were Puritan gentlemen of the first rank who could not be ignored. The questions asked were pointed. Did the settlers from Massachusetts Bay acknowledge the rights of the gentlemen, and were they willing to submit to the governance of John Winthrop, Jr., since they were certainly out of the jurisdiction of the Bay Colony? The records contain no reply, but the General Court of Massachusetts Bay fashioned a compromise solution.

On March 3, 1636, the General Court on its own behalf and on behalf of John Winthrop, Jr., appointed a commission of eight authorized to hear and determine such disputes as might arise among the settlers and to issue orders respecting the affairs of the new plantations, even to the point of declaring defensive war. Mention was made of the commissioners' power to call the inhabitants of the several towns together in a General Court for purposes of government; yet their authorization to act was limited to one year, and the whole arrangement would be concluded sooner if the settlers, Winthrop and his co-agents, and Massachusetts Bay agreed upon a permanent form of government. The commissioners named were Roger Ludlow, who had already led Dorchester people to Windsor, and William Phelps, who also intended to settle at Windsor; William Pynchon, who had led a few settlers from Roxbury and founded a trading post at Agawam (Springfield), and Henry Smith, who joined Pynchon; John Steele and William Westwood, who were committed for Hartford; and William Swaine and Andrew Ward, who went to Wethersfield. John Winthrop, Jr., despite his designation by the Warwick patentees as governor, was not even listed as a commissioner, let alone as governor. Apparently his intention to construct a fort and buildings at the mouth of the Connecticut River was looked upon as an enterprise separate from the up-river settlements.

Several considerations concerning this commission need mention. Clearly it was a temporary expedient designed to serve until the rights of Winthrop's employers could be better established; nor was Massachusetts Bay conceding to others jurisdiction over these Connecticut towns. All the commission said about jurisdiction concerned misdemeanors that would require "speedy redresse"; "in regard of the distance of place, this state and government cannot take notice of the same as to apply timely remedy, or to dispence equall justice to them and their affairs." The categorical statement of young Winthrop and the agents that the Connecticut settlements were out of the Bay's jurisdiction was not formally recognized; indeed, in 1641 the General Court of Massachusetts Bay declared that the commission "was not granted upon any intent either to dismise the persons from us, or to determine any thing about the limits being as then unknowne."

Finally, one should not read too much into the provision that allowed the inhabitants to be called together for a General Court, or legislature. Professor Charles M. Andrews, for example, saw significance in the use of the word *inhabitants* because at this time in Massachusetts freemanship was accorded only to church members. To Andrews this word suggested the seemingly more generous definition of freemanship Connecticut would adopt later under the Fundamental Orders.* Still, at the time the commission was drafted, ministers in Massachusetts had only just begun to limit church membership to those who could demonstrate saving grace. Heretofore, the distinction between inhabitants and church members had probably not been very sharp, membership going to all those who tried to live decent Christian lives. It seems unlikely that the new stricter test for membership was so well established by March 3, 1636, that the language of the commission, supposedly drafted by Roger Ludlow, deliberately mentioned inhabitants as a broader group than church members. People settling in new Connecticut communities were not apt to welcome all to a General Court, decent Christians and loose-livers alike. In opposition to this view, it might be argued that also on March 3 the General Court reaffirmed its restriction of freemanship to members of a church, adding that the church must be an approved one; but Ludlow and his associates almost certainly did not know in advance of this tightening of the Massachusetts system. The word *inhabitants* at this stage simply cannot bear all the weight that some would put upon it.

Soon after the commission was sanctioned, new streams of migration flowed to Connecticut. Before March was out, the Reverend John Warham led his congregation from Dorchester to Windsor, among them Roger Ludlow and some of those who had fled back to the Bay the preceding December. To Springfield went William Pynchon and others from Roxbury. Additional settlers went from Watertown to Wethersfield, both by land and sea, and a few went from Newtown to Hartford to settle among those already there—the advance contingent of the much larger group that was to follow. On the last day of May Thomas Hooker set out with his flock from Newtown.

---

* Charles M. Andrews, *The Colonial Period of American History,* 4 vols. (New Haven: Yale University Press, 1934–38), vol. 2, pp. 78–79.

Warham believed that members of the church could include the godly and the "openly ungodly," leading Professor Edmund Morgan to suggest that Warham left Massachusetts to be nearer to Hooker, who he knew was going to migrate and whose views on church membership were closer to his own.* Warham, soon after his arrival at the Bay from England, had had discussions with a Plymouth deacon who made it plain that Warham's standards for admission were far too lax, and it is possible the newcomer sensed that a tightening of the qualifications for church membership was under way.

Meanwhile workmen were beginning to build a fort and other buildings at the mouth of the Connecticut, carrying out the instructions that John Winthrop, Jr., had received from his employers. By the summer of 1636, a new colony was in the making. The meadows offered an inviting prospect, the Dutch had been forestalled, and church and lay leaders would find ample opportunity to exercise their talents.

*   *   *

Apart from the open meadows along the river, what did the country offer to the migrants who had come to it through one hundred miles of forests or by a sea voyage that could be hazardous in rounding Cape Cod and navigating past the shoals that marked the entrance to the Connecticut River? A waterway teeming with fish, particularly salmon, and navigable for fifty miles from its mouth; better than adequate soil, at least for most of the towns established before 1650; heavy hardwood forests abundant with large and small game; and sufficient isolation to allow self-development without interference from either Massachusetts Bay or England. Legally, of course, the settlers had no right to their lands, but, then, the charter of the Bay Colony had recently been voided in the English courts without serious effect upon that colony. Connecticut was even more remote from English control.

Trade with the Indians, as has been mentioned, was the attraction for some, and the valley Indians were ready to welcome it; in fact, these Indians had sought to encourage the opening of trade, for they were looking for allies to support them against two powerful tribes that

---

* Edmund S. Morgan, *Visible Saints: The History of a Puritan Idea* (New York: New York University Press, 1963), pp. 107–8.

threatened and harassed them: the Mohawks and the Pequots. The Pequots, enemies of the Mohawks, had their chief fort on the Pequot (later Mohegan, then Thames) River and extended their dominion along the shore westward as far as Guilford. The Mohawks were part of the Iroquois Confederacy and held tributary the Indian tribes in the western part of Connecticut. The Indians who suffered at the hands of these two powerful rivals were divided into many tribes. Benjamin Trumbull, historian of Connecticut, claimed that there were ten distinct tribes in the area of Windsor alone, but historians refer collectively to the valley tribes as river Indians, perhaps the best known tribe being the Podunks in the vicinity of Hartford. Along the shore of the Sound were the Western Niantics, tributaries to the Pequots, and the Eastern Niantics, usually under the sway of the Narragansetts of Rhode Island. The Mohegans, who figure so largely in Connecticut history, were a splinter group of the Pequots, who took the old tribal name that the Pequots had had before they migrated from New York to Connecticut.

Claiming that Connecticut Indians had been relatively less affected by disease and war than other New England tribes, Trumbull asserted that they were more numerous in proportion to area than were Indians anywhere else in New England. Yet except for the bloody Pequot War and events associated with it, which came soon after the river towns were established, the Connecticut colony enjoyed generally peaceful relations with the Indians within its borders. Lands for the river towns were purchased from the tribal chieftains, who presumably expressed satisfaction with the prices paid, although individual Indians did not have the white man's conception of land ownership. Land not under cultivation could still be hunted over, they believed, regardless of the passage of title. On the other hand, whites frequently found excuses to encroach on lands set aside for the exclusive use of Indians. In Connecticut such violations led to quarreling and appeals to the authorities rather than to violent skirmishes, however.

For two of the river towns—Windsor and Hartford—the churches, both pastors and members, migrated, leaving new churches to be organized in the Massachusetts towns they had left. But for Wethersfield, only a handful of communicants came from Watertown. Thus an important part of the business of the commissioners authorized by the Massachusetts General Court and young Winthrop, five of whom met in April 1636, was to confirm the act of six members from the Watertown church who covenanted to form a new church at Wethersfield. Actually the six agreed to renew the covenant under the approval of members of the other churches, presumably because it took seven to found a church. The action of the commissioners tells us something about the kind of communities these Puritans were establishing in the Connecticut wilderness. First of all, the six men from Watertown had been officially permitted to leave their church; one did not simply leave a Puritan church and go elsewhere. The founding of a new church required certain procedures, worked out over a period of time, and the approval of existing churches had to be sought.

The priority given to establishment of a church in a new community must be particularly noted. Puritans went to the frontier in groups so that they could carry civilization with them. The lone Puritan was not encouraged, indeed, not allowed, to strike off on his own, for he would be out of reach of a church and out of sight of the watchful eyes of neighbors. In fact, the temporary government of Connecticut forbade any young man to keep house by himself without first securing permission from his town; and no young male could even be taken in by the head of a family without town consent—all to ensure family discipline reinforced by the weight of neighbors' approval. Covenanting to form a church was virtually the first order of business in new areas. Whether saved or not, settlers on the frontier must hear the Word, preached as soon as possible by a pastor called to serve them, and regulate their lives according to the laws laid down in the Old Testament lest God destroy a community sunk in wickedness.

The other business of the commissioners in this meeting on April 26, 1636, was to provide for the control of stray swine, to name a constable for each one of the three towns, and to forbid sale of arms to the Indians. Despite the general friendliness of the river Indians, the settlers feared seeing them as well armed as themselves. When the commissioners met in June, they ordered that each soldier in the three plantations keep in readiness two pounds of powder and twenty lead bullets, to be exhibited to the constable upon demand. This measure was probably aimed at the Dutch as much as the Indians, for the Dutch claimed prior rights in the Connecticut Valley and resented the intrusion of the English. Soon the men of each plantation were required to train every month, oftener if they were unskilled in the use of arms.

During the year that it lasted, the commission saw to various other matters: the probate of John Oldham's estate, which occupied much of their attention; the fixing of the bounds of Windsor, Wethersfield, and Hartford, which were given their names by the commissioners; the regulation of indentured servitude in two instances; and the proper supervision of single young males in the communities. Five of the commissioners met with Thomas Welles of Hartford in March 1637 in what was called a court and issued directions to an employer of indentured servants, requiring him to fulfill his promise to teach them the trade of carpentry. This court also set the pay for jurymen. A General Court consisting of five original commissioners and Welles plus nine men separately listed as "committees," presumably deputies from the three towns, met in May 1637 for the purpose of declaring offensive war against the Pequot Indians and imposing a levy of troops and supplies on each of the three towns. For the rest of 1637, the General Court met three more times, twice in June and once in November, all its business concerning the Pequot campaign and the gains that were secured from the war. Connecticut was determined to claim the lands "that God by Conquest hath given to us."

The causes of the Pequot War are controversial, but it had its roots in the Indians' killing of English traders in retaliation for their brutal murder of a sachem, or chief. Severe reprisals by whites followed. Then the slaughter and mutilation of John Oldham in his boat off Block Island in 1636 brought a retaliatory raid on the island by John Endicott from Massachusetts Bay. Endicott next proceeded to Pequot country to demand surrender of the murderers of Oldham and other Englishmen killed earlier. Met with evasion and delay, Endicott's forces looted at will and inflicted casualties on the inferiorly armed Pequots. Most fair observers would concede that the English had ignored the Indian version of events and, even given the settlers' version, had far exceeded the bounds of just punishment. The consequence was Pequot attacks in September 1636 and February 1637 upon the Saybrook settlement at the mouth of the Connecticut River. When reinforcement of the fort made Saybrook less vulnerable, the Pequots chose to go up river, where in April they attacked a work party in a meadow at Wethersfield, killing nine and seizing two young women. Meanwhile Massachusetts diplomacy, greatly aided by Roger Williams of Rhode Island, had defeated an effort of the Pequots to bring to their side the Narragansetts, heretofore an enemy of the Pequots but lately at peace with them. The message of the Pequots to the Narragansetts was the more urgent in that the Pequots were unable to effect reconciliation with the Mohegans, who had split off from them. Further, the Pequots, hated masters of the river tribes, feared the latter might join in to help the English. The Narragansetts, however, chose not to believe the Pequot assertion that the English intended to eliminate the Indians and take all their lands; instead, the Narragansetts entered into an understanding with Massachusetts Bay to join the war against the Pequots.

Although Massachusetts had initiated the punitive raid of 1636, Connecticut suffered the reprisal and launched the campaign that broke the morale of the Pequots. After the slaying of Connecticut men and women and under pressure from river tribes, which urged a strike at the ancient enemy, Connecticut named John Mason to head an expedition of ninety men, drawn from the three river towns, against the Pequot stronghold. His force was joined by a contingent of sixty from the Mohegans led by Uncas. They proceeded down river to Saybrook, where the Mohegans proved their loyalty by capturing some Pequots in the vicinity. At Saybrook a small company of Massachusetts men led by John Underhill took the place of Connecticut men not fit for duty. From Saybrook the troops went to Narragansett country by water to engage some scouts to aid them in a flanking assault on the Pequot fort, which they expected to attack from an unexpected direction, the east.

On May 26, having camped the night before only a mile or so from the stockaded Pequot village on Mystic River, the English force with its Indian allies launched a surprise attack at dawn. They charged into the village, set it on fire, and then drew a tight ring around it so that the Pequots could be killed as they tried to flee the flames. The Indian allies formed a second ring to catch any who slipped through the first. Many Pequots never even got out of the village; they perished in the flames. Although the English and their allies suffered relatively few casualties, the Pequots, many of them women and children, died by the hundreds. Puritans gave thanks to God for so glorious an outcome. Yet it should be noted that this was not a war of one race against another. All the surrounding Indian tribes had chosen to support the English against the Pequots to punish them for their past arrogance and cruelties. So devastating was the victory that Mason was able to march his forces right through the rest of the Pequot country back to Saybrook.

Mop-up operations became the responsibility of Israel Stoughton of

Massachusetts, who rounded up Pequots still in the vicinity of their second stronghold on the Pequot River. Many, however, had fled westward along the shore. Pursued on land by Mohegans and Narragansetts, as well as by some English forces, and under watch by the main colonial force by sea, the Pequots were finally trapped in July 1637 in a great swamp at the site of modern Southport. Those incapable of combat were allowed to surrender; some warriors successfully fled to freedom, but most were slaughtered as they sat on the ground awaiting their fate. After this, stray Pequots became fair game for Indians who sought to prove their loyalty to the English and their mighty weapons. Even those who managed to escape to New York to what they thought would be the protection of the Mohawks suffered death, the scalp of their chief Sassacus being sent back to Hartford. Captured Pequots who remained alive were parceled out among the Indian allies—to Mohegans, Niantics, and Narragansetts. The Pequots ceased as a distinctive tribe.

This war, fought with chilling efficiency, gave Connecticut and New England years of security from serious Indian threats, but the cost for the new settlements on the river was heavy. The requisitioning of supplies for the troops and the loss of manpower for agriculture brought food shortages and a burdensome debt; but lands gained from the victory seemed some compensation. Even before the swamp fight a Connecticut General Court made provision for sending an occupying force into the Pequot country to maintain Connecticut rights; the river plantations early recognized that there might be a quarrel with Massachusetts Bay over claims to newly won territory. The court sent John Haynes and Roger Ludlow at the end of June "to parley with the Bay about our setting down in the Pequot Country." Obviously these towns already saw themselves as a separate entity, whatever Massachusetts had intended in providing them with temporary government.

At the General Court convened in November 1637 only four of the original commissioners were listed, along with eight other names, but none was labeled a committeeman. In March 1638, only one of the original commissioners was designated as a committeeman; thus one may assume that the people of the river towns were choosing whom they wished to represent them. Some of the original commissioners apparently functioned as magistrates on the Massachusetts model, sitting as a particular court, and other names were added to their company as people saw fit. A new election was ordered for a General Court in the spring of

1638. A brief reference in a letter by Hooker intimates that the towns elected committeemen, who in turn chose commissioners or magistrates.

These general courts took on more and more governmental functions, most of them legacies of the recent war. To manage the war debt, the General Court appointed a treasurer and tax collectors and levied a tax of £620 among the towns of Hartford, Windsor, Wethersfield, and Agawam, payable in money, wampum, or beaver skins. For further revenue, the court exacted tribute from several Indian tribes in the form of so much wampum per man and placed a tax of one shilling on each skin in the beaver trade. To control trade better with the Indians, the court restricted it to seven men, two in each of the three river towns and one in Agawam. All but one of the seven were public officials, a first instance of the government's largess to those with influence.

To secure the defense of the settlements, the court regularized its militia system by requiring all men over sixteen, except commissioners and church officers, to train ten days each year under the general direction of Captain John Mason and to keep powder and shot ready in their homes. Each town was to maintain a magazine of powder and lead in stated amounts and furnish itself with a designated number of "costlets" (corselets) on pain of fine for failure to comply. Perhaps also in the interest of defense as well as justice, the court laid down regulations covering relations with the Indians. No commissioner or other person was to take it upon himself to restrain or punish Indians for wrongdoing unless he was assaulted or caught Indians in the act of destroying property. Wrongdoers were to be brought before a magistrate for a hearing and punished only for cause. Any tribe of Indians that took up residence near an English settlement was to give an account of itself, naming its sachem, or chief, who was to be liable for trespasses and damage to livestock.

But the prime concern of the General Court was to overcome the great shortage of food resulting from the war. It contracted with William Pynchon for the delivery of corn at fixed prices and named others to go as far as the Narragansett country to seek it. Individuals were forbidden to make their own bargains with Indians for fear prices would be driven up. Pynchon, who against his wishes had been given the beaver trade monopoly for Agawam, although it was the tax rather than the monopoly he probably disliked, pleaded that he could not supply the corn at the prices fixed. When the river towns sent the redoubtable Captain Mason up river to deal directly with the Indians for corn, it was alleged that Pynchon did all he could to thwart the mission. Ultimately this elected commissioner was put on trial at Hartford and charged with bad faith. After hearing his defense, which sounded plausible enough, the court sought the advice of the Reverend Thomas Hooker, who imputed to Pynchon the worst of motives. The result for Pynchon was a fine of forty bushels of corn, treatment that helped him to decide to have nothing more to do with the Connecticut colony.

This was not the first source of antagonism between Pynchon and the river towns. During the war, the General Court had impressed his shallop, and the tax levied afterwards probably rankled, for he delayed paying it and was ordered to Hartford to explain his delinquency. Although Pynchon chose to cast his lot with Massachusetts, jurisdiction over his town was not so easily settled. The issue of who had the rightful claim to Agawam or Springfield became a bitterly contested question between the Bay Colony and Connecticut. At stake were taxes and the right to regulate the economy of that area.

Although Pynchon was one of the original commissioners named by the Massachusetts General Court for Connecticut's temporary government, Agawam had not been regularly represented in Connecticut. Pynchon met with the commissioners during the year only once so far as the records disclose, and his name does not appear again until March 1638, as one of the elected commissioners. At the outbreak of the Pequot War no levy of troops was made upon Agawam; it was explained that Pynchon and his settlers would be responsible for their own defense. Yet, as already noted, Agawam was taxed with the river towns for its share of the war debt. Probably from Pynchon's point of view Connecticut was seeking to make a tenuous connection a closer one with regard to taxes and the regulation of trade—at Agawam's expense. Moreover, Agawam was included in the defensive measures decreed by Connecticut in 1638, being expected to maintain a magazine and provide seven corselets or suffer fines.

The dispute over which jurisdiction could claim Agawam came to have a larger significance, for it was partly to blame for the delay of the New England colonies in forming a confederation. As early as the summer of 1637, when Hooker, Samuel Stone, Pynchon, Ludlow, and others were at the Bay for a conference, a proposal was made for such a confederation, with an invitation being extended to Plymouth to join in; but no agreement was reached. Either then or at some later date the Massachusetts magistrates proffered a set of articles for Connecticut's consideration, it being Connecticut's understanding, according to Hooker, that each side would consider them and perhaps suggest changes. In 1638, Connecticut sent John Haynes, Pynchon, and John Steele to negotiate with the Bay on the changes it desired. The stumbling block was Massachusetts's insistence that a majority vote of the representatives should have binding force on the confederating colonies; Connecticut held out for reaching a consensus after repeated consultations with the several governments.

In the discussion that followed, according to Winthrop, one of the Connecticut commissioners, identified by Hooker as John Steele, said that "they would not meddle with any thing that was within our [that is, Massachusetts's] limits." The Bay General Court seized this opportunity to claim Agawam, and Winthrop states that Connecticut's commissioners accepted the decision. There followed an exchange of ill-tempered letters between Winthrop, protesting Connecticut's continued exercise of jurisdiction over Agawam, and Ludlow, who broke off negotiations. Winthrop then wrote upbraiding letters to Haynes and Hooker and was answered in kind. Hooker called Pynchon a covenant-breaker; there is little doubt that Pynchon had willingly acquiesced in the Massachusetts ploy despite the official office he held in Connecticut. Winthrop dismissed the Connecticut leaders as deficient in learning and judgment in affairs of state, too reliant on ministers who, however godly, were out of their element in this business—a jibe at Hooker. After that, Agawam went its own way for a time, too distant from Boston for representation there, and too close to the river towns for William Pynchon's desires. The United Colonies of New England did not come into being until 1643.

What, in sum, had the river towns accomplished during the short period of their existence? They replaced the temporary commission with a General Court composed of committees chosen by the towns and of magistrates or commissioners chosen by the committees. They fought a successful Indian War and laid claim to considerable new territory as a result. They established a system of taxation and defense, and their magistrates saw to the correction of wrongdoers. They regulated trade in the general interest and began to formulate an Indian policy. Clearly, whatever the intentions of Massachusetts Bay, the river towns had become a separate colony, a fact which the Bay Colony implicitly recognized by entertaining discussions on a confederation. But Connecticut had no written frame of government, no political covenant to match the covenants on which their churches were founded. Perhaps this deficiency explains Hooker's reference to the Bay as a state and to Connecticut as "magistrates and people." Some have seen here more evidence of Hooker's "democratic" leanings as compared with the aristocratic preferences of John Winthrop. But Hooker was as much a Puritan as Winthrop. Although the people elected their rulers and even set limits on their powers, they acted "according to the blessed will and law of God." To become a state they needed a written instrument, such as Massachusetts had in its charter. That instrument was drafted in the closing months of 1638 and adopted in January 1639.

2

THE EVOLUTION OF GOVERNMENT

With the adoption of a frame of government the initial phase in the political evolution of Connecticut came to an end. No records remain to tell us precisely how the Fundamental Orders came into being, who drafted or ratified the document, or why it took the exact form that it did. Informed speculation holds that it was drafted by a committee named by a General Court and put into its final shape by Roger Ludlow, the only man in Connecticut at the time with significant legal training, and that it was accepted by the General Court. The document itself offers few surprises.

In the preamble, the inhabitants of the three towns, acknowledging God's will that orderly government be established among men, declared that they were joining together "to mayntayne and presearve the liberty and purity of the gospell of our Lord Jesus" and the discipline of His churches, and to be guided and governed by the laws, which are then set forth in eleven numbered statements. As Congregationalists, these people along the Connecticut River were adapting for civil purposes the familiar covenant used to bring their churches into being. As long ago as 1620, the Plymouth people had covenanted in the Mayflower Compact to establish civil government. The Fundamental Orders represented some advance in the idea, for here the people of three plantations, not just one, covenanted together, and the orders spelled out the basic arrangements under which the Connecticut settlers were to live.

Much ink has been wasted in debating whether the orders can properly be considered a constitution. The question is, however, anachronistic, since American ideas on the nature of constitutions did not evolve until some generations later. Certainly the Connecticut General Court never thought that interpretation of the orders or amendments to them required special machinery or anything more than the decision of the court itself, or, in some instances, of the freemen. The specific provisions were modeled in part, as one would expect, on the commercial charter under which Massachusetts Bay was governed. The very terms *governor, general court, freemen*, for example, had been employed by companies chartered by the king.

Thus the Fundamental Orders decreed the meeting of two general courts each year, the spring meeting to be a Court of Election in which a governor and six magistrates were to be chosen by the admitted freemen. In the commercial charter, similarly, reference was made to a governor and assistants (in Massachusetts Bay the magistrates were still called assistants). The freemen of the company would be called the stockholders today. Obviously in Connecticut, where a government was being created, freemen had to be thought of in other terms—as residents within the jurisdiction, those who had taken an oath of fidelity, those who had then been admitted to freemanship by the General Court.

The orders went on to describe the mode of nomination and election of officers, the qualifications for the governor, the method of convening meetings of the General Court, the mode of election for deputies to the court, their qualifications, and their collective powers when assembled. That the orders went beyond their origin in a commercial charter is apparent from several provisions: magistrates were to administer justice according to established law "and for want thereof according to the rule of the word of God"; no governor was to be elected more than once in any two years, and he had to have served as a magistrate prior to his election and to have been a member of an approved congregation; a representational system of deputies coming from each town and newly elected for each of the two regular sessions of the General Court was to replace the primary assembly of freemen-stockholders except for the election meeting each spring. (Massachusetts Bay had gone over to representation in 1634.) And, of course, the powers of the General Court went beyond those of a chartered company.

The Fundamental Orders served as the basis for government until Connecticut received its royal charter in 1662. The orders made no mention of the king; in every way, Connecticut was a self-governing colony, yet one that expected English aid in confrontations with external enemies like the Dutch. The locus of power was the General Court, now defined as the governor, magistrates, and deputies chosen by the several towns. In the court the governor acted as presiding officer, having no vote except in case of a tie. He had no veto power; and although he could, with the concurrence of the major part of the magistrates, call the court into special session if circumstances warranted, he could not adjourn or dissolve it without the consent of a majority. The orders made no mention of a deputy governor, but the records of the first court after the adoption of the orders listed Roger Ludlow as deputy, and deputy governors were regularly chosen by the freemen thereafter.

Although the magistrates sat with the deputies, the General Court did not long remain a truly unicameral legislature. Early in 1645 the court ruled that "no act shall passe or stand for a law, which is not confirmed both by the mayor parte of the said Magistrats, and by the mayor parte of the deputyes there present in Court, both Magistrats and deputyes being allowed either of them, a negative voate." Massachusetts had adopted this principle in 1635. Besides ample legislative powers, the court exercised judicial authority. It acted as a court of appeal and even as a court of first instance, although the orders placed the administration of justice into the hands of the magistrates, who with the governor, or his deputy, came to constitute a Particular Court. Except for the governor, none of these officials was required by law to be a church member, but a study of five towns shows "a rather close correspondence between church membership and office-holding throughout the first forty years of the Connecticut colony."* All such officials, of course, had to be freemen.

The Fundamental Orders distinguished two kinds of voters: freemen and "admitted inhabitants." The latter could vote for town officials and deputies to the General Court, the orders stipulating that the voting for deputies be by ballot; but only freemen could vote for magistrates and other officials, including the governor. In 1643, the General Court interpreted the term *admitted* to mean accepted by "a generall voate of the Mayor parte of the Towne that receaveth them." Approval of one's neighbors or, later, local officials remained a fixed requirement throughout the colonial period. Apparently those born in the town as sons of inhabitants and living in it won acceptance without formal scrutiny. In 1657, the court defined admitted inhabitants as "householders that are

---

* David H. Fowler, "Connecticut's Freeman: The First Forty Years," *William and Mary Quarterly* 15 (July 1958): 333.

one & twenty yeares of age, or have bore office or have £30 estate." Here is the first explicit mention of an age limit and a property qualification, though whether of real or personal property or both is not clear. No reason was given for this change; one can only conclude that the court was not satisfied to leave the decision solely to the majority in a town without setting some standard.

Without knowing the assessment rate on lands and personal property, it is impossible to say how much property a man would have to own to qualify. The printed records do not furnish assessment rates on lands until 1676, although land was certainly taxed from the beginning. The Code of 1650, described later, gives specific assessments only for animals over one year old, the assessment increasing with age to a category of four years and older. Amounts ranged downwards from £12 for horses to £5 for cows, heifers, and steers. Four-year-old bulls and oxen were assessed at £6, and all sheep, swine, and goats over one year at 30s., 20s., and 8s., respectively. The printed records do give for 1657 the total taxable estate and the number of persons, that is, males sixteen years and older, for Hartford, Windsor, and Wethersfield. For what it is worth, according to a standard estimate that one fourth of polls were under twenty-one, the average assessment per adult male in the three towns was £123, £107, and £140, respectively. The property qualification probably denied the vote to few adult males in the town.

Before charter government, Connecticut added one final requirement for admitted inhabitants. In 1660, the General Court ruled that "none shalbe receaved as Inhabitant into any Towne . . . but such as are knowne to be of an honest conversation, and accepted by a Major part of the Towne." The phrase *honest conversation* implies upright behavior in accordance with Puritan standards. Connecticut did not, like Massachusetts, require voters to be church members, but given the small communities and the multiplicity of means for overseeing conduct, there was probably no great difference in this respect between the two colonies in the first years. Modern research has shown that in Massachusetts, before 1647 at least, towns often ignored the absolute requirement of church membership, and certainly in Connecticut under the Fundamental Orders there was no room for religious dissenters of any kind.

The other kind of voter, the freeman, could achieve his status only through act of the General Court or of those magistrates to whom it might delegate the power of making men free, as the phrase went. The oath of fidelity taken by a freeman and presumably by admitted inhabit-ants meant that he had to be a Trinitarian, although it is not likely that the authorities in 1640 thought that swearing in the name of "God in our Lord Jesus Criste" would prove any obstacle to anyone in the colony. And a prospective freeman swore fidelity to Connecticut, not to the king.

In 1646, the General Court stipulated that no one convicted of a scan-dalous offense should be allowed to vote in town or commonwealth until the court removed his disability, and at the same time it turned over to any three magistrates the power to administer oaths of fidelity and admit freemen "uppon certificatt of good behavior, as is provided by former Order." Even though the records do not mention such certificates for freemen, apparently the court was already requiring some local approval before admission to freemanship. In 1657, the court became more specific. It now required a prospective freeman to have a certificate from all or a major part of the deputies of his town stating that he was a man of peaceable and honest conversation. Moreover, the court now decreed that only those whom the court itself approved should be admitted to freemanship. This was the same month in which the court attached property and age qualifications to the requirements for admitted in-habitants. Obviously the meaning of the court's action was to bring admission to freemanship more closely under its own control. Now men known to the court were asked to give testimony bearing witness to the candidate's character. The lack of fixed requirements seems to have left all discretion in the hands of the sponsoring deputies and the court as a whole.

Two years later, in 1659, the court decided to follow the pattern it had laid down for admitted inhabitants: a legal age of twenty-one and a property qualification or experience in office. But there were differences, for the freeman had to have thirty pounds of "proper personal estate," and he still could be admitted only by the General Court. Personal estate included not only cattle, but also goods for sale, ships, and so on, and an estimate of his income as a trader or artificer, if he were not simply a farmer. The Code of 1650 called upon listers to assess smiths, carpenters, butchers, bakers, and the like, in accordance with income and in propor-tion to those whose income was from real estate. Thus such workers were rated on their "faculty," or business or profession, as part of their personal estate. To illustrate the principle, in the eighteenth century the least active lawyers were assessed (not taxed) fifty pounds on their faculty.

There may have been objection to the complete discretion the court had heretofore exercised in admitting freemen, for in noting that it would admit them only in October, the court remarked that it wished "to prevent tumult and trouble at the Court of Election," which was held in May. The freemen may have complained when men were denied admission to freemanship without specific reasons. Two requirements for freemen—personal property and the approval of the General Court— now remained to distinguish their qualifications from those of admitted inhabitants. Since only freemen could be deputies and officers, the court determined who could hope to rise to those positions. In our own day, a rough equivalent would be that only state legislators could decide who could run for legislative, executive, and judicial office in the state. Such arrangements in Connecticut were in keeping with the Puritan principles that only the most able should hold positions of leadership and that ability was to be judged by those demonstrably able themselves.

Until an analysis of tax lists has been made, and their scarcity may make results inconclusive, one cannot know whether the personal property qualification sharply limited the number of freemen.* One recent study claims that the freemen listed in the records before 1662 must have represented only a fraction of the total number, since undoubtedly magistrates, when they were authorized to admit men to freemanship, did not report all the names to Hartford. An older study, noting the sharp decline in the number admitted after 1659, argues that the drop was owing to the personal property qualification, but this judgment remains conjectural.†

One must guard against the assumption that men eagerly sought the freemanship just because today we view the right to vote at all levels as

---

* Jackson Turner Main, "The Distribution of Property in Colonial Connecticut," in James Kirby Martin, ed., *The Human Dimensions of Nation Making* (Madison, Wis.: The State Historical Society of Wisconsin, 1976), pp. 54–104, uses probate records to determine the distribution of personal and real property. Main's study takes account of variables such as region, age, time period, occupation, and marital status, but his concern is not with the relationship between property and social class or political power. His use of estate inventories means that nontaxable personal property is included in the total figures for estates, but in determining the right to vote only *taxable* personal property could be included.

† Fowler, "Connecticut's Freeman," p. 323; Albert E. McKinley, *The Suffrage Franchise in the Thirteen English Colonies in America* (Philadelphia: University of Pennsylvania, 1905), p. 388.

supremely important. In seventeenth-century Connecticut making the trip to Hartford to vote in the Court of Election no doubt seemed a hardship to many (although some towns may have sent the ballots rather than their freemen), to say nothing of going before the General Court in October to be admitted to freemanship. It has been estimated that, by 1669, 70 to 80 percent of adult males were eligible for freemanship but that perhaps only 40 percent actually took the trouble to qualify. In 1702, when the requirements for freemanship were easier to meet and when travel to Hartford was no longer necessary, the General Court ordered town clerks to assess fines of two shillings on those absent from properly announced freemen's meetings if they could not show good cause for their absence. Voter apathy is obviously no new disease.

In voting for governor and magistrates, freemen used a slip of paper. For governor, each freeman wrote down the name of his choice, election going to the one who had the most votes. For magistrates, as the secretary called out the name of each nominee, each freeman handed in a paper—with the man's name on it if the voter favored him, blank if he disapproved of him. Those men to the number of six who received more written than blank ballots won election. If six were not so elected, then those candidates with the most number of written ballots were counted elected until the total of six was reached. Nominees for the office of magistrate had to be chosen at a General Court prior to the Court of Election in the spring. They could be nominated either by their towns or by the General Court itself. The actual voting took place at the Court of Election with most voting freemen physically present, but at some point, without statutory authorization, freemen from the remoter towns were permitted to send in their ballots as proxies. The only mention in the printed records of this practice is found for the year 1660.

In the spring of that year the General Court asked the freemen to consider whether they wished to alter the Fundamental Orders so that a governor could succeed himself. The governor in question was John Winthrop, Jr., who was personally popular and respected for his accomplishments. It had been customary for governor and deputy governor to alternate in officeholding each year. Thus Winthrop had been governor in 1657–58, with his deputy, Thomas Welles, taking over the governorship in 1658–59. Welles however had died in January 1660, leaving Winthrop with no one to change places with in 1660–61. Not surprisingly, the freemen were enthusiastic about continuing Winthrop;

indeed, he served until he died in 1676. Thus began a pattern in Connecticut, only twice broken, of steady reelection of governors as long as they could serve.

Only twice before had the freemen rather than the General Court made changes in the Fundamental Orders. In 1646, they had shifted the date of the Court of Election permanently from April to May for greater convenience; and in 1654, the freemen had provided that when both the governor and deputy governor were absent, a majority of the magistrates could call a General Court, which could then choose a moderator from among magistrates and deputies to preside. All other changes in the orders were made by the General Court itself. Only one change proposed to the freemen seems not to have been acted upon, a proposal to reduce the size of the General Court to lessen the cost of so large a representation. The original three towns were to send four deputies each and other towns in proportion. No action was taken, probably because steps were already under way to get a charter from the Crown, in which the matter of representation might well be settled.

*   *   *

Governor John Winthrop, Jr., was sent to England to obtain a charter, and a better choice could not have been made. Urbane, learned, a man of engaging warmth, and an astute politician, he made an effective and attractive representative for the interests of Connecticut at the royal court. In early 1661 Connecticut had decided to petition the newly restored king, Charles II, for his favor and for continuation of Connecticut's privileges. The awkward fact, of course, was that the colony lacked a proper legal foundation. The Fundamental Orders, however useful to the people of Connecticut, had no legal standing in the eyes of English authorities. While the mother country had been engaged in civil war, Connecticut had pursued its way unmolested; but the new king had many at his court who wanted New England brought to heel. It behooved a prudent people to establish friendly and well-defined legal relationships with the mother country. Yet there was no joy in Connecticut at the restoration, no hurry to proclaim the new king.

Winthrop had early recognized the need to secure friendly intercession with the Crown. Writing privately to family connections in England, Winthrop urged that Connecticut be presented in a favorable light to

JOHN WINTHROP, JR. (1606–1676). This portrait was probably painted in the 1640s by an artist not now known. Governor of Connecticut from 1657 to 1676 and the first American colonist to be elected to the Royal Society, Winthrop was a man of great charm and was popular with his constituents, not only for his personality but also for his medical skill. *Courtesy of the Massachusetts Historical Society.*

Charles II; and after the General Court had approved in principle a petition to the king, the governor wrote a fulsome address to Charles II intimating that Connecticut's loyalty had never been in doubt. The choice of Winthrop to go to England to secure a charter was a logical outcome. He went armed with instructions to seek out Lord Saye and Sele, Lord Brook, the Earl of Manchester, and others, so that he might find a copy of the Warwick patent, which Connecticut desired should be amended to include the sort of immunities and privileges enjoyed by Massachusetts under its charter. If an entirely new instrument had to be sought, Winthrop was to get one as much like that of Massachusetts as possible and with ample boundaries, running from Massachusetts and Plymouth to Delaware Bay.

The men Winthrop was to seek out were well chosen, for not only had they been connected with Warwick but some of them had also been active in the king's restoration and held high office under the Crown. The negotiations were long and were threatened at several points by the rival activities of Rhode Island, but Winthrop succeeded in getting a most generous charter, which made Connecticut virtually a self-governing colony with sea-to-sea boundaries. If those boundaries were ambiguously stated and conflicting, as they proved to be, still Connecticut had been put upon a secure legal foundation. Negotiation and compromise over many years would serve to establish the colony's boundary lines. It has been suggested that Charles II was the more willing to give Connecticut wide latitude in self-government, as he also did for Rhode Island a year later, because he saw these colonies as a counterweight to the overweening conduct of neighboring Massachusetts, whose charter Charles's father had sought to void.

The governmental provisions of the charter of 1662 made little change in the way Connecticut had been managing its affairs. The number of deputies to be sent from each town was now limited to two, a limit that obviously favored the small towns, giving them greater weight in the legislature than their population warranted. As the colony matured, only rarely did a town fail to send the two representatives it was entitled to have. As before, deputies were newly elected for each of the two regular sessions of the General Assembly (the official name now for the General Court)* each year, but turnover seldom occurred. The governor re-

---

* The charter introduced the term *General Assembly*, and, for a time at least, the secretary consistently used it at the head of his notes for each session. But old habits die

mained essentially a presiding officer with very little power, but the number of magistrates was raised from six to twelve. The charter made no mention of voters other than freemen, who still became such by action of the General Assembly. In 1664, the assembly ruled that the meaning of the charter was that only freemen could vote for deputies, a right that had belonged to the admitted inhabitants under the Fundamental Orders. Freemen still assembled in person at the Court of Election to cast their votes for colonial officers if they chose, but in 1670 the assembly clearly made proxies, or sealed written votes, an alternative to actual attendance.

Although the charter did not recognize admitted inhabitants as voters, they continued to have status in Connecticut as voters for town affairs, with the old qualifications continuing until 1678, when the assembly made a new stipulation: a fifty-shilling freehold estate. At the same time the assembly made it clear that this new requirement should bar no freeman from voting in town affairs; freemen had always had that privilege. In 1750, the assembly permitted a forty-pound personal estate as an alternative to the fifty-shilling freehold. Charles Grant has argued persuasively that although property qualifications for admitted inhabitants were retained in the printed laws, in practice after 1727 or so, the towns made no distinctions in allowing adult males to vote in town affairs if they were recognized as inhabitants of the town.

The General Assembly in the years after the charter tinkered even more with the requirements for freemanship. In the very month the charter was first publicly read, October 1662, the assembly changed the property qualifications from thirty pounds personal to twenty pounds estate "in addition to their persons." The meaning of this last phrase is that all males sixteen years and older were assessed at eighteen pounds, a figure that had been arrived at in 1651 and that remained constant throughout the colonial period. The ruling of 1662 included two other innovations: a certificate from the majority of townsmen that the candidate for freemanship was of sober conversation; and presentation of the candidate at the October session of the assembly, actual admission to be

hard. By the 1670s he had reverted to the old term, which was regularly used by him until 1697. After the formal division of the legislature into two houses, *General Assembly* was the common term. J. Hammond Trumbull and Charles J. Hoadly, eds., *Public Records of the Colony of Connecticut, 1636–1776,* 15 vols. (Hartford, 1850–1890), vol. 1, pp. 384, 392; vol. 2, pp. 43, 115, 136; vol. 4, pp. 221, 282; hereafter cited as *Conn. Col. Records.*

delayed until May. Thus freemanship was finally to depend in great part upon town rather than upon deputy approval, and a probationary period of some months was instituted. In 1673, the property qualification was altered to twenty pounds estate in housing and lands besides personal estate, and in 1675 that was reduced to ten pounds. Approval of the majority of selectmen was also required.

Finally, in 1689 Connecticut adopted the traditional English requirement of a forty-shilling freehold, which meant one producing an income of at least that amount per year, as Connecticut put it, "in country pay." Country pay was the values assigned by the government to crops and other commodities acceptable for payment of taxes. For example, in 1689, wheat was acceptable at four shillings and sixpence per bushel, corn at two shillings and sixpence, and peas and rye at three shillings. Shifting the definition of the value of an estate from assessment to income represented a great easing of the franchise restrictions, and it has been suggested that one reason for this was a desire to please English officials in the period of the Glorious Revolution. A man could now qualify for freemanship if he held land that produced, say, less than ten bushels of wheat or eighteen bushels of corn. In contrast, the law of 1675 would have required a freeman to have, in addition to a three-acre house lot, a minimum in most towns of eleven acres of cultivated land, which would yield far more than the bushels of grain mentioned in the law of 1689.

The law of 1689, moreover, maintained the requirement of the candidate's approval by the selectmen rather than a majority of the whole town. A certificate of approval presented to a local judge (commissioner or assistant) would bring admission, thereby at last eliminating the role of the General Assembly and with it the probationary period. In 1702, the property qualification became a forty-shilling freehold or forty pounds personal estate, but the most significant change came in 1709.

In that year the assembly defined property qualifications in terms of the applicant's listing in the year he presented himself. Starting in 1676, the assembly had begun to assign assessed values to different kinds of land in various locations. This first effort produced complicated variations among several groups of towns, with older towns having much heavier assessments for house lots and improved meadowlands, for example. The discrepancies tended to narrow in subsequent assessment changes made in 1692, 1701, 1712, and 1714. By 1737 the assessments were stabilized; no further changes were made in the colonial period. By then, plowed and mowed meadowland in Hartford County was assessed at fifteen shillings per acre, elsewhere at seven shillings and sixpence. All other types of land—mowed boggy meadows, plow lands, pasture, fenced land unfit for pasture, and home lots up to three acres—were assessed the same everywhere: five shillings, ten shillings, eight shillings, two shillings, and one pound, respectively, per acre. Meanwhile the assessments on livestock had declined from the values stated in the Code of 1650, largely stabilizing by 1670.

The meaning of the law of 1709 was that property qualifications, tied now to fixed values for land and livestock, would be less affected by market conditions or by the inflation of money values, such as occurred in the eighteenth century, than property qualifications tied to income. A person's right to vote would be tied to a set number of acres of land or of livestock of various kinds, the assessment of faculty or business aside for the moment. With respect to acquiring the right to vote, the impact of inflation would be felt only by those without lands or livestock and seeking to purchase them at rising prices. Thus Albert E. McKinley's belief that inflation would make the vote easier and easier to come by seems partly in error. One can surmise that the effect of the suffrage laws was to exclude from the vote those families lacking a heritage to start with, possibly a small number of the adult males if Connecticut reveals upon greater study the pattern that research has disclosed in other colonies. Charles Grant's investigation of Kent reveals that nearly 80 percent of adult males possessed enough property to qualify for freemanship. Chilton Williamson's analysis of East Guilford finds a similarly high proportion of males who could vote. Inflation *would* have the effect of making personal property qualifications easier to meet since they were tied to income. A lawyer's faculty assessment became fixed at fifty pounds minimum as early as 1725, but not until 1771 were listers given any guidance in assessing merchants, shopkeepers, and artificers.

Poor families struggling to subsist, however, would hardly fall into such categories. If without lands, they would find it difficult to acquire a two-acre home lot or four acres of plow land to meet the forty-shilling requirement. Ezra Stiles in a letter to Benjamin Gale in 1766 estimated the number of freemen in Connecticut at only one-ninth of the adult males, an estimate that seems very low.* Extensive analysis of taxable

---

* Edmund S. Morgan, *The Gentle Puritan: A Life of Ezra Stiles, 1727–1795* (New Haven: Yale University Press, 1962), p. 251.

property holdings might yield some clues if used in conjunction with lists of freemen, but those estimates, based on the actual number of votes cast in an election, omit, of course, those who chose not to vote. And many chose not to vote, or even to become freemen, except when a real contest loomed, for example, that between Jonathan Trumbull and Thomas Fitch in 1770.

The last change in the procedure for becoming a freeman was made by the assembly in 1729. In noting the inconvenience of having to register the names of all freemen in the secretary's office, the law stipulated that the names were to be enrolled by the town clerk in an open freemen's meeting; the implication is that, in the future, such meetings, rather than the selectmen, would determine admission to freemanship. For the rest of the colonial period, then, both types of voters were created by local action, presumably in accordance with standards defined by the General Assembly.

From time to time the colonial government stepped in because of complaints about illegal voting. In Lyme in 1714 the moderator and selectmen allowed unqualified men and noninhabitants to vote for town officers, and the governor and Council (the executive and magistrates empowered to act between sessions of the General Assembly) ordered new elections to be held in accordance with the law defining voters. The governor and Council heard a similar case in 1727, this time in New London, but held that the complainants had failed to establish their charge that unqualifed persons had been permitted to disturb the meeting and to vote. The disappointed petitioners had to pay charges. A few months later the General Assembly ruled invalid Voluntown's admission of some inhabitants and nullified all votes taken after their admission.

The method of having deputies select nominees for colonial office remained virtually unchanged for some years after the granting of the charter, but in 1670 the assembly prescribed a voting precedure that left itself with some influence over the freemen's choice in the actual elections. The nomination list, made up by the assembly in October as before, was read out by the constable to the freemen at their local meetings, and out of the list the freemen cast separate votes for governor, deputy governor, treasurer, and secretary. Then the constable went down the whole list of twenty-odd names, name by name, in the order prescribed by the assembly, each freeman casting a written or blank ballot for each nominee on the entire list. The law of 1670 concludes, "and at the time of election [the counting of votes at Hartford in May] those that stand for nomination shall be put to election in the same order that they are propownded, untill the number required by Charter are elected, and then they shall cease."

The order of the list was critical. The first twelve men who got more written ballots than blanks would be declared elected as magistrates. Obviously those at the top of the list would stand the best chance of election. Examination of nomination lists after 1670 shows at once that the ordering of the list favored those already serving as magistrates, but examination of the lists before 1670 shows the same pattern, a circumstance that must mean the law was merely spelling out old practice. The assembly probably thought it useful to do that because it had just made explicit provision for freemen to vote by proxy in their towns, where the assembly wanted the order of the voting on the names to be the same as the order of the counting of the votes.

Ideally, the governor, his deputy, and the twelve magistrates should come from the first fourteen names on the list, since separate voting for treasurer and secretary did not deny them seats as magistrates as well. Study of the nomination lists and election results for the ten years 1671 to 1680 shows that 70 percent of the time successful candidates came from the first sixteen names. Clearly, for a nominee, the hazardous spot was toward the bottom of the list. Once a new man won election as magistrate, he became number fourteen, below all those who had served in the office already.

In 1689 the General Assembly modified the voting procedure in important respects. The nomination list was now limited to twenty and was to be made by the freemen voting on the third Tuesday in March, each voter handing in his list of twenty names at his local meeting. Except for a brief interval, allowing the voters to choose the nominees remained the practice for the rest of the colonial period. Those twenty men getting the most votes would make up the nomination list. The voting on the list in April proceeded as before, each name being taken up in the order set by the assembly. When the votes were counted in May, however, the twelve men getting the most votes would be declared winners. Now the order of the nomination list was less important than it had been. Under the former procedure, to win election one had only to be among the first twelve to get more written than blank ballots; now one had to be among the twelve getting the most votes. But the order of the nomination list was not without significance; we know that even today voters tend to prefer those on the top of any list of candidates. The assembly continued to order the list to favor incumbents, and that tradition was to list incumbents by seniority of service and nonincumbents in descending order of the total votes they had received in the nomination. This system of ordering the list accounted in great part for the very slow turnover of the body of magistrates, or upper house, as it was called after 1698. A new man who received even a very heavy vote in the nominations remained well down the list after every incumbent, and he might remain there through four or more elections. A sudden change of order was a very rare occurrence.

A recent study of nominations for colony office made by voters in their separate towns shows much less unanimity in voting than is revealed by the official nomination lists and the choice year after year of the same men to high office. "Anywhere from thirty-nine to sixty-two individuals received more than one hundred votes for governor and assistants each year. . . ."* But, of course, most voters chose the holdovers in making up their nomination list.

In 1697, the day for nominations was changed from March to the third Tuesday in September to allow a longer time between nomination and the voting in April. The assembly announced the nomination list in October. In 1708, the requirement that the freemen must make their choices for governor and deputy governor from the list of twenty was dropped. They now had "libertie to choose . . . where they see cause, of all or any of the freemen within this Colonie." The practical meaning of a free choice for governor was probably not great; any man not prominent enough to be in the nomination list would hardly stand a chance of being elected governor.

The printed laws of 1750 show that the freemen could vote for only twelve names out of the twenty, a change that seriously impaired the secrecy of the ballot, for now a voter by handing in a paper when a name was called gave public notice of whom he was supporting for magistrate. The only way he could keep his choice secret was to cast a blank ballot; but if he did that, he would sacrifice one of his twelve votes, since he could come up to the constable or selectman with a ballot only twelve times.

Lack of secrecy would discourage maneuvers to make a dramatic

---

* Robert J. Dinkin, "The Nomination of Governor and Assistants in Colonial Connecticut," Connecticut Historical Society, *Bulletin* 36 (July 1971): 92–96.

change in the composition of the magistrates, for one would be defying tradition, and failure would lay one open to scorn. The tradition became so strong that in later years when an attempt was made to win an election by circulating a private nomination list, the newspapers were filled with outraged protest.

The many changes in the law governing the procedures for voting for colony officials contrast glaringly with the practice of voting for deputies. The Fundamental Orders had required a ballot for deputies, but neither the charter nor the statutes passed after 1662 make mention of the method of voting for them. Choice of deputies by acclamation at the freemen's meetings became the usual practice. But even here, when no agency outside the town sought to arrange nominations for a predisposed result, the freemen tended to choose many of the same men year after year. A recent study by Bruce C. Daniels covering a span of eighty years and drawing its data from all the towns in existence for the entire period shows what he calls "family-dominated oligarchy."* That is, a few men from prominent families served a remarkable proportion of all the deputies' terms in each town. Almost one-half of the terms were served by five men; five families served nearly two-thirds of them. Obviously campaigning was not the key to success in winning election to colony office. In fact, according to Samuel Peters, the candidates were not permitted "to give a dinner, or a glass of cider, on the day of the election, to the voter."

The many revisions in the election laws during the seventeenth and eighteenth centuries show some easing of voting restrictions. Emphasis on moral approval of prospective voters, whether by towns or elected officials, declined. Charges of illegal voting commonly alleged that those improperly allowed to vote were deficient not in character but in adequate residence or property qualifications. If these requirements were met, registration of freemen in open meetings must have been virtually routine. The status of admitted inhabitant could be acquired, the laws on property requirements notwithstanding, if one had economic resources to avoid becoming a charge to the town. Careful study remains to be done on whether the linking of the franchise to fixed assessments on land reduced the percentage of voters as increased population made land

---

* Bruce C. Daniels, "Democracy and Oligarchy in Connecticut Towns: General Assembly Officeholding, 1701–1790," *Social Science Quarterly* 56 (December 1975): 465.

harder to obtain. Not enough Connecticut towns have been analyzed to permit generalization. Finally, voters enjoyed greater freedom of choice after the General Assembly permitted them to make the nominations, decreed that those on the list getting the most votes would win election, and ceased prescribing the order in which candidates would be voted upon.

Yet none of these changes lessened the disposition of the majority to remain with familiar leaders. It is well known that Connecticut reelected its colonial governors beginning with John Winthrop, Jr., year after year until poor health or death dictated another choice. Such loyalty helped earn the colony the nickname of the "Land of Steady Habits," a term more colorful than useful for what it implies. But governors did continue long in office—Winthrop for seventeen years continuously, Gurdon Saltonstall for seventeen, and Jonathan Trumbull for fifteen, right through independence. Yet events could make a difference and freemen could arouse themselves. In 1754, the freemen rejected Roger Wolcott as governor in favor of Thomas Fitch. Wolcott, who had served as deputy governor under Jonathan Law since 1742, and who had been elected governor in 1751 on Law's death, was dropped from the governorship in 1754 because of scandal. He was thought to share responsibility for the shabby treatment that a Spanish merchant in distress had received at the hands of New Londoners when he put into their port. The Spaniard's stored cargo had been plundered, and his complaints came to the attention of British authorities, who demanded that Connecticut restore his property. Some years later the freemen dropped Fitch from the governorship in the election following his taking of an oath before the magistrates in accordance with the provisions of the despised Stamp Act. By that date, 1766, political factions had begun to form, and the action of the freemen was not quite so spontaneous as it had been in 1754.

Despite the governor's lack of real power in the legislative process, he had important duties, great prestige, and frequent special responsibilities. The governor presided over the Council, which was made up of magistrates and, later, of freemen as well, who, with the governor, were given power to act between sessions of the legislature. The first Council was authorized in 1663 and recreated in 1675, and met intermittently thereafter, especially in times of emergency. Under the Fundamental Orders, the governor sat with some of the magistrates to form a Particular Court, which met quarterly as a court of appeals and as a court to try criminal cases and important civil suits with a jury in attendance. Under the charter the governor and magistrates were constituted as the Court of Assistants, which had original jurisdiction over crimes involving life, limb, or banishment, as well as appellate jurisdiction in all other cases. In 1711, this court was replaced by the Superior Court, consisting of a chief judge and four others. Meeting originally twice a year, the Superior Court, with the press of business, became more of a circuit court, meeting twice a year in each county seat. Beginning in 1715, the deputy governor was regularly named chief judge of this court. All magistrates had the powers of a justice of the peace in a specific county. By 1728 the governor, the highest magistrate, could exercise such powers in every county throughout the colony. The governor was commander-in-chief of the militia and signed all military commissions. From time to time the legislature asked him to undertake additional duties. He might be named as one of the commissioners to the United Colonies, before its demise in King Philip's War; it has been mentioned that Winthrop went to England to secure a charter. And of course the governor was ceremonial head of state, he handled official correspondence, and he called important matters to the attention of the General Assembly for action.

In their legislative capacity, the magistrates, also called from earlier days *assistants,* were known after 1698 as the Council, not to be confused with the Council that acted with the governor when the legislature was not in session. Without authorization from the charter, the General Assembly in 1698 constituted itself a two-house legislature, the magistrates or Council with the governor or his deputy being called the upper house, the deputies or representatives, the lower house. The latter was now allowed to choose its own speaker. The enacting style for legislation became "be it enacted by the Governor, Council and Representatives in General Court assembled," but informal references continued to be made to the enactments of the General Assembly.

Besides being legislators and members of the Superior Court, magistrates functioned as chief judges in the several county courts, which first came into being in 1666. They met quarterly, the number of judges in each court varying over the years, a chief judge sitting with two to four others. As justices of the peace, single magistrates tried cases involving no more than forty shillings. In 1698 the assembly first appointed freemen to act in this capacity. For a brief period, 1701–2, candidates were nominated by their fellow freemen, but the assembly withdrew this privilege because nomination was "found to be an occasion of Strife and

Debate in the severall Townes." Fees paid by litigants, set by law, were put in local or colony treasuries, and compensation for judges and justices was set at a per diem rate by the assembly, with the more important judges sometimes being awarded a salary as well. County courts tried civil cases and criminal ones not "extending to life, limb, banishment, or divorce." Most actions required a jury.

The jury system itself underwent changes over the years. In the 1640s a judge was permitted to demand that a jury reconsider its verdict if he felt that it had not paid sufficient attention to the evidence, or he could impanel a new jury, but by the 1690s the judge no longer had this right. By the eighteenth century a more careful system of selection of jurors by lot from the freemen had been instituted. Town officials were to write on paper slips the names of freemen who were able and judicious, the slips to be drawn from a box when a jury was required. The assembly stipulated the number of such veniremen for each town in each county.

Thus Connecticut paid no attention to the niceties of separation of powers. The chief executive and his deputy as well as the members of the upper house all had judicial powers, and the General Assembly itself continued to function as the highest court of appeal in Connecticut. It frequently overturned judgments of the Superior Court, ordered new trials, or reduced judgments. To reduce the burden of appeals, the General Assembly in 1773 gave equity jurisdiction within stated monetary limits to the county and superior courts. Individual members of both legislative houses often held more than one position. It was common for upper-house members to be treasurer or secretary of the colony, at least before the work of the legislature became too heavy. For example, John Allyn served as magistrate and secretary from 1668 to 1695, when a new secretary, not a magistrate, was elected by the freemen. Magistrates were named by the assembly not only to head county courts but also to serve simultaneously as probate judges. Many members of the lower house could expect to be named justices of the peace.

Under the charter, as before, the locus of power was in the legislature. In contrast to Massachusetts, for which a recent scholar has argued that the eighteenth century saw the towns virtually independent of real control by the colonial government, Connecticut, through its General Assembly kept a tight, if benevolent, rein on its towns, and the towns were quick to turn to the assembly for solution of even the pettiest of problems.

Thus, the assembly ordered townspeople complaining of irregular elections to hold new ones; required boundaries in dispute between towns or between ecclesiastical societies (those bodies authorized to levy taxes to support a church) to be rerun under the direction of a legislative committee; and when local authorities were deemed neglectful, might request the building of highways or bridges to promote public worship or to increase trade. Towns were told how to control swine, where to locate their meetinghouses, and how to curb tumult in their local meetings. The assembly regulated Indian affairs within the colony and exercised oversight over religious matters, the economy, and the welfare of citizens caught up in a thousand trying situations. Any reader of the legislative records cannot help being struck by the multitude of petitions asking for the legislature's consideration, which was favorably bestowed more often than not. Routine were hundreds of petitions from widows or administrators of estates requesting permission to sell real estate when the deceased's personal property would not settle his debts. Petitions came from the lame and the halt asking relief from poll taxes and militia duty. Relatives of idiots sought authorization to dispose of property to provide support for their helpless charges. Now and again a woman whose husband was long since gone petitioned for divorce, or a deserted husband asked for the same consideration. Men complaining of the way their lawsuits were handled in the courts sought to overturn judgments or stay executions.

On a larger scale, the General Assembly was ready to embargo shipments of foodstuffs from the colony in the face of shortages or impending war; loan money from the public funds to encourage business enterprise; establish the rates for ferry service; set wages or prices if they were thought excessive; stipulate the time of year for gathering bayberries, which were used for tallow; levy import duties in favor of Connecticut citizens and discourage noninhabitants from bringing trading goods into the colony; set standards of quality for meat, tobacco, and other commodities exported from the colony; grant monopolies or subsidies for a set period of years to encourage the mining of copper, the making of silk, hemp, and linen products, and the manufacture of iron, steel, potash, glass, and salt; and, of course, grant lands and lay down the conditions for settlement of new townships.

A legislature with this kind of immediate effect upon those whom it represented was careful to maintain the most correct relations between itself and its constituents. Petitions in this period in Connecticut and elsewhere had to be filed in the most humble language; never could there be a suggestion that the august General Assembly might not know what it was about. One acknowledged that its deliberations were careful and wise; one hoped that it would deign to consider a personal plight by making an exception or by giving permission to do what had to be done. Occasionally an impetuous petitioner forgot his manners, or an irritated citizen had the temerity to suggest that the legislature was "a parcel of rogues." The assembly was quick to take offense at any slight upon its dignity or that of the governor as well. An impolite petitioner would have his petition thrust aside and be perhaps called upon for an apology before he could resubmit his plea. Those daring enough to resort to slander might be fined and disfranchised, as happened to several.

Normally the assembly met twice a year, in May and October, but the press of business or emergency might bring a special session or two. In the early years the assembly held many such additional sessions. In the 1640s, for example, five to seven sessions in the year were common. Beginning in 1701, the October meeting was held in New Haven and only the spring meeting in Hartford. To avoid additional sessions, the legislature could delegate responsibility to the governor and Council. After the formal establishment of bicameralism, assistants, or members of the upper house, were paid a shilling or two more per diem for attendance and a penny or two more per mile for travel allowance than were members of the lower house. Legislators had perquisites, besides, that had monetary value. When on public business, they could use the ferries free, as could others, like the governor and judges. The assistants paid no poll taxes, although the deputies had no such exemption.

How much did this governmental establishment cost the taxpayers of Connecticut? Relatively little, except in times of war. Trumbull estimated the cost of colonial government at not more than £800 per year in the early 1700s. In 1756, the colony reported to the Board of Trade that the cost was £4,000 lawful money, of which £490 went to the schools. These low costs can be variously explained. Salaries were low. In that year, for example, the governor was paid £132 plus a bonus of £80 for "extraordinary service." The deputy governor received £66, and the treasurer a total of £68 10s. 6d. for nine months. At this time the meanest lawyer was assessed £50 for his faculty in the common list, a sum supposedly equal to his annual income as a lawyer. Another reason was that the salaries of many officials, like judges, sheriffs, constables, and the like, came in large part from the statutory fees and fines of those who resorted to them, although the fees went into treasuries from which these officials received per diem allowances set by the assembly. Further, many services that today would fall to executive agents to perform were handled by legislators acting in committees appointed by the assembly. Such committeemen received their expenses for traveling to view a boundary or locate a meetinghouse site, but the expenses were paid by local people who benefited directly. Finally, the assembly was careful to insist that responsibility for care of the poor, the elderly, and the handicapped remain local. Only rarely, and in a few well-defined circumstances, did the colonial government expend money for such purposes.

The costs of government were met mainly by taxes on polls and estates, although some revenue in the eighteenth century came from the sale of land (earlier, land had been granted to prospective settlers or given as a reward to deserving men) and from import and export taxes. The polls, including all males sixteen years old and over (sixteen to seventy beginning in 1720), were assessed at eighteen pounds apiece. By the assessments established in 1737, which lasted to the Revolution, the assessment on a poll was equivalent to that on twenty-four acres of the best plowed or mowed meadowlands in Hartford County, or thirty-six acres of ordinary plow land anywhere in the colony, or six cows three years old or older. Thus the poll tax was no inconsiderable part of a man's total taxes. A man having two or three grown sons not yet independent or a servant or two not receiving wages would have to pay a formidable poll tax, relative to other taxes, though we must always keep in mind that unimproved land, not used or fenced, was not taxed for colony purposes. Certain people were automatically exempt from poll taxes. Besides the assistants, already mentioned, the governor, deputy governor, ministers, schoolmasters, and the rector, tutors, and students at Yale enjoyed such exemption. The injustice of the poll tax, which put an unfair burden on the poor, became a matter of protest during the Revolution. In 1778, Norwich called the tax "an insupportable burden on the poor," and Samuel Peters's *History* described it as cruel. Typically the tax rate was a penny on the pound, but in time of war it could rise to two or three or even more pence in the course of a year. Colony taxes were in addition, of course, to town rates and taxes for the support of the minister.

The making of assessments was the work of the listers, local officials who collected from each town inhabitant a list of his taxable property as of August 20 each year. On receiving each list, the lister would set a value on those taxables not particularly provided for by law but left to his discretion, such as the value of a man's trade. The sum total of all the lists would be sent to the General Assembly in October. Between that time and December, the end of the taxable year, the lister would go over his lists to make sure nothing had been left out, perhaps even going to a man's farm to check his livestock or acreage. Taxable property omitted was to be assessed at fourfold value, and anyone failing to submit a list would have the assessment of his whole estate quadrupled. Such additions had to be submitted to the May session of the assembly. For his trouble the lister after 1737 was to receive one half of the taxes arising from the fourfold additions. Thus he would be highly motivated to turn in an accurate total. Any taxpayer overcharged could seek relief from the lister, or, failing that, from a justice of the peace assisted by selectmen. Despite the incentive, listers were sometimes content with their old records and had to be warned to look to the real nature of fenced land. Undoubtedly the job was unpopular; old records made it easier to live with one's neighbors, their affection being worth more perhaps than tax money from fourfold assessments. Yet the records show at almost every legislative session a list by towns of some fourfold assessments.

The lister was but one of many local officials chosen by town inhabitants and saddled with duties spelled out by the General Assembly. A recent study estimates that by 1750 towns were choosing sixty to seventy local officials and that by 1776, owing to population increases, the number had risen to between seventy-five and ninety. Some of these offices were originally created by the towns, any regulations of the General Assembly coming after their establishment. Town treasurers and moderators are examples. Local elections for clerk, lister, townsmen or selectmen, haywards, fence viewers, constables, surveyors of highways, grand jurors, and other functionaries were held annually; those elected who refused to serve and could not demonstrate before a magistrate or justice of the peace good reason for refusal paid a substantial fine. Officeholding was a duty not to be shirked, however onerous. Only if one were overburdened with offices, or if there were others who had not done their fair share, could one escape without penalty.

Edward M. Cook's recent study of New England towns, including Connecticut ones, finds that in the lesser towns access to office was relatively open for those who were respected for ability and judgment, that only in important places did the higher offices become a monopoly of the elite based on wealth and family. Normally a man served in a succession of lower offices before obtaining a higher one, such as that of representative, but in the commercial and political centers those of the "better sort" gained high office earlier and enjoyed longer tenure. Yet their longer service often simply reflected their greater ability to stand the expense of officeholding. However, Bruce C. Daniels, who examined tenure in the office of deputy or representative for far more Connecticut towns than did Cook and analyzed the holding of important local offices in three of the largest towns, doubts whether a monopoly of officeholding was more likely in large than in small towns. He found, for example, that small old towns were marked by family dominance.* But, refinements aside, research confirms the existence of elites that enjoyed repeated election to important local offices.

The selectmen acted for the town in dozens of ways, sometimes in conjunction with other officials like justices of the peace, constables, or town treasurers, but in so acting they carried out the wishes of the town as expressed in the annual meeting and in special meetings. The town voters decided whether a new road should be laid out, the schoolhouse repaired, or an additional pound built. With the passage of time the General Assembly through its enactments added to the duties of selectmen a variety of responsibilities, including military protection of their towns, supervision of care for the poor and abatement of their taxes if necessary, and, with the revolutionary crisis, policing of the loyalty of local citizens. Some town meetings increased the selectmen's burdens by assigning to them specific tasks, such as entering into negotiations with neighboring towns and handling problems formerly left to specially elected committees.

Yet these local decisions took place within a framework established by the General Assembly and further refined by it from time to time. All able-bodied men were required to work on the highways, for example, and each town had to care for its own poor. The duties and procedures of local officials whose activities directly affected the colonial government were carefully spelled out and modified from time to time; and towns

---

* Bruce C. Daniels, "Democracy and Oligarchy in Connecticut Towns: General Assembly Officeholding, 1701–1790," *Social Science Quarterly* 56 (December 1975): 460–75.

were even left no choice about many small things—for example, erecting stocks for the punishment of offenders or providing milestones on the postroads to show the distance from the county seat. Yet a recent study of the relationships between towns and the colonial government in the seventeenth century has shown that within limits towns exercised some discretion in obeying General Court directives to the letter.* Town privileges were conferred by the assembly at an appropriate time, and until that moment, settlements could not claim them. Willington, for example, had a poor family with an idiot child settled in its midst. Too poor to bear this burden, the settlement nonetheless had not been able to warn out the family (that is, order it to leave before it became a public charge) because it was not then a recognized town; its only recourse was to petition the legislature, which appropriated six shillings per week for the child's support.

Years of study devoted to towns have obscured the significant role that the counties played in the lives of New England colonists. Modeled on the English example, the counties fulfilled in New England some of the functions that they did elsewhere in the American colonies, but some functions were unique to Connecticut, particularly those concerned with education. The four counties of Hartford, New London, New Haven, and Fairfield were created in 1666. Windham was established in 1726 and Litchfield in 1751. The counties were mainly judicial districts, the county courts being the most important agents at the county level. For a time they were military districts as well, since each county had its regiment and regimental officers, but that system was soon superseded in favor of a larger number of regiments. Besides its judges and justices each county had a treasurer, a sheriff, and grand jurors. The latter were elected by the several towns and through the presentment process were given oversight over enforcement of laws, particularly such as those designed to promote morality and education. Sheriffs were the peace officers in the counties, as constables were in the towns; they quelled tumults, served writs, and handled other matters. Sheriffs were appointed by the governor and Council. Counties maintained jails, workhouses for the poor and idle, and Latin grammar schools for training boys to enter college.

---

* Thomas Jodziewicz, "Dual Localism in Seventeenth-Century Connecticut: Relations between the General Court and the Towns, 1636–1691" (unpublished Ph.D. dissertation, College of William and Mary, 1974).

Besides fees, fines, and the like, county income depended upon a small tax on polls and estates and occasionally upon special excises.

The ordinary Connecticut inhabitant could know where he stood with respect to the laws by consulting printed collections of them furnished from time to time to each town clerk. Collections were published in 1673, 1702, 1715, and 1750, but Connecticut's first code was compiled in 1639 for the use of the towns. Unfortunately no copy of this earliest codification is extant. Quite likely the opinion of Thomas Hooker that magistrates should not be allowed too much discretion and the knowledge that Massachusetts Bay people were agitating in vain for a code prompted the General Court to request a review of the laws and a recording of those "necessary for publique concernement."

The earliest extant code is that of 1650, largely a borrowing by Roger Ludlow from the Massachusetts laws of 1648. The code lists fourteen capital crimes, all of them based on Biblical texts. Long as the list was, the number was lower than in England at the time. Death was prescribed for worship of strange gods, witchcraft, blasphemy, willful murder, murder through guile, bestiality, sodomy, adultery, rape, kidnapping, false testimony resulting in death, insurrection, the striking or cursing of parents by children over sixteen years old, and stubborn disobedience to parental wishes by sons of at least sixteen years. The listing of such punishments, of course, does not mean that they were all carried out. Almost certainly disobedient children, for example, were not put to death. The printed laws show some omissions from and additions to this old code. Capital felonies by 1750 do not include worship of strange gods, witchcraft, adultery, kidnapping, cursing of parents and stubbornness on the part of children, and one or two other crimes, although not all capital offenses are listed in this compilation. Meanwhile, Connecticut had taken from Parliament the capital offense of high treason, and had made capital crimes of certain mutilations of others and concealing the death of a bastard child.

While the capital laws of the Code of 1650 are nearly an exact transcription of the Massachusetts laws (murder arising from anger is not mentioned in the Connecticut version), the rest of the code has fewer categories than the Massachusetts laws. A number are omitted, of course, because of different circumstances and some because they are covered in the Fundamental Orders—the method of voting, for example. But some differences are significant; for the Connecticut code lacks a number of the protections or rights spelled out in the Massachusetts laws. The rights of children, widows, servants, voters, noncitizens, and criminals are either passed over or less explicitly provided for in the Connecticut laws.

Massachusetts stipulated that no one could deny children the right to marry at an appropriate time, and it protected the right of both children and widows to share in a man's estate. Servants were protected against abuse, and noncitizens were to enjoy the same application of the laws as citizens. The accused and criminals enjoyed guarantees against double jeopardy and inhumane punishment. No one was to be made to confess to a crime through torture except in a capital case where the accused had been proved guilty and confederates in the crime were suspected. No one was to be put to death without the testimony of two or three witnesses or the equivalent (none being specified), and at least four days had to pass between sentencing and execution. Voters were protected in their right to remain silent and also to have their dissent from the majority view, whether in speech or writing, entered in the records of "any Court, Council or civil Assemblie," even in important matters like religion, capital offenses, the waging of wars. Some of the Massachusetts freedoms possess economic meaning. No monopolies were to be granted except on new inventions for a limited time, and no one was to demand excessive wages or prices. Thus the Massachusetts laws were more comprehensive than the Connecticut code and in many respects took on the character of a bill of rights. Connecticut's laws were more concerned with prohibitions than with guarantees, although later enactments filled some of the gaps.

Some provisions found in Connecticut's code and lacking in the Massachusetts laws include a prohibition against divulging the secrets of the General Court or the words of any member of that body, explicit tax support for ministers, impartial appraisal for debtors' goods seized to satisfy a judgment and for damages done by stray animals, a requirement that home lots must be settled if title to them was to be maintained, and prohibitions against the use of tobacco and trading by foreigners within Connecticut.

The development of government in Connecticut in the seventeenth and eighteenth centuries reflects the tension between two Puritan principles: that the fittest should rule and that rulers must be responsible to the people. Thus the system of nominations for office and the procedures for counting votes were gradually designed to favor the retention in office of incumbents, men of experience. Those exercising judicial powers at the highest levels were executives and legislators or were appointed by the latter from a relatively small pool of talent. Yet those who enjoyed even the highest offices had to undergo annual testing by the voters; and though Connecticut is noted for the relatively little change that occurred, the system did permit the voters to reject a long-term officeholder if they were so minded, as they were on occasion. Although what was said in legislative debate remained secret, the legislature itself was open to the humblest petitioner, and if he had good reason to seek exception to the laws or special consideration, he usually won a sympathetic, if prudent, response. The meanest wretch was entitled to minimal care at some level of government, every child was entitled to minimal education, and every citizen had recourse if dealt with unfairly by listers or other officials.

If government was responsive, it was nevertheless far from what we would call democratic. Connecticut and its neighbor Rhode Island were more nearly self-governing than any of the other colonies, for their governors were elected, not appointed by the king or a proprietor, and their laws were not routinely scrutinized by English officials for a possible royal veto. But as in other colonies only white males could vote, and voters were never allowed to forget that even elected officials were a class apart to whom deference was due. There is more to democracy, of course, than elections. One must consider class structure, social attitudes and pressures, and other matters—subjects for later discussion.

3

EXPANSION

The expansion of Connecticut is a story of the acquisition of jurisdiction over areas within the state's present bounds, as well as temporary control over areas now outside them, and a remarkable growth in population, arising more from natural increase than from heavy immigration. Starting from the nucleus of the three river towns, the colony expanded southward to the shore, then eastward and westward along it, later filling up the country back from the coast east and west of the Connecticut River. For a time in the seventeenth century the colony laid claim to towns on the eastern end of Long Island; and during the revolutionary period, Connecticut extended its jurisdictional sway to the Wyoming Valley in Pennsylvania.

The three towns comprising early Connecticut acquired their first additions with relative ease. In 1644 George Fenwick, who was the only settler of a group that had obtained a patent from the Earl of Warwick to establish a plantation at the mouth of the Connecticut River, sold to Connecticut the fort that he had constructed and the land adjacent to it (Saybrook). He even offered to sell all the land eastward to Narragansett Bay if he could demonstrate his right to do so. Although the sale proved to be without legal foundation, Connecticut exercised jurisdiction over Saybrook and would later claim the purchase from Fenwick as the basis for obtaining a charter. Soon after this purchase, Connecticut acquired, with the consent of the United Colonies, a settlement on the Pequot River (now Thames) that was made in 1646 by John Winthrop, Jr., under the authority of both Massachusetts Bay and Connecticut. These two colonies had conflicting claims to the Pequot country. Originally called "Faire Harbour," the Winthrop settlement eventually won approval from Connecticut authorities for the name New London.

In the 1640s Connecticut was expanding in other directions as well, westward along the coast to include the newly founded towns of Fairfield and Stratford, and later Norwalk, and across the Sound to Long Island, where Southampton and Easthampton were absorbed. Long Island had originally belonged to William Alexander, Earl of Stirling, by way of the New England Council. Connecticut and New Haven Colony acquired presumed legal rights there by foreclosure on a mortgage given by Stirling's agent after the Earl's death. The United Colonies encouraged Connecticut and New Haven to establish settlements, particularly to offset the Dutch, who were expanding to the island from Manhattan. Southampton and Easthampton preferred Connecticut's jurisdiction to New Haven's, as did Huntington and Setauket (Ashford or Brookhaven) in 1660 and 1666. When Connecticut received its charter, which included within the bounds of the colony the adjoining islands, Connecticut claimed the whole of Long Island "except a precedent right doth appear, approved by his majesty" and proceeded to name officers for all the towns, even those heretofore under Dutch jurisdiction. His majesty, of course, had meanwhile made Long Island part of the magnificent 1664 grant to the Duke of York.

The next step in the expansion of Connecticut's political jurisdiction was its absorption of the New Haven Colony, a step that New Haven leaders resisted bitterly. The New Haven Colony began with the founding of New Haven itself in 1638 by the Reverend John Davenport and Theophilus Eaton, merchant, friends of the grantees of the Earl of Warwick, who knew there was empty land west of Saybrook. They made arrangements to purchase land from the Indians, and each subsequent addition was acquired through such purchase either by them or associates or friends. The site of New Haven attracted them both because it was a natural harbor suitable for commerce and because Davenport and the members of his church who came from England with him were not satisfied that the religious atmosphere in Massachusetts was pure enough.

For its form of government New Haven adopted the scheme of the Reverend John Cotton, then under discussion in Massachusetts Bay. Cotton's scheme, called *Moses His Judicials* (1636), brought together the current practices of Massachusetts Bay with appropriate material from the Scriptures, particularly the Mosaic Code. At first only those settlements that obtained land grants directly from the town of New Haven were subject to its political jurisdiction and sent representatives to its General Court—Stamford, for example. Other towns like Guilford and Milford kept politically separate at first, thrown into the arms of New Haven only with the establishment of the United Colonies of New England in 1643, which promised a united front against the menace of Indians and the Dutch. Accepting New Haven's political control meant, of course, accepting its fundamental law with later modifications, and particularly the provision that one must be a member of an approved church to vote and to hold office, a requirement that did not sit well with many.

The leaders of New Haven Colony well knew that under English law they had no proper title to the area they claimed. Fearful that their friendship with the Warwick patentees gave little real security, they sought through an agent in 1644 to obtain a patent from Parliament, then under Puritan control. The enterprise failed because their agent was lost at sea. They took no further steps until the Restoration, except for trying unsuccessfully in 1651 to get a patent to lands on the Delaware River, where they were seeking to establish a colony.

The Restoration made their position even more precarious. In England powerful supporters of the colony had been executed, and as a Puritan colony, New Haven shared with others in New England the fear that the new king would deal harshly with outposts of his former enemies, especially those that lacked the legal support of a charter. New Haven had additional causes for concern: it had obstinately refused to cooperate with crown agents seeking to arrest regicides William Goffe and Edward Whalley, who were known to have taken refuge in that colony; and it had failed properly to acknowledge the restoration of Charles II to the throne. For a time New Haven considered seeking the protection of the Dutch, but New Netherland rejected terms that would have given the colony control over its own government and religious practices. In this crisis several of the colony's towns broke away to join with Connecticut—Guilford, Stamford, and Southold on Long Island —dissatisfaction with the franchise being part of the reason.

Up to this point, relations between Connecticut and New Haven had been generally amicable. The two shared a common fear of the Dutch and the Indians and supported each other's expansionist moves—Connecticut's into the Pequot territory, New Haven's into the Delaware River region. As often as not, they had jointly resisted the overbearing behavior of Massachusetts Bay within the confederation. But the need to obtain a patent from Charles II made them at once rivals, although on the surface they seemed to seek cooperation. New Haven wanted a single charter spelling out separate political jurisdictions, while Connecticut hoped to absorb the smaller colony. John Winthrop, Jr., governor of Connecticut and its agent at the London court, hoped that New Haven would voluntarily join Connecticut, and he disowned any plot to take over that colony through legal maneuver. But Hartford leaders exerted heavy pressure on New Haven to accept the inevitable, provoking men like Davenport to frustration and anger. In London Winthrop managed to block New Haven's separate bid for a charter, and in 1663 the disillusioned and annoyed New Haven leaders sought once again to reach an accommodation with the Dutch, who came around too late.

The boundary provisions of the charter granted to Connecticut in 1662 described its bounds as running from Narragansett Bay on the east to the South Sea on the west between the southern line of Massachusetts Bay and the Sound. The grant was ample enough to include the whole of New Haven Colony; and when Connecticut received a copy of this charter before Winthrop had finally worked out an agreement with Rhode Island's agent in London, Connecticut politicians tried at once to exert political jurisdiction not only over New Haven's towns, by naming officials and accepting oaths of allegiance, but also over the whole of Long Island. Under the leadership of Davenport and with the towns of New Haven, Milford, and Branford standing firm, the New Haven Colony voted to reject union with Connecticut until further consultation could be had among all parties.

A spur to agreement was the arrival in the colonies of a royal commission in 1664, which was to secure the submission of the Dutch and examine the affairs of New England. Now Massachusetts Bay added its voice to those urging that New Haven yield to Connecticut lest all New England suffer the unwelcome intervention of the king's commissioners. A united front was necessary to forestall any threat to New England's semiautonomy. The United Colonies, which met in September 1664, counseled the two colonies to reach an understanding, even though Connecticut protested the presence of representatives from New Haven, a colony allegedly no longer in separate existence. The United Colonies ignored its own charter, which required the body's formal consent to any such union, promising instead to recommend to the Massachusetts and

Plymouth governments acceptance of an altered membership for the confederation. In October 1664, the royal commissioners finally recognized
New Haven as part of Connecticut. In December the New Haven Colony
capitulated, Connecticut some time since having offered freemanship
and official positions to men in New Haven's towns. The town of New
Haven itself surrendered a few weeks later.

Connecticut's charter of 1662 put to rest two other disputes over terri-
tory, although one of these cropped up periodically to fray the nerves of
Connecticut's leaders. For some years after the conquest of the Pequots,
Connecticut and Massachusetts had disputed their share of the spoils, a
strip of territory running from the Niantic River to Weekapaug in present day Rhode Island. In the 1650s a division had been made at the
Mystic River, giving Massachusetts title to the area east of that river.
Here Massachusetts Bay established the colony of Southerton, which it
relinquished when Connecticut's charter set its eastern bound at Narragansett Bay.

More troublesome was the Duke of Hamilton's claim to all the land
from the Connecticut River to Narragansett Bay, running back from the
coast sixty miles. This was yet another grant from the Council of New
England. Made in 1635 to the Marquis of Hamilton and periodically
revived by his heirs, it overlapped, of course, the grant to Lord Saye and
Sele and his associates. Rejected by the English authorities in 1665, it
was revived in 1683, only to be rejected again in 1697 by the Board of
Trade. When Connecticut's charter came under scrutiny and attack in
the 1740s, the heirs of the Duke once again sought to resurrect the old
claim to no avail.

The rest of the present bounds of Connecticut had to be established by
long and nagging disputes with its neighbors: Massachusetts Bay, New
York, and Rhode Island. For those who lived at the time, agreement on
boundaries was of great importance. Once established, political jurisdiction affected the validity of land titles and could determine what taxes
landowners paid and whether quitrents would be imposed. The line between Connecticut and the Bay Colony had been run to the Connecticut
River in 1642 by Nathaniel Woodward and Solomon Saffery to the satisfaction of Massachusetts Bay, but there had been no formal acceptance of
this line by Connecticut. The old map in the Massachusetts Archives
shows the southern boundary running due west along 41° 55' of north
latitude. On its eastern end it crossed the "path from the Bay to

Providence," and it ended in the west at the Connecticut River at "Windsor fery place, the house of John Bissell being on the west side and the widow Gibbs her house on the east side of the river." In the years thereafter Connecticut had extended the bounds of Windsor northward (the original town lay on both sides of the Connecticut and comprised all the land north of Hartford) and west of Windsor had established the town of Simsbury. Massachusetts Bay had extended the bounds of Enfield (then including Somers) and Suffield southward so that the towns of the two colonies overlapped. Town grants of land to individual holders naturally provoked disputes. Connecticut in 1708 accused Enfield and Suffield men of seizing barrels of turpentine belonging to settlers in Windsor and Simsbury. In 1713, after protracted negotiations, Massachusetts Bay and Connecticut agreed to accept the old line to where it reached the Connecticut River and to run it westward from there, despite Connecticut's earlier complaint that Woodstock at the eastern end of the line ran too far south also. Connecticut was probably amenable to compromise because in this period the chartered colonies were coming under heavy attack in England; Connecticut preferred a settlement with her neighbor without stirring up the English authorities. Private soil rights were left intact, and political jurisdiction remained as it had been even though the line put some Massachusetts towns south of it.

The survey showed that Massachusetts Bay had granted over one hundred thousand acres more than it should have in the area belonging to Connecticut. To redress this wrong Connecticut received an equivalent amount of land within the bounds of western Massachusetts, although Connecticut alleged later that much of this equivalent actually lay in New Hampshire. Nevertheless Connecticut sold the equivalent land at auction for £683 in 1716. Compensation for past error did not end the matter, however.

In 1747, the towns of Woodstock, Suffield, Enfield, and Somers (created out of Enfield in 1734) petitioned the General Assembly of Connecticut to be put under that colony's jurisdiction, declaring that since they lay within Connecticut's charter bounds they were being denied their charter rights and that they had never given their assent to the arrangement of 1713. In all likelihood the real reason why the four towns sought to live under Connecticut's jurisdiction was that its taxes were lower than those of Massachusetts Bay. Connecticut's initial response was to seek the advice of three prominent New York lawyers, who questioned whether Connecticut could legally have ceded jurisdiction over territory belonging to it by the king's charter grant.

After a prudent interval, Connecticut in 1749 accepted the four towns on the ground that the agreement of 1713 had had no royal sanction, and it prepared to take its case to England if Massachusetts Bay refused to accept this decision. While each side was preparing its case for the king, Connecticut paid the expenses of a Woodstock man seized by a Worcester County sheriff, granted the usual privileges to the ecclesiastical societies of the border towns, and designated brands for the towns' livestock. Connecticut not only attacked the validity and even the honesty of the Woodward-Saffery line, but also asserted that the Connecticut commissioners had been imposed upon in 1713, and reiterated that jurisdictional right could be established by the king alone. The colony won a favorable judgment from the crown in 1755, when the four border towns became part of Connecticut.

The two other protracted boundary disputes, those with New York and Rhode Island, grew out of the Connecticut charter. Connecticut had hardly secured its sea-to-sea grant when England undertook the subjection of New Netherland, sending over the already mentioned royal commission for the purpose. With conquest of the Dutch holdings went the handsome grant to the brother of Charles II, the Duke of York—all the territory between the Delaware and the Connecticut rivers and between the Kennebec and the St. Croix, as well as Long Island and other islands. Obviously, imperfect understanding of geography had sliced away a good part of Connecticut's bounds, and the colony had to reach some understanding with the Duke if it was to flourish.

After several false starts, Connecticut reached an agreement with New York in 1683 on how the boundary line ought to be run, but the actual survey and agreement upon the results took years of frustrating maneuvering. Generally speaking, the line was to run twenty miles east of the Hudson River, but in the southwest corner the agreed-upon division brought Connecticut much closer to the Hudson than twenty miles, and an equivalent along Connecticut's western border had to be offered. This strip, which was only a little over one and three-quarters miles wide and comprised 61,440 acres, was called the Oblong. Laying out the southwestern boundary precisely and surveying the Oblong was a quarrelsome business, Connecticut having to appeal to the king more than once to persuade New York to act jointly with her in the survey. When it stood to gain, Connecticut was quite ready to appeal to the Crown; other times it found it convenient to say that mutual agreements should be sufficient. In any case, appeals to England were risky because Connecticut feared attacks upon its charter and the consequent loss of her virtual freedom from British control. All surveys were finally completed in 1731, when the Oblong was formally ceded to New York, although controversy continued long afterwards.

The disputes with Rhode Island arising out of charter boundaries were but a continuation of long-standing quarrels. Neither Connecticut nor Massachusetts Bay had ever respected the boundaries claimed by Rhode Island. That colony was a pariah in New England, considered wrong-headed in its religious toleration and unfit to join with the other colonies in their defensive league. The statement in the charter of Connecticut that its eastern bounds ran to Narragansett Bay would have reduced Rhode Island to unviable size; only the alertness and negotiating skill of John Clarke, Rhode Island's agent in London, saved the colony from being almost swallowed up.

When John Winthrop, Jr., sailed for England to obtain Connecticut's charter, he carried with him the high hopes of a speculative company, of which he was a member, that Connecticut's boundaries might be so described as to assure the safety of its investment in lands claimed by Rhode Island. At the start legality might have seemed to rest with Rhode Island, for it had obtained a patent from Parliament in 1644, and Connecticut had only the Fenwick purchase based upon the Warwick patent. At stake were four hundred square miles—the southwestern one third of modern Rhode Island. This area was known as the Narragansett country, and it was claimed by the Atherton Company.

Humphrey Atherton and his partners—Winthrop was at first a passive one, but he paid for his share—purchased from the Indians in 1659 that portion of the Narragansett country lying twelve miles along the western side of the Bay, part of it known as Boston Neck; it was good upland pasture land. Several months earlier, Rhode Island, like all the New England colonies, had decreed that purchases from the Indians had to have prior approval from the authorities, but Atherton called his tract a gift, ignoring Rhode Island's charges of fraud. This land grab whetted appetites for more. In 1660, the United Colonies laid the blame for disturbances in eastern Connecticut and on Long Island on the Narragansett Indians and assessed a fine of 595 fathoms of wampum, a princely

sum, payable to Connecticut within four months and secured by a mortgage of the Narragansett country to the United Colonies. Posing as a
friend of the hard-pressed Indians, Atherton came forward and paid the
wampum to Connecticut on condition the mortgage be transferred to his
company. When the Indians could not redeem the mortgage in the
allotted time of six months, Atherton foreclosed. The entire Narragansett country now belonged to the Atherton Company, which was determined to have a more sympathetic government under which to live.
What better one than Connecticut, whose perennial governor was an
Atherton partner?

In London, Winthrop secured approval of his colony's charter with its
generous boundaries before Rhode Island's agent was aware of what was
going on. But aware at last, Clarke had the charter recalled until he had
wormed from Winthrop a formally sanctioned agreement between them
that Narragansett Bay, the eastern boundary of Connecticut, was really
the name of Pawcatuck River. This fiction would secure to Rhode Island
its traditional western boundary, one named in its patent of 1644.
Winthrop managed to insist, however, that no property owners were to
be disturbed in their titles and that the Narragansett proprietors specifically might claim the jurisdiction of Connecticut if they chose. This
was in April 1663. Although the authorities were skeptical that the
boundaries were settled, the agreement freed the Connecticut charter
and helped ease the Rhode Island charter through official toils. The latter, however, named the Pawcatuck River, the Connecticut charter notwithstanding, and omitted any mention of proprietors' rights. Here
were all the ingredients of future squabbles.

Because London authorities were uneasy with these arrangements,
Winthrop had been pressured to accept the idea of a royal commission
that would, among its many tasks, make alterations in boundaries if
it thought them necessary, alterations to be binding on both colonies.
The instructions of the commissioners reminded one and all that Winthrop had promised "the same submission to any alteration . . . as if no
Charter were then passed to them."* But this maneuver reckoned
without the intransigence of Connecticut, which had received the patent
from Winthrop before the other two copies in London had been recalled.
In the colony's view, Winthrop's commission as agent had ended the

---

* British Museum, Egerton MSS, 2395, f. 393.

moment the charter passed the seals, and thus he could enter into no binding agreement with John Clarke. Within a few months of this very agreement, Connecticut upon application from inhabitants on Narragansett Bay appointed selectmen and a constable for them and named their settlement Wickford.

When the royal commissioners arrived in New England to consider a variety of problems, they finally took up the boundary dispute between Connecticut and Rhode Island. Before leaving England, they had been instructed by the Earl of Clarendon, Lord Chancellor, to assert the king's claim to the Narragansett country. The basis for this claim was that in 1644 the Narragansett Indians had been persuaded to submit to royal protection. When the King's Province was created, Connecticut refused to recognize it on the technicality that the chief of the commissioners had not been present when they announced its creation in March 1665. In Connecticut's eyes, her writ still ran to the Bay.

Despite Connecticut's stubborn attitude, it saw dangers in its course, for it might provoke further English meddling and a consequent reexamination of the charter. Thus Connecticut entered into negotiations with Rhode Island at various times after 1664, though without being able to reach agreement. During King Philip's War many Rhode Island settlers moved out of the Narragansett country because their government, under Quaker influence, did not afford adequate protection. Connecticut people took the opportunity to move in, and the Atherton Company called for a shift in jurisdiction from Rhode Island to Connecticut.

During the period of the Dominion of New England, Sir Edmund Andros took Rhode Island's side in the dispute, but his regime did not last long enough to effect a settlement, and in 1697 the English government began to review the whole matter. This stirring of interest prodded the two colonies to resume talks, with Connecticut taking the line that no agreement should affect any man's property, as Winthrop had agreed with Clarke so many years before. Mention of this agreement probably signified that Connecticut was willing to discuss a boundary at the Pawcatuck River. In fact, the agreement reached by the two colonies in 1703 settled upon the middle channel of that river as the boundary, to be followed till the point where the Ashaway River emptied into the Pawcatuck. From there the line was to run to the southwest corner of Warwick's grand purchase and then due north to the Massachusetts line.

Winthrop's original agreement had called for following the Pawcatuck to its source and then north, which line would have deprived Rhode Island of a considerable part of its present territory. Thus Connecticut had made a genuine concession.

Agreement on a line was one thing; running it was another. Connecticut appointed a committee to do so in 1714, only to suspend any further action a few months later. Rhode Island appointed a committee in 1719 for the purpose, only to meet frustration once again, and the matter ended up in England yet another time. In 1723, the Board of Trade, noting the great length of time the dispute had gone on, recommended that Connecticut and Rhode Island voluntarily submit themselves to the government and be annexed to the royal province of New Hampshire. The surrendering of charter rights, to say nothing of the impracticality of the solution, stimulated the two colonies into further efforts in 1724 and again in 1726. In the latter year a committee of the Privy Council in its report approved the line agreed upon in 1703, the king and Council endorsing its report. The line was accepted by the colonies, and the running of it was completed in 1728.

Outside of the present limits of the state, Connecticut claimed the northern one-third of Pennsylvania on the grounds of the sea-to-sea clause in its charter, which antedated the charter of William Penn by nineteen years. In this instance, the territorial claim was initiated not by the government, however, but by private land speculators, who had organized themselves in 1753 as the Susquehannah Company without benefit of the colony's sanction. The initiators included some of the substantial men in the eastern part of the colony like Eliphalet Dyer, Jedidiah Elderkin, and Jabez Fitch. Attracting many others throughout the colony, as well as some subscribers from New York, the company in 1754 clandestinely and illegally purchased from some sachems of the Six Nations a tract of land in Pennsylvania lying between the latitudes of Connecticut and running 120 miles in width, its eastern boundary being a line roughly paralleling the eastern branch of the Susquehanna River but lying ten miles east of it. Similar purchases were made shortly thereafter by the First and the Second Delaware companies, their grants lying along the Delaware River. These purchases came at a time when the General Assembly had received a number of petitions complaining of the lack of land within Connecticut for growing families and calling upon the assembly to make grants out of its ample sea-to-sea extent.

To all these pleas for grants or for recognition of purchases made from the Indians the assembly turned a deaf ear for nearly two decades. In official reports Connecticut had mentioned that her western border was the New York line, and the assembly saw no sense in claiming more. But the pressure continued to mount, particularly from the Susquehannah Company, until the western lands became a key political issue in the colony. At last, in 1771, the colony adopted the claim so long urged upon it and began the necessary legal moves to validate it. At the outbreak of the Revolution the matter was before the Privy Council for decision; but when the colonies broke away from Great Britain, the forum for judging between Connecticut and Pennsylvania became the Continental Congress. This story continued for many years, embroiling thousands of people in a succession of legal maneuvers and in outright violence. Full settlement of the dispute was not achieved until the first decade of the nineteenth century.

Despite Connecticut's tardy recognition of her claim to western lands, the organized land companies made plans to establish settlements along the Delaware River and in the Wyoming Valley region, site of the modern city of Wilkes-Barre. Delayed by the outbreak of the French and Indian War and then by the Proclamation of 1763, actual settlement did not begin until 1769. The Pennsylvania proprietors protested this invasion of their domain, looking upon the charter granted to William Penn in 1691 as perfectly valid and citing the illegality of the Connecticut speculators' purchase from the Indians. Since compromise was rejected by both sides, each being convinced of its own essential rightness, force became the only answer. The first "Pennamite War" was fought sporadically between 1769 and 1771, with the Susquehannah Company settlers managing to gain a permanent foothold when they drove out the Pennamites. Constant pleas from the settlers finally brought the Connecticut General Assembly to organize the town of Westmoreland in 1774, which ran from the Delaware River to a north-south line fifteen miles west of Wilkes-Barre. This gargantuan town was given all the privileges of a Connecticut town, which it proceeded to exercise by sending delegates to the legislature. In 1776, the General Assembly made Westmoreland into a county with the usual complement of officials and courts. All during the revolutionary fighting, Westmoreland functioned as a Connecticut county, raising militia and contributing companies to the Connecticut line. Loss of political jurisdiction did not come until 1782, when a special court set up by the Congress of the Confederation decided in favor of Pennsylvania, but disputes continued long after that even though no reversal of jurisdiction was ever secured.

*   *   *

Extension of Connecticut's political jurisdiction by purchase, merger, and boundary settlements is, of course, only part of the story of the colony's expansion; the other part is the peopling of the land and the decisions determining how it should be parceled out to towns, individuals, and families.

Englishmen recognized that the soil belonged to the Indians and that justice required some means of legitimately acquiring title. At the same time, Englishmen never doubted their right to enter upon the country and to trade with the people they found there; the rights of trade were internationally recognized. The simplest procedure was to buy land from Indian leaders in the confident belief they could dispose of lands for their tribes. Usually sachems were willing to sell, partly because they did not fully understand the Englishman's notion of passing a land title and partly because they wished to cultivate the friendship of people who could be powerful allies against their Indian enemies. When some Indians proved hostile, either because they resented the imposition of English laws or the air of superiority Englishmen affected, or because, more practically, they saw dangers in the encroachment of ever increasing numbers of Englishmen, open warfare between the two races offered another way to secure title to the land—by right of conquest. In this way Connecticut acquired title to the Pequot territory. In either case, conquest or purchase, it was the colony that obtained the title, at least ideally. Connecticut, like other New England colonies, very early forbade private citizens to acquire title to Indian lands by purchase; later, the General Assembly permitted such acquisition only with its prior approval. The records make it abundantly clear, however, that many private purchasers ignored these strictures.

Officially, land obtained from the Indians and not yet granted by the General Assembly belonged to the colony and was intended for those in need of it. Given its Puritan background, Connecticut granted most of its lands, at least in the beginning, to groups of people intending to found new towns. The very maintenance of civilization depended upon the creation of communities that could provide the churches and the schools necessary for orderly, sober lives on earth and salvation after death. Puritans feared the lone wolf, the isolated settler unable to attend church or to educate his children to read the commands of Gods for themselves. Thus, empty land, Puritans felt, should be settled by whole groups of families starting out together and under the vigilant eyes of the authorities. And for good measure, there was a practical as well as a religious motive: communities could better defend the frontiers than isolated settlers. In 1704, for example, the General Assembly named seven frontier towns that could not be broken up without its permission. Individuals who deserted would forfeit their estates in such townships.

New towns came into being in various ways. Usually the initiative came from a group that wanted to remove itself to a new area because of beckoning opportunity. In 1650, the General Court permitted a group from Hartford to plant a town at "Norwaake" on condition that sufficient numbers went and that they provided for their own defense, divided their lands justly, and paid their fair share of the public charges. More frequently the move was neither too far away nor to an exposed location. Inhabitants of Guilford and Killingworth were permitted to start a new plantation at Cockinchaug (Durham), to cite just one instance. Frequently new towns came into being by a process like cell division: some of the inhabitants who were separated from the others by a geographic feature might petition for creation of a new town. Thus Canterbury was created out of Plainfield and Mansfield out of Windham in 1703, the dividing line in each case being a river. But always the General Assembly had to be reassured that there were sufficient numbers to start a viable town. Preston, however, came into being because settlement of the boundary lines of New London and Norwich left inhabitants there outside any town.

By law, boundaries between towns had to be marked by heaps of stones or ditches dug six feet long by two-and-one-half feet wide and of "ordinary" depth. Or sometimes specified trees were named as markers. Despite the praise that has been accorded the New England colonies for careful prior survey of lands intended for settlement, the casualness with which bounds were described after survey produced many disputes over lines of division between towns. Connecticut records offer many examples of towns hotly contesting their boundaries and appealing to the General Court for settlement of their disputes. Even the annual perambulation of bounds that the law required the selectmen or their agents to perform each year to renew the markings did not eliminate intertown quarrels. Where a man's lands lay could make a real difference in his taxes and the church he had to attend. Lines presumably settled once were sometimes challenged many years later, often to the annoyance of the General Assembly.

Sometimes the initiative for starting new towns came from men with speculative interests, or from the General Assembly itself, which was glad to see the land divided up and settled, for unimproved land paid no taxes. In 1697, to take just one of many examples, a group of ten petitioned for permission to purchase a tract from the Indians with a view to starting a town. In such a case, an assembly committee usually approved the suitability of the tract before the project went ahead, and a committee oversaw disposal of the lands to settlers afterward. Those who initiated the development got compensation from those who came to settle—perhaps double the cost of purchase from the Indians as well as compensation for surveying and laying out lots. The assembly itself acted when it learned of ungranted lands that were suitable for towns, again naming a committee to undertake the work of investigation, purchase from the Indians, surveying, and the like. Such committees were paid for their efforts just as private developers were, although they might receive their compensation from the first taxes raised by the town.

Until the early eighteenth century the General Assembly probably saw itself as accommodating the wishes of those who wanted new homes and more land, colony revenues benefiting indirectly from the enlarged tax base. But by the second decade of the century, the assembly began to sell land to produce revenue directly. In 1715, the assembly required proprietors of two townships claiming land from the Indians to pay the colony for quitclaim deeds. In 1718, the legislature directed that the lands in Stafford be sold to provide money for a statehouse at Hartford, and the next year ungranted lands north of Voluntown were added to that town and sold to promote the same purpose. The biggest sale came in 1737, when the colony auctioned off the northwest townships, seven in all. Yet even when the assembly was seeking direct revenue, it did not lose sight of the purposes of community building.

At auctions, there was no guaranteed group that planned to migrate to a new location, but the assembly laid down conditions designed to assure the maintenance of community life: the auction townships were to be divided into fifty-three rights (in one smaller township into only twenty-five), three of which were to be reserved for public purposes—for the first settled minister, for the ministry in perpetuity, and for a school. The remaining rights were to be auctioned to individuals who would settle and stay for at least three years, build houses of a minimum size, and fence at least six acres of land, on pain of forfeiture of their right for failure to meet these conditions. Each successful bidder had to post a bond for double his purchase price to insure performance. Moreover, the auctions themselves were held in different towns in successive months to allow as many as possible to participate and to discourage the monopolizing of this opportunity by a few.

Comparison of this Connecticut land auction with a similar one in Massachusetts in 1762 is instructive. The latter laid down conditions of sale for nine townships plus a large tract, reserving three rights for public purposes and requiring the building of houses and the improving of land within a specified time. But Massachusetts disposed of all its townships on a single day in Boston, and whole townships, not rights, were offered to bidders. The upshot was that about three dozen men acquired these lands, assuming the obligation to settle sixty families in each township within five years. Failure to fulfill the conditions meant forfeiture not of individual rights, as in Connecticut, but of a whole township. Laxness in enforcing the forfeiture provision—and there was some in Connecticut but more in Massachusetts—meant in the former case an unoccupied homestead here and there; in the latter, it could mean townships half or three-quarters empty.

In the interest of viable communities, Connecticut very early adopted the principle that a right must be settled by either the owner or a substitute if it was to be maintained. Hartford adopted the principle in 1635, and the Code of 1650 presumably required that a home lot be built on within twelve months, although the law may not have been part of the original code. In the 1670s, forfeiture provisions were decreed for the towns of Woodbury and Simsbury, and between 1708 and 1719, the General Assembly in seven separate instances provided time limits ranging from three to five years, in all cases stipulating fines or forfeitures (sometimes both) for noncompliance by individual holders of rights in townships.

Forfeiture provisions curbed but did not stop speculation in land. Those who purchased rights in a township could and did sell their rights to others, and a right might be sold several times over before the time limit for settlement expired. After the time had elapsed, rights might remain unimproved, for enforcement of the law was never perfect. Even in the earliest years, time limits were sometimes ignored with impunity, but the forfeiture provision was not an empty gesture. The assembly took back a tract of land west of Coventry and Tolland that had been acquired by legatees of the Indian Joshua on sufferance of the assembly because they had not settled it "to the mind of" the legislators. The principle of having to settle a right to maintain it was carried over into the Susquehannah Company territory, where the requirement brought some Pennsylvania people to support the intruding Yankees against Pennsylvania speculators who were interested merely in engrossing the land.

Although Connecticut emphasized creating thriving communities, the assembly also made grants and sales of land to individuals—tracts, extensive though some were, generally not large enough to sustain a town. These were perhaps inconsistent with the important settling principle, but they were made for a variety of reasons and with the unspoken assumption that some day they would be part of a town. In the beginning, since land was abundant, it was natural to reward important public officials for services rendered. Thus the assembly made grants in gratitude to Captain John Mason and to governors John Haynes, John Winthrop, Jr., and Gurdon Saltonstall. The latter recieved the largest single grant—2,000 acres—in 1714; Haynes obtained 1,000. Mason and Winthrop acquired several grants apiece, totaling well over 1,000 acres for each. Members of the legislature were rewarded with 200- and 300-acre plots from time to time, and the assembly used empty lands to compensate soldiers for their service in Indian wars and occasionally persons suffering from various afflictions.

All such grants were made on condition that they not conflict with other grants or impede the establishment of a new town. Before land actually passed into the recipient's hands, the assembly had to order someone to lay out the tract; and after that, it might be several years before the survey was actually made. Thus John Bishop obtained a grant for 200 acres of land in 1674, and six years passed before the assembly ordered a survey. The tract was actually surveyed in 1684. Bishop's case was not at all unusual. A grant made to a man might very well be laid out for his heir, a son, or even a grandson. A grant made in 1673 to Alexander Bryant was finally surveyed for his grandson in 1714. A grant from the assembly could pass from one person to another several times before the actual survey, so that a right to land became negotiable. Such delays sometimes meant that when the assembly had specified the particular area of the grant, compensation had to be offered elsewhere because in the meantime a town had been founded and all shares disposed of.

Such land grants to individuals were made chiefly in the seventeenth century. In the late 1680s when Connecticut was fearful for its charter—the Massachusetts charter was voided in 1684—and worried about the new administrative arrangements planned for New England by the king, the assembly granted land wholesale to get it into private hands lest ungranted lands be claimed by the king's agents. In January 1687, the assembly granted to the towns of Hartford, Windsor, Wethersfield, Middletown, Farmington, and Killingworth all the vacant lands between the Connecticut and Housatonic rivers. The intention of the assembly was that these towns should hold this land until further direction was given for its disposal; the legislature did not intend to lose control over it. Many years later, in 1719, when permission was given to plant the town of Litchfield, the assembly specifically reserved the land around it for future disposal. But Hartford and Windsor people took the position that the grant of 1687 had been bona fide and insisted upon settling towns in the western country. Ultimately the assembly gave up its right to the eastern portion of this ungranted land, and Hartford and Windsor each laid out four towns in their areas.

The desire to transfer land to private hands may also account for assembly approval in the 1680s of other large grants. In 1686, it approved without the usual conditions an eight-mile-square tract of land along the Connecticut River given by a Niantic Indian to six well-known men, four of them members of the legislature at the time of the approval. At the same time the assembly granted a patent to a group of proprietors who wanted to start a town in an area north of Norwich in a large tract Captain James Fitch had obtained from the Indian sachem Oweneco two years before. Fitch, one of the biggest seventeenth-century speculators, was one of the petitioners and an assistant at the time. No mention was made of his having received prior approval for obtaining Indian land nor of the exact conditions of settlement that should prevail. The southeast corner of the patented tract went to an Englishman, John Blackwell, his holding comprising 5,750 acres, which was confirmed by the assembly in 1687. Blackwell's son sold it to Jonathan Belcher in 1713. Because it continued to remain unsettled, the assembly added it to the town of Pomfret in 1752. In May 1687, the assembly granted to Governor Robert Treat all the land north of Milford twelve miles from the sea. All these grants were out of character and were made in a moment of panic.

In the eighteenth century outright grants became fewer as sales became the pattern, but, even so, favoritism is apparent. In 1720, the assembly sold 16,000 acres for £510 current money to eight men, all but one of them members of the legislature at the time of the sale. The land was used to establish the plantation called Willington.

*   *   *

Within the towns the actual parceling out of lands to individuals reveals several interesting and significant patterns. The closest student of Connecticut town planning, Anthony Garvan, has discerned three modes of laying out towns. The earliest was the village with a single center. Modest-sized home lots were laid out along a central street on which the meetinghouse and the minister's home were also situated. This plan comported with Puritan notions of a close-knit community of neighbors under the constant scrutiny of the minister and the authorities, but Garvan, arguing that Irish colonization was well known to many Englishmen, sees the model for it in Ulster. Planting fields were laid out around this center and roads built to provide access to these fields. The village might practice an open-field system, in which the planting fields were worked in common during the cropping season even though each man owned a designated plot. Norwalk, an example of this type of village, only very slowly divided up its common lands; the total going to individuals was relatively small with each division. Norwalk made twenty-four divisions to parcel out some 14,000 acres, only about half the town's total acreage. One man in Norwalk who participated in every dividend got only a total of 300 acres.*

A contrasting pattern of land division was that of Fairfield. This town, a center of trade, rather rapidly parceled out its common lands into individual holdings with no disposition to try to maintain an open-field

---

* Erna F. Green, "The Public Land System of Norwalk, Connecticut, 1654–1704: A Structural Analysis of Economic and Political Relationships" (unpublished M.A. thesis, University of Bridgeport, 1972).

system. There was also active trading of lands within the town to consolidate holdings. Fairfield seemed to lack the community sense that Norwalk strove to maintain. Fairfield people were individualistic, up and doing. Rarely did this town grant lands to those acquiring property and settling after the original founding, but in Norwalk newcomers were permitted to share in land dividends. In neither case, of course, could late arrivals settle without town permission, as decreed by Connecticut.*

The earliest towns laid out their planting fields in long narrow strips, the allotments of an individual being scattered to give everyone a fair share in the best and poorest lands. Most historians have thought that this method of allotment was essentially medieval in origin, but Garvan has noted that American strips were much longer than the traditional furlong—in Wethersfield three miles long, in Fairfield, ten miles long. The model, he feels, is to be found in the fens stretching southwest from Boston in Lincolnshire, where the drained land was parceled out to proprietors in large amounts.

In early typical settlement the first division of land held in common would be followed at intervals by a second, third, and so on, until eventually the entire township had passed into the hands of individual holders. Norwalk probably was slower than many towns in that it made so many divisions, each yielding to the holder a relatively small amount of land—as little as eight acres in outlying fields. In fifty years Norwalk still had nearly half of its common acreage. Most seventeenth-century towns were completely divided by 1700, Windsor being an outstanding exception in not proceeding to a general division until 1726. The method of division was usually by lot, the area to be divided having been surveyed and the allotments numbered. Those eligible then drew corresponding numbers. Towns varied as to whether all shared alike or whether distinctions were made according to taxes paid, size of family, and other factors.

Obviously a farmer who had scattered strips of land would spend a good part of his time traveling to and from his home lot and his holdings. In time, some found it more convenient to move closer to the land they were working and to sell off their holding in the town's center, where

---

* Joan Ballen, "Fairfield, Connecticut, 1661–1691: A Demographic Study of the Economic, Political, and Social Life of a New England Community" (unpublished M.A. thesis, University of Bridgeport, 1970).

land prices had risen. Thus the centralized village tended to break down and with it the original Puritan conception of a single close-knit and supervised community for each town. As more families moved to the fringes and found themselves an inconvenient distance from the church and the school, they sought to organize themselves as separate ecclesiastical societies with their own church and school. The loss of tax revenue to the town's center caused resentment of such separations, so that appeal to the General Assembly had to be made officially to allow the formation of new societies. What began, then, as a centralized village might wind up as a town with several separate centers. This change did not necessarily destroy community spirit as such but created several foci of such spirit.

In the later seventeenth century some new towns started out with more than one center. Windham, for example, laid out in 1686, had three centers almost from the start—one at Pond Town and one at Willimantic, as well as the present center of Windham. In such towns the home lots ran much larger than two to four acres: in Windham, thirty-one acres; in Woodstock, from ten to thirty acres; in Lebanon, up to forty-two acres. The meaning of these changes is that from the first the farms tended to be isolated because of the difficulties of cutting and maintaining the needed roads.

With large home lots went larger divisions of the land. In the eighteenth century the general divisions subsequent to the first tended to be so large that complete division occurred in a few years. In Kent, for example, the proprietors in two years divided among themselves 32,000 acres of good land. The ultimate, of course, was complete division of a whole township before settlement. Voluntown, created to reward veterans, was carved up into 150 farms in 1706 with no provision indicated for future divisions or even for roads—a far cry from the centralized village with its scattered strips of land.

Further evidence that considerations other than establishing a close-knit community affected town planning in the eighteenth century is furnished by the action Hartford and Windsor took in the western towns reluctantly granted to them by the assembly in 1726. Large home lots were laid out, the land in each town was completely divided at the start, and no provision was made for public purposes. The idea was quick sale to investors for speculative profit with no thought given to the need for roads or for future land use of actual inhabitants. These results in a sense were an aberration; because of circumstances, the assembly had lost control of the situation. As we have seen, when in 1737 the assembly ordered the auctioning off of the northwest townships, it insisted upon division of the land into rights and the reservation of three of them for public purposes. The assembly was trying to maintain the pattern of the centralized village and all that this implied for the maintenance of community. Even where the original grants were large and land was surveyed not in strips but in polygons in the modern manner, so that plots and roads were accommodated to the contours of the land, the auction towns generally managed to retain their centers and kept their population from being too widely scattered. These towns grew more rapidly in population than the Hartford and Windsor towns because their provision for ministers and schools made them attractive.

Not all the land parceled out in the towns was by general division. From the first, towns made grants to individuals as encouragement to keep a ferry, establish a mill, or open a smithy. Such grants might be a hundred or two hundred acres; much smaller grants of two or three acres might be given for support to a poor person for a limited time. These grants were made by the town when there was no distinction between town inhabitants and proprietors of the land. Towns were at first considered corporations, and those officially admitted as inhabitants, that is, those who could vote in local elections, determined grants and divisions and shared in the latter. Yet in English law it was highly irregular for the towns to have been given this power. The colony, itself a corporation, could not under common law create subcorporations.

When Connecticut began to have fears about its charter in the 1680s, it decided to vest the ungranted lands in the towns in proprietors, that is, the admitted inhabitants as of that date.* The ungranted lands now belonged to a fixed group, and the rights of an individual in this group could be sold or passed to an heir. While newcomers to the town might obtain the status of admitted inhabitants, they would no longer have an automatic share in the undivided land. Over time, the inhabitants and the proprietors would become two separate entities. Eventually the as-

---

* Apparently some towns, like Hartford, had a separate group of proprietors before the colonial government acted. See Richard L. Bushman, *From Puritan to Yankee: Character and the Standing Order in Connecticut, 1690–1765* (Cambridge, Mass.: Harvard University Press, 1967), pp. 42–46, esp. p. 43, note 8.

sembly gave specific identity to the proprietary group, allowing it to hold separate meetings, to tax itself, and in all ways to see to the management of its common lands. Yet some towns clung to their old ways, dividing land by vote of the town meeting, in which, of course, proprietors could participate. In 1723, the General Assembly validated such land divisions even though they had occurred after the act that had vested ungranted lands in proprietors only. At the same time the assembly gave full validity to proprietors' meetings, and where they functioned, no mere inhabitant could claim land without their consent.

Vesting proprietary rights in a fixed group and permitting sale or inheritance of such rights made possible absentee proprietorship. A proprietor no longer had to live in the town where he held his right, although Connecticut law did require him to provide a substitute settler if he lived elsewhere. Absenteeism, of course, would be an additional threat to the sense of community that the colony tried to promote. How serious a threat was it? Grant's study of Kent suggests that absentees were no serious problem. Typically they were men who held only a relatively small part of the acreage of the town, and in their social position they formed no elite group antagonistic to the actual settlers. Many absentees were relatives or neighbors of Kent settlers, living in nearby towns. Most of those not in this category were small investors, living at some distance, but seen as customers of Kent settlers rather than exploiters. The most active speculators lived in Kent, not outside it. Richard Bushman has accepted the judgment that absentees in Connecticut posed no danger. The critical difference between Connecticut and Massachusetts Bay, where absentees were rightfully accused of impeding settlement, was that Connecticut auctioned rights, rather than whole townships, and required settlement on a homestead to maintain a proprietary right.

Still, the records reveal many instances of complaint about absentees, usually in the form of a petition to the assembly to allow taxation of their unimproved lands, for without such taxation towns complained that they could not support the ministry. In 1719, the assembly had given constables blanket authority to collect colony taxes and other rates from owners of property within their towns who lived elsewhere; but the taxing of property not appearing in the lists compiled each year, that is, unimproved land, required special permission from the legislature. One of the most common problems was failure to pay taxes by proprietors who had not yet settled in the town. They took full advantage of the grace period allowed before settlement had to take place if a right was to be maintained. Thus complaint about delinquent absentees came from Windham in 1694, Coventry and Durham in 1712, Newtown in 1714, Bolton in 1720, and Salisbury in 1741. All of these complaints came relatively soon after settlement of the town.

Only a few towns long after they had been founded complained about nonresidents. New Milford, which was granted town privileges in 1712, petitioned to tax the unimproved lands of nonresidents in 1753 in order to build a meetinghouse. Other such petitions came from "Hartford towns," like Hartland and Winchester, where no time limit had been established for settlement to maintain a right. Additional petitions to tax nonresidents came from ecclesiastical societies in towns where more than one such society existed, and here it is difficult to tell whether the absentees lived in the town but not within the society's limits or whether they lived outside the town entirely. A law of 1735 explained the obligations of such absentees. If they lived in the town and also had lands within the bounds of an ecclesiastical society to which they did not belong, but had no tenants there, they were to pay their taxes on such lands to the society within whose bounds they lived. If there were tenants, the owner had to pay taxes to the society within whose bounds the lands were located. Absentees also had to pay taxes on property within an ecclesiastical society's bounds if they lived in some town other than the one in which the society was located. Frequently, the assembly upon being petitioned allowed an ecclesiastical society to tax the unimproved lands of residents and nonresidents alike, but in a number of instances action was aimed solely at nonresidents, permitting taxation on unimproved or improved lands, or sometimes both.

At any rate, nonresidents who shirked their obligations do not seem to have threatened any town's existence, as happened in western Massachusetts. In 1738, a law required nonresidents with an interest in common fields to appoint agents to act in their behalf in maintaining fences; noncompliance left the nonresidents liable for charges from the fenceviewer. In one or two instances when nonresidents lived outside the colony and beyond the reach of local courts, the assembly authorized leasing of the lands of delinquents in lieu of tax money. Taxation of unimproved lands and of nonresidents became less of a problem as the colony filled up.

By 1774, the estimated white population was 191,392, that of nonwhites, 6,464, a figure that is too large by 16 according to the figures for each county. Growth to this figure was neither spectacular nor steady. In population, Connecticut remained one of the smallest of the original colonies, but it had a high density of population per square mile, a fact that accounts for much of the migration from Connecticut into Massachusetts Bay, Vermont, New Hampshire, New York, and Pennsylvania. The colony grew at a rather steady rate from 1640 to 1700, an average gain per year of 408 persons. But between 1700 and 1710 the average increase rose to 1,348, and between 1710 and 1720, jumped to 1,938. Then the rate of growth declined between 1720 and 1740, only to spurt ahead again in the period 1740 to 1750 and again in the two subsequent decades.* The greatest increases in population, then, occurred between 1700 and 1720 and between 1740 and 1770. Connecticut's population, apart from blacks and Indians, was homogeneous. There were few Irish and Scots and no French, Germans, or Dutch to speak of. Most of the immigration into Connecticut was from Massachusetts Bay, so that the overwhelming predominance of the English was little disturbed. Blacks remained under 3 percent of the total population throughout the colonial period.

---

* *Historical Statistics of the United States, Colonial Times to 1957* (Washington, D.C.: U. S. Government Printing Office, 1960), p. 756.

4

CONNECTICUT AND NEW ENGLAND

Although much of the energies of colonial Connecticut were absorbed in meeting the demands of growth—regulating the economy, parceling out lands, and establishing institutions—the colony played its role on a larger stage as well. It joined with its neighbors in discussion and deed to promote the common welfare, to settle disputes, to present a united front against enemies, although not always successfully; and it took into account the larger requirements of the empire by accommodating itself, to, though occasionally challenging, the wishes and rulings of the home authorities and by joining with other colonies to protect the empire against its enemies. It acted, as all states do, out of its perception of self-interest, but with an admixture of loyalty, too, that induced it at times to strain its resources to the limit in serving its sovereign. But Connecticut's loyalty was that of a people ever mindful of their rights, rights enshrined in the colony's charter and beyond the tampering of any parliament or king.

*   *   *

Outside its bounds, Connecticut expected to promote the same good order as it sought within; consequently, its closest associations were with the Puritan colonies that followed the right way—with Massachusetts Bay, Plymouth, and New Haven. Rhode Island, unorthodox in religion, was the pariah of them all.

The efforts of the Puritan colonies to form a closer union for defense and for mutual support in other ways has been mentioned earlier. In

1638, the conflicting jurisdictional claims of Connecticut and Massachusetts Bay to Springfield and their differences over the powers that any confederation should have prevented the formation of a union. Connecticut particularly feared giving binding powers to the majority of any confederation's commissioners. Still, in August 1639, the Connecticut General Court directed the governor, John Haynes, to write to Governor Winthrop of Massachusetts Bay stating Connecticut's continuing interest in a confederation, "a firme combinacion for a defencive and offencive warr." Apparently nothing came of Haynes's letter to the Bay. The next initiative came from Massachusetts, which in 1642 appointed a committee that stood ready to meet with representatives from any of the other three Puritan colonies, but Massachusetts Bay laid down the condition that it would take no part in an offensive war unless its legislature assented. The colonies agreed to confederate on the terms set, and the United Colonies of New England came into being in 1643.

Although Massachusetts reserved the right to judgment in the case of offensive wars, the Articles of Confederation remained ambiguous on the point. The second article mentioned a "firme and perpetuall league of Friendship and amytie for offence and defence, mutuall advice and succour upon all just occasions," but no definition of *just occasions* was attempted, nor were any means described to determine them. Yet the sixth and ninth articles seemed to leave all power respecting war and peace in the hands of the eight commissioners, six to be sufficient to reach a binding decision. This vagueness about where ultimate power lay would some years later drive a wedge between Massachusetts Bay and the other colonies.

The confederation, of course, was not solely designed for war but was meant to settle disputes among its members as well as to advance their common interests in religion and other matters. Connecticut and Massachusetts Bay divided sharply in the early years of the confederation over two issues: the validity of Connecticut's right to tax goods coming down the river from Springfield and proper division of the lands conquered from the Pequot Indians.

In 1645 Connecticut levied a tax on grain, biscuit, and beaver skins shipped on the river, the revenue to be used for maintaining a fort at Saybrook and meeting the payments owed to George Fenwick for the purchase agreed to in 1644 (Chapter 3). William Pynchon of Springfield, who had thrown in his lot with Massachusetts Bay, and whose allegiance had been accepted, refused to pay such taxes despite Connecticut's argument that the fort was a benefit to Springfield as much as to the Connecticut towns. In 1647, the question came before the commissioners. The line the Massachusetts commissioners took was that Springfield should not have to pay for the Fenwick purchase, that it derived no benefit from the fort, that Connecticut could not of its own volition tax settlements outside its jurisdiction, and that Springfield had been unfairly singled out, for Connecticut made no attempt to tax the goods of New Haven or Plymouth, which could also be said to enjoy benefits from the fort if Springfield did. The arguments of Massachusetts Bay, however, did not prevail. The commissioners of Plymouth and New Haven insisted that Connecticut's action was legitimate, although they cautioned that the levies were not to be perpetual and that the question should be reviewed a year later.

When Massachusetts Bay reopened the dispute in 1648, it reiterated the belief that Springfield derived no more benefit from the fort than did untaxed New Haven, but, more than that, its commissioners asserted that Massachusetts Bay would not "yealde up any Lawefull Liberty god hath given us to the will and discresion of others." The Massachusetts commissioners then accused Connecticut of blocking cooperative action in the confederation and sought to throw that colony off balance by demanding to see the Connecticut patent. These tactics were meant only to be a cover for the determination of Massachusetts Bay, the largest and most powerful of the confederates, not to be overruled by the lesser members in any matter it deemed vital to its interests. Springfield was a part of the Bay Colony; it was intolerable that any outside government should presume to tax its trade. But in 1648 Massachusetts Bay argued in vain; the other commissioners reiterated their support for Connecticut, insisting that Springfield enjoyed a greater and different benefit from the fort than did New Haven. Moreover, a question was raised about the southern boundary of Massachusetts Bay and whether Springfield was truly within that colony's bounds.

The next year Massachusetts Bay imposed a retaliatory tax on goods entering Boston harbor from any of the confederated colonies, noting that the vote of the commissioners the preceding year had ignored the destruction of the Saybrook fort by fire, which obviated any justification for taxation. In 1650, Connecticut apparently stopped collecting the duties, for Massachusetts Bay repealed its retaliatory tax in the belief that Connecticut had yielded. The episode was more than just a petty quarrel;

it was a test of the cohesiveness of the United Colonies. The Massachusetts interpretation of the binding character of confederation decisions was not pursued at the time, but the meaning of the covenant remained unresolved and would come up again when Massachusetts Bay felt threatened.

At the root of the controversy were the conflicting claims of the two colonies over which had contributed most to the defeat of the Pequots. Connecticut's position that its role in the war was the major one and that it had purchased the land from George Fenwick caused it to refuse to recognize any right of Massachusetts Bay to conquered Pequot territory. When John Winthrop, Jr., founder of the settlement that became New London, pleaded in 1646 for a ruling from the commissioners of the United Colonies, they divided the disputed territory at the Pequot River, all land west of it, including Winthrop's settlement, going to Connecticut and all east of it, to Massachusetts Bay. Despite this ruling, Connecticut within a few years was encouraging settlement on the Pawcatuck River, well within the area recognized by the commissioners as belonging to the Bay Colony, which protested in 1658. A new division then set the dividing line at the Mystic River. When Connecticut was disappointed by the rulings of the United Colonies, it did as other members did, bided its time and interpreted confederation decisions to suit its own interest. Within a few years Connecticut won its entire claim by a different route. The charter of 1662 set its eastern boundary at Narragansett Bay.

In the matter of defense against enemies, the United Colonies allied themselves against the Indians and Dutch. What they feared most was cooperation between the two that might drive the Puritans from their lands. The Dutch and the English, of course, were rivals in trade with the Indians and stoutly defended, verbally at least, overlapping claims to territory. More particularly, the Dutch claimed priority in the Hartford area and were not at all satisfied with the thirty acres that Connecticut people were willing to acknowledge as theirs, nor was the situation eased by Massachusetts's urging Connecticut to grant an additional amount. Another locus of dispute was Long Island, where both Connecticut and the New Haven Colony established towns in defiance of Dutch claims. The Dutch even looked upon that stretch of coast on the mainland settled by New Haven people as part of New Netherland. When that colony expanded westward to the region of Derby, the Dutch threatened force, claiming the new settlement would be within a few miles of the Hudson. The New Haven Colony clashed with the Dutch on the Delaware as well, where the Dutch saw New Haven's attempts to establish a trading post as an outrageous intrusion into an area already preempted.

Aside from conflicting territorial claims, another source of grievance for the English was the willingness of the Dutch, and the French for that matter, to sell arms and ammunition to the Indians. Almost from the beginning Connecticut had forbade the sale of arms as a safety measure, and the United Colonies applied the prohibition to traders in all its member colonies. Dutch officials from time to time denied that such sales were being made and occasionally made a show of confiscating arms from greedy Indian traders willing to get their furs at any price. Dutch law, like English law, forbade sales, but policing was another matter. In English eyes the Dutch were willing not only to arm Indians but also to urge them on in hostilities against the English. Underlying these fears, of course, was sharp trading rivalry. The English resented, furthermore, impositions laid on English ships trading at, or merely passing by, Manhattan.

Finally, after many a charge and countercharge of greed, bad faith, and downright lying, the United Colonies and the Dutch in 1650 signed a treaty at Hartford designed to establish boundaries and ease grievances. The heavily outnumbered Dutch were in no position to spurn compromise, nor could they hope for settlement of differences through diplomacy in Europe, for England was too distracted by internal trouble to pay much attention to Dutch overtures. As for the New England colonists, they had nothing to lose by attempting peaceful resolution of long-standing quarrels. The Dutch governor, Peter Stuyvesant, was moved to action by threat of reprisals against Dutch traders and seizure of guns and ammunition. After tedious negotiations, the treaty signed at Hartford set boundaries for Long Island and the mainland and confirmed Dutch holdings in the Hartford area. Both sides agreed to return fugitives from justice. But no resolution of New Haven's claim to trade in the Delaware region nor settlement of other vexing problems was effected.

Thus the treaty only laid the groundwork for future altercations. Charges of collusion between Indians and the Dutch filled the minutes of the meetings of the United Colonies. By May 1653, the commissioners were considering what apportionment of troops among the four colonies would be equitable if God called upon them to declare war on the Dutch.

As matters got more serious, Massachusetts Bay drew back, calling into question the right of the commissioners on their own to declare an offensive war. In September, despite the interpretation Massachusetts Bay had given the Articles of Confederation, the commissioners conceived themselves called by God to make war on Ninigret, the eastern Niantic sachem, and they apportioned troop quotas for the purpose. A few days later, on the initiative of New Haven, the six commissioners declared they had "just grounds of a warr against the Dutch." The action of New Haven, backed strongly by Connecticut and less enthusiastically by Plymouth, nearly destroyed the United Colonies; and Connecticut seemed willing enough to consider going it alone, without Massachusetts Bay. The latter was accused of breaking the covenant, but its firm refusal to furnish its quota of troops for any offensive war, since it had to supply by far the largest number, hamstrung any action by the confederation. The crisis was eased only because the war between England and the Netherlands, which had broken out in 1652, ended in 1654, but not before Connecticut had seized the Dutch trading post on the Connecticut River. In September of that year, the danger past, Massachusetts acknowledged the power of the commissioners to determine the justness of all wars.

The greatest crisis faced by the confederation, of course, was King Philip's War, which broke out in 1675. Connecticut suffered less in this war than did its neighbors, but its contribution was significant.* Although Connecticut troops sustained their greatest casualties in Narragansett country, the colony's chief theater of action, apart from raiding forays, was western Massachusetts, for the Connecticut Valley offered a natural invasion route into the colony's heart. Thus a pattern of defense was established that Connecticut resorted to later, time and again, during the French wars—sending troops northward to aid Massachusetts towns. In the early stages of the war Connecticut favored a cautious approach to Indian negotiations, critical at times of what it regarded as the too rigid and rigorous methods of Massachusetts negotiators. But when fighting broke out, Connecticut wanted vigorous offensive action; it resented guard duty for Connecticut troops in Massachusetts neigh-

---

* Connecticut's role in King Philip's War has been described in Douglas Edward Leach, *Flintlock and Tomahawk: New England in King Philip's War* (New York: Macmillan, 1958).

borhoods. If guard duty was their function, they might better do it in their hometowns. Connecticut's fixed notions about the conduct of the war were to be a source of severe disagreement within the United Colonies, reducing the effectiveness of that body at a time of the gravest peril.

In a sense, Connecticut had become obligated as early as 1671 to fight against Philip, leader of the Wampanoags, if he broke his word to the Plymouth colony, for Connecticut had sent commissioners to the meeting at which the treaty between the Indian leader and Plymouth had been signed. When war did come, Connecticut interests were involved for other reasons as well, for there was a question whether the Narragansett and Mohegan Indians, themselves bitter enemies, would support Philip or not. The Mohegans were a sizable force within Connecticut itself, of course, and the Narragansetts were in a position to ravage Connecticut's sparsely settled and defensively weak eastern frontier. When Uncas, the Mohegan sachem, declared for the English, it was almost certain that the Narragansetts would take Philip's side. But during the period of uncertainty, Connecticut favored the most careful and unprovoking discussions with the Narragansetts, and it was annoyed by Massachusetts's willingness to resort to force unless the Narragansetts gave a firm pledge of neutrality and signified their willingness to turn over to the English any Wampanoags they captured. Connecticut pressed for delay in the talks, and ultimately Massachusetts Bay accepted the pledge of the Narragansetts despite their supposed insolence and devious ways.

Connecticut's commitment to moderation had another cause besides the weakness of its eastern frontier. At about the time negotiations were going on with the Narragansetts, Sir Edmund Andros, governor of New York, was trying to assert the claim of his master, the Duke of York, to a large part of Connecticut territory. Since the Duke's patent gave him the land between the Delaware and the Connecticut rivers, Andros was laying claim to Connecticut shore towns and even to Hartford itself. Andros chose this moment of impending Indian warfare to appear at the mouth of the Connecticut River with two sloops carrying armed men. Happily, the fort at Saybrook was well manned with men being readied for possible trouble to the eastward, and in the ensuing confrontation Andros, after some blustering, decided to back down. All during King Philip's War, however, Connecticut remained ever mindful of the threat from New York, and the antagonism between the two governments prevented any cooperation from that quarter as the war intensified.

Within a few weeks of the outbreak of hostilities, Connecticut sent a force under Major John Talcott up the river valley to search for Wampanoags who had escaped from their home ground on Mount Hope Peninsula to seek the support of the Nipmucks of Massachusetts Bay. Here again, Connecticut stressed moderation for fear that any other course would needlessly turn the river Indians against the English. It soon became apparent that the Nipmucks would join Philip and that the river tribes could not be trusted, however peaceful their past relations with whites. For the Indians, the war had become one of survival in the face of the stifling spread of white civilization.

To meet the growing danger, the commissioners of the United Colonies assigned troop quotas—among them, 315 for Connecticut. Of these, two hundred were to form part of a western army, first under the command of Major John Pynchon and then under Major Samuel Appleton. Major Robert Treat of Connecticut served as second in command. Treat successfully evacuated the people of Northfield after one attempt made earlier by Massachusetts men had failed, and he aided in the defeat of Indians who had ambushed people evacuating Deerfield. But Treat found himself helpless on the wrong side of the Connecticut River when Indians put the torch to Springfield in October of 1675. As the weeks wore on, uneasiness grew in Connecticut that prolonged operations of its militiamen in western Massachusetts were leaving the colony poorly defended despite the Connecticut government's order that at least one quarter of the militia was to do guard duty in Connecticut towns every day and to patrol the roads between towns to guard against surprise attacks. Mutterers began to say that Massachusetts Bay was not furnishing its proper proportion of troops and that it had unnecessarily antagonized the river Indians.

These complaints, official and unofficial, affected cooperation in the field and produced quarrels in the meetings of the United Colonies. The commissioners had issued orders that no troops were to leave an assigned area except upon their direct command or that of a council of officers; but when rumor spread that hostile Indians were lurking in the vicinity of Hartford and Wethersfield, Major Treat marched back to Connecticut with sixty of his men. Moreover, Treat countermanded an order of his superior that would have sent remaining Connecticut men off on a mission; Treat wanted them kept within reach. Massachusetts charged before the confederation that Connecticut was damaging the war effort by such behavior. Somewhat later, Treat, once again back in western Massachusetts, requested Major Appleton's permission to return to his colony, for he was convinced that the Indians, no longer discoverable in the upper Connecticut Valley, were moving southward. When Appleton rejected Treat's request, Treat challenged the validity of Appleton's commission as commander, saying it had not been ratified by the commissioners of the United Colonies. By mid-November the Connecticut General Court was notifying Appleton that if Connecticut troops were kept in garrisons, they would initiate their own maneuvers.

Friction within the confederation and in the field over command responsibilities was not the only source of trouble. In the fall of 1675, Connecticut had clamped controls on the export of grain and breadstuffs and refused the appeals of Massachusetts Bay for more food. All three colonies, of course, faced food shortages because men had been drawn from the fields at a critical time. Massachusetts merchants were even prevented from removing Connecticut supplies they had purchased before the embargo and kept in warehouses. When the matter came before the confederation, Bay Colony commissioners pointed out that their colony was having to import food from as far away as Bermuda in order to supply troops, but not until May 1676 did Connecticut ease its restrictions in response to its neighbor's importunities. Connecticut was also accused of violating the purposes of the confederation when its lone commissioner, Governor John Winthrop, refused to act for his colony until he was joined by a second commissioner. At stake was action to be taken against the Narragansetts for failing to live up to agreements reached earlier.

Despite the delay that Governor Winthrop forced upon his fellows, Connecticut did join the expedition of 1,000 men into Narragansett country in December 1675, Robert Treat serving as second in command under Governor Josiah Winslow of Plymouth. Connecticut furnished 300 troops and 150 Indian allies. Connecticut more than the other two colonies consistently used friendly Indians in support without the racial animosity that afflicted so many Massachusetts people, who came to see virtually all Indians as enemies. The Connecticut contingent was much delayed in getting to the rendezvous point on the western shore of Narragansett Bay, and this delay was an important factor in the hardship and limited success of the campaign against the Narragansetts. The high point was the Great Swamp Fight, in which the English attacked a fortified position in the middle of a swamp. Nearly one-half the Connecticut forces suffered casualties, far more than those of Massachusetts and Plymouth. In mid-January 1676 the Connecticut men were allowed to return to their colony for recuperation.

Very reluctantly did Connecticut raise men and furnish supplies for a second strike at the Narragansetts, who were escaping to Nipmuck country in central and western Massachusetts. The assigned quota of 315 men was declared too high in view of the losses the colony had recently sustained. As it was, Governor Winslow's second effort failed to engage the enemy, and his army was disbanded. In February 1676, Connecticut sent fresh troops for a new joint force under Major Thomas Savage, once again Major Treat leading the men to the rendezvous point at Brookfield, Massachusetts. Although Treat's men, aided by a Massachusetts company, held off an Indian attack on Northampton in March, the spring campaign was generally a failure. Quarreling over the numbers of men each colony furnished (Plymouth had sent none) caused the army to break up, Connecticut withdrawing its troops when Major Savage took most of his back to Boston.

Connecticut did not participate in joint operations again until the summer of 1676, but its soldiers were not idle. When Indians returned to Narragansett country seeking food, the colony made a number of forays in that direction, the men encouraged by the government's willingness to let them keep what they could plunder from the parties of Indians. One such excursion, led by Captain George Denison, captured the important Narragansett leader, Canonchet, who was executed at Stonington by Indians on their own demand. Connecticut sought to promote peace by trying to arrange a conference with the Indians at Hadley, Massachusetts, where Indian grievances were promised a hearing. The colony failed to understand that survival, not grievances, was at issue. The Indians replied to Connecticut's invitation, but no conference ever met.

In June 1676, under the command of Major John Talcott, Connecticut sent 440 men including Indians to rendezvous with Massachusetts troops at Hadley; Connecticut forces already there brought Talcott's command to over 500 effectives. While he awaited the arrival of Massachusetts forces, Talcott easily beat off an Indian attack on the town. When combined forces finally moved northward, they found no Indians, and Talcott returned to Connecticut with his men. Soon he was leading sweeps into Narragansett country, where he and his men killed and captured well over 200 Narragansetts. Obviously the heart had gone out of the Indian uprising, and as increasing numbers of Indians surrendered, the colonies had to decide what to do with them. Those deemed guilty of encouraging the war and of inflicting inhuman cruelties on its victims were put to death. Among the three colonies, Connecticut was alone in forbidding the sale of other Indians into foreign slavery. Instead, the colony sentenced captives to ten years of domestic servitude if they were sixteen or over at the end of that term; those under sixteen served until age twenty-six. After service they were free to work for themselves, presumably putting to use whatever skills they had acquired. Indians who ran away from service, however, could upon capture be sold abroad.

Although none of Connecticut's towns was destroyed during King Philip's War, the financial costs to the colony were high, estimated by one historian at a total of eleven pence on the pound in three years.* The war virtually destroyed the effectiveness of the United Colonies, since the three members had been unable to put aside suspicion and a selfish outlook. Although Connecticut certainly must carry a full share of the blame for promoting dissension and for consulting its own interests at the expense of others, it was not alone in intransigence. Massachusetts Bay and Plymouth also were stubborn and uncooperative. None of the three readily yielded its sovereignty in matters it deemed crucial.

*   *   *

The period immediately after King Philip's War, when New England lay in weakened condition, presented itself to the English Crown as an ideal moment to bring to heel the most important and obstreperous of the New England colonies—Massachusetts Bay. This colony was thought to be seeking virtual independence and violating the Acts of Trade and Navigation in wholesale fashion. The move to exert greater imperial control over the colonies had begun soon after Charles II ascended the throne in 1660, but attempts faltered through the ineptness of royal agents, renewed war with the Dutch, and internal troubles in England. Moreover, Massachusetts Bay took advantage of circumstances. It be-

---

* Benjamin Trumbull, *A Complete History of Connecticut, Civil and Ecclesiastical . . . to the Year 1764*, 2 vols. (New Haven, 1818), vol. 1, p. 351.

came adept at finding excuses to avoid giving an account of itself before the Privy Council. Thus despite stepped-up efforts after 1676, the Bay Colony managed to delay any legal process that threatened its charter. But the will of the imperialists was not to be denied. In 1684 the charter of Massachusetts Bay was revoked.

Although Connecticut was not directly concerned in this struggle between the Crown and its neighbor, it could not help feeling that the stubbornness of Massachusetts Bay would encourage a hostile mood in England toward all chartered colonies. Success in voiding one charter would lead to actions against others. And Connecticut assessed the situation correctly. A king who was determined to exert his prerogative in many different directions at home would not abide autonomy in the colonies. Just before his death Charles II discussed with others what sort of government the colonies should have. The upshot, under James II, was the Dominion of New England, first conceived as a consolidation of Massachusetts Bay, New Hampshire, and Maine, later expanded to include Plymouth, Rhode Island, and Connecticut; and, later still, New York and New Jersey.

On orders of the Lords of Trade, Edward Randolph, who earlier had been appointed Collector of Customs for all New England, in July 1685 prepared articles on which to base a *quo warranto* proceeding against the Rhode Island and Connecticut charters. Against Connecticut, he alleged violation of the laws of England, citing laws affecting capital punishment, forbidding sale of lands and houses without town consent, and affecting the conduct of jury trials and the performance of marriage ceremonies. He also pointed out that fines were appropriated by the colony, that oaths of fidelity were administered by the colony without also requiring the oath of supremacy and allegiance, and that members of the Anglican church were not given freedom of worship.

The writ of *quo warranto* had already lapsed when Randolph brought it to Connecticut for an answer, and Connecticut began a waiting game, refusing to be joined to the consolidated government without being pushed into it by the king. In fact, Connecticut leaders were divided on how the colony ought to proceed. Council members for the most part favored accepting the inevitable, confident that they would have positions of some dignity in the new government. James Fitch, himself a councilor but supported by a group in the lower house, successfully urged delay in submitting, the ostensible reason being that the colony

awaited word from the king. Actually Connecticut was in a good position to hold off, for it made no secret of its possibly joining with New
York, whose governor, Thomas Dongan, was offering generous terms for
a merger—minimal taxation, freedom of religion, and continued use of
Connecticut ports for clearances. If it could not keep its independence,
Connecticut really preferred to join Massachusetts Bay, but it played
along with Dongan. As long as he urged upon the Lords of Trade the
necessity for New York to be enlarged, Connecticut could keep free of too
much pressure from Sir Edmund Andros, governor of the dominion.
When Connecticut finally wrote to the lords that it preferred Massachusetts Bay to New York, the message was taken as an act of submission,
and Andros was told to take over the colony. He assumed control on
October 31, 1687, without, however, Connecticut's surrendering its
charter. Legend has it, of course, that it was hidden in the Charter Oak.*

Governor Andros soon appointed Robert Treat, who ceased to be governor of Connecticut, colonel of the militia in New Haven County and
gave him, former colony secretary John Allyn, and former councilor
Nathan Gold commissions as judges of common pleas in Connecticut
counties. Treat and Allyn also served as members of Andros's council, as
did Fitz-John Winthrop, son of the former governor, who technically
represented the Narragansett country, although his home was in New
London. Thus the old pattern of prominent men holding several offices
continued, and the inclusion of Connecticut in the dominion was hardly
a wrench in the careers of those at the top.

But the laws of the dominion as applied to Connecticut did promise
some significant changes. For example, selectmen, or townsmen, were to
be ineligible for reelection after two years in office, and their terms were
so staggered that one-half the total number in each town was to be newly
chosen each year. Moreover, in future, town meetings were to be held
only once a year for the sole purpose of electing local officials; any other
purpose was unlawful. Obviously direct participation by the voters in
decision making was decreed ended. And in the act for "settling the

---

* There is no contemporary narrative of this event, and the official records are silent
about it. Benjamin Trumbull was the first to tell the Charter Oak story, and he probably
obtained it from the Wyllys family. Thus a legend was born. See Albert C. Bates, "Expedition of Sir Edmund Andros to Connecticut in 1687," American Antiquarian Society,
Proceedings 48 (1938):289–90.

militia" no mention was made of the men's right to elect their company officers; instead, officers were named by Andros, who might or might not follow local advice in making his appointments. Exemptions from militia service continued to be multifarious, but the dominion law made some interesting changes, most notably the exemption of one servant for each member of the Council. On the other hand, Negroes and Indians were not named as exempt, as they had been since 1660 under Connecticut law. Perhaps most important, inclusion in the dominion meant that all laws favoring the approved churches were done away with, leaving all Protestant churches on the same footing; this condition threatened to undermine the whole basis of the Connecticut colony as leaders had conceived it, for it meant the end of tax support for Congregational churches. With the repeal of all colonial laws, tax support terminated for schools, too, potentially a severe blow to the Puritan concept of education.

In practical terms, however, the impact of the dominion upon Connecticut was minimal. When, in the wake of the Glorious Revolution in England, Massachusetts Bay revolted in the spring of 1689 and imprisoned Governor Andros, it was an easy matter for Connecticut to resume its old ways pending word from the new king. The manner of the resumption of the charter disturbed some people nonetheless, for there was a dispute over whether to call for new elections or whether simply to restore to power those who had been in office when Andros took over the colony. James Fitch, land speculator and leader of a popular faction that challenged the conservatives in the Council who had too readily accepted inclusion in the dominion, wanted elections in May that might sweep the traditional leaders from office. Gershom Bulkeley, a justice of the peace under Andros, issued a tract in 1692 entitled "Will and Doom," opposing resumption of the charter by any method that did not recognize the legality of the Andros government. Bulkeley criticized both Connecticut's Glorious Revolution and its interpretation of its charter and asserted that several votes had to be taken and the freemen manipulated before the old leaders were returned to power. Bulkeley and several others persisted in their belief that until the king moved positively, Connecticut's government was illegal.

But in May 1689, the reinstated government of Connecticut blandly stated that "wheras this Court hath been interupted in the management of the Government in this Colony of Connecticutt, for neer eighteen

months past, and our lawes and courts have been disused," all the laws
and the machinery for justice were to be reestablished "that there may be
no damage accrue to the pub[lic] hereby." The General Court continued
all militia officers and provided for nominations by the men to fill va-
cancies; it then proceeded to name justices of the peace for those towns
that were not already well provided for by having assistants living in
them.

Despite this apparent confidence that resuming charter ways was legal, a measure of doubt remained. Increase Mather, agent for Massachusetts in England, obtained opinions from the attorney general and the
solicitor general that Connecticut's charter had never been surrendered
and was therefore still valid and its privileges intact, but misgivings
remained. A letter to Connecticut from King William dated March 3,
1693, was addressed to "such as for our time being, take care for preserving the peace, and administering the laws in our colony of Connecticut"
—hardly royal recognition that the colony was lawfully operating under
its charter. Matters came to a head in the fall of 1693, when Governor
Benjamin Fletcher of New York sought to execute his royal commission
to take control over the militia of Connecticut, a clear violation of charter
rights as Connecticut leaders saw it. Before Fletcher even arrived in Connecticut from New York to inspect the militia, the General Court had
polled the towns to see whether they were willing to support the costs of
an appeal to the Crown to continue their charter rights and, with them,
control over the militia. Earlier the Privy Council, in the interest of a
unified command during King William's War, had given Sir William
Phips command of the entire militia of New England, but Connecticut
had refused to recognize the validity of Phips's commission without a
direct order from the Crown. Now here was Governor Fletcher with a
new commission that threatened Connecticut's integrity. The people
voted overwhelmingly to appeal to England; and when Fletcher tried to
read his commission, the assembled militia drummers, on direct orders,
drowned out Fletcher's voice with their drum beating.

Fitz-John Winthrop was named agent to proceed to England with
Connecticut's petition for recognition of its charter liberties and
privileges and especially of its right to control its militia. Connecticut
took the line that its militia was quite different from the militia described in acts of Parliament under which the king had issued the commission to Fletcher. In Connecticut all males between 16 and 60 were,

with certain exceptions, automatically members of the militia, but in England membership was tied to specified property qualifications. Thus the king's militia and Connecticut's were two different organizations. Control of Connecticut's militia according to the charter lay with that colony's duly constituted government. This argument, lubricated by an expense fund of some £1,000 that Winthrop had at his command, was persuasive with the king in Council. His majesty contented himself with assigning to Connecticut a quota of 120 men who were to be under the command of New York's governor—a reasonable quota Connecticut was perfectly willing to accept. Thus the period of uncertainty ended; Connecticut's charter and its liberties had successfully survived the Dominion of New England, and Connecticut continued to operate under its charter until 1818.

5

THE ECONOMY

In Connecticut, as in other mainland colonies, over 90 percent of the people were engaged in agriculture, but scarcity of capital and labor along with inadequate transportation kept most farmers at the subsistence level of production. For most of the colonial period only those farmers who lived sufficiently near navigable rivers to make carting feasible were readily able to send surpluses to towns and ports. The consequence of widespread subsistence farming was low per capita income and limited demand for manufactured goods. The narrow market, in turn, discouraged domestic industry from reaching the point at which economies of scale could be achieved. Since colonial manufacturers could not gain satisfactory profits by large-scale production of items on which the individual profit was small, they could not compete in most products with British manufacturers. These conditions were only intensified by high labor costs and lack of adequate development capital. Of course, some agricultural surpluses were produced, significant trade was carried on, and domestic manufacturing did exist, but the condition of agriculture in general largely explains the colony's relatively slow economic growth.

* * *

Connecticut had three important navigable rivers, none of them permitting carriage into the interior as far as greater rivers to the west and south, like the Hudson, Delaware, or James. The Connecticut River was navigable for some fifty miles from the mouth—to Hartford—by small vessels of no more than eighty to one hundred tons capacity. Somewhat larger ships could move up the river as far as Middletown. Shoals and sandbars at the mouth made navigation difficult for the largest ships, and in 1772 the General Assembly agreed to permit a lottery to raise money for buoys marking the channel. The Housatonic River in western Connecticut was navigable for twelve miles to Derby, and the Thames River in the eastern part of the colony was navigable for fourteen miles to Norwich. Of course these and other rivers could be used for floating rafts; and timber products could be floated where ships could not travel.

But rivers could be a hindrance as well as an aid to transportation and communication. Ferries across large streams and bridges over small ones had to be maintained if people were to travel overland very far. Very early the General Court assumed the power to authorize and regulate ferries, setting rates for men and animals and establishing hours and conditions of operation. A ferry over the Connecticut at Windsor was authorized as early as 1649, and by the eighteenth century many were in operation. The convenience of the public was always the first consideration. Where bridges would serve, the General Assembly saw to it that towns built and maintained them. If two towns separated by a river could not agree to build a bridge, any citizen could bring suit in court to compel the selectmen to do their duty. The court would then order a survey made and empower the selectmen to raise the money by an appropriate tax. Failure to comply could bring court-imposed fines. If a bridge was washed away, that the town was poor was insufficient excuse for not building another.

As noted earlier, the first roads built were laid out within the town—a main street and secondary roads to allow farmers to get to their outlying fields. If a town neglected a farmer, an appeal to the General Assembly might compel a town to lay out a road so that he could get from his farm to the center. In 1638, the government gave the first order to lay out a highway from Hartford to Windsor and soon thereafter stipulated that able-bodied men and sufficient teams should be called out by surveyors of highways to work at least one day in the year to keep highways fit for use. The Code of 1650 increased compulsory service to two days, and by 1674 the assembly defined the able-bodied to include those between sixteen and sixty years of age. Throughout the colonial period, compulsory work on the highways remained an obligation, which a man could escape only by paying a fine so that a substitute could be hired. It was the obligation of each town to oversee the condition of intertown highways within its own borders. Still, the work was often neglected, at least in the early days, "the ways being incumbred with dirty slowes, bushes, trees, and stones, etc." Neglect was encouraged by the small fines imposed for missing work, so the assembly stiffened the fines and remonstrated with the delinquent towns. Those who encroached upon the highways also had to be reprimanded and warned off, being assessed damages for non-compliance.

Public transportation over these highways began as early as 1717, when Captain John Munson of New Haven started a wagon service for both passengers and goods between that town and Hartford. For the monopoly he was granted over this route, the assembly required him to make at least one trip per month except during the winter. By the pre-revolutionary period, regular stage routes were established, and postal service had improved over the fortnightly trips of post riders of the early eighteenth century. Still, overland travel remained hazardous and slow.

*   *   *

Except where settlers found meadows along rivers, as did the settlers of the first three towns in Connecticut, land had to be cleared to be worked. The Indians had regularly burned underbrush to open up planting areas, but such cleared land was insufficient for the more numerous whites. They had to resort to the back-breaking work of clearing forested lands, using a method learned from the Indians. To allow needed sunshine to penetrate the thick forest cover they girdled trees to kill them, making their first plantings among the naked trunks. Later they felled the dead trees, burning branches and using the timber for firewood and fences. Grubbing out the stumps was a long and painful process. In Connecticut, as elsewhere in New England, the fields yielded each year their crop of stones, heaved to the surface by frosts, from which farmers in the eighteenth century constructed stone fences to mark off planting and pasture fields. Fences were also made of poles and split rails.

The most important early crop grown was Indian corn, which the General Court made legal tender as early as 1641. Also mentioned in the first records are wheat, rye, and peas. The government provided encouragement for the growth of hemp and flax, and, for a time, even tobacco, by assessing users of the latter a fine if they imported it instead of using that locally grown. By 1745 Connecticut was sending tobacco to the West Indies and to Boston and exporting large quantities of flaxseed, much of it to New York for transshipment to Ireland. Oats and barley also find mention in the records; but apart from onions, of which there were "great quantities raised," root vegetables like carrots, potatoes, and turnips found little favor as crops for export. Potatoes, introduced early in the eighteenth century, became a favorite for domestic consumption. Fruit was used chiefly for making cider and brandy, the former a common drink with meals. According to the contemporary historian Samuel Peters, the watery part of fermented fruit juice was separated from the alcoholic part by freezing, the latter then being colored with corn and stored in vessels for three months. He declared that the finished product tasted so much like Madeira wine that Europeans could not tell the difference, no doubt the exaggerated claim of a local booster. "They make peachy and perry, grape, cherry, and currant wines, and good beer of pumpkin, molasses, bran of wheat, spruce, and malt."

Peters asserted that the pumpkin was "held very sacred in New England." Its seeds, boiled to a jelly, were a remedy for strangury, and its meat was used for not only beer but also "bread, custards, sauce, molasses, vinegar, and . . . pies." The shell served as a lantern, and, placed on the head, as a guide for cutting hair, if Peters is not pulling the reader's leg. In each corn hillock it was customary to plant, besides the five kernels of corn, two pumpkin seeds, and between the hillocks, beans—a pattern of planting learned from the Indians. But Englishmen by the 1670s were using the plow to run furrows at right angles to form the corn hillocks instead of using only hoes as did the Indians.

The tools of the farmers remained about what they had been for centuries: plow, hoe, harrow, scythe, sickle, and flail. Reliable information about crop yields is difficult to find. On fair soil, twenty to twenty-five bushels an acre was about the average yield for corn, although Peters claims from thirty to forty bushels on hilly land and from forty to sixty on level. For wheat, perhaps an average yield was fifteen to twenty bushels, although here again Peters claims yields of twenty to thirty bushels. In Connecticut, wheat was grown on only the most fertile soils and virtually disappeared from the older towns with the passage of time. All New England suffered from wheat "blast," or black stem rust, which first appeared in Connecticut in the 1660s. This disease was increasingly destructive with repeated plantings of wheat in the same ground. Rye yields were ten to fifteen bushels per acre. Constant cropping reduced yields of all grains, and poor methods of husbandry generally took their toll. Farmers paid insufficient attention to fertilization or rotation of crops, allowed the quality of seed to decline, had little concern for the best times to plant and harvest, and hoed inadequately. Indeed, seed and methods used were well below the best European practices of the time. Pioneer reformers like Jared Eliot tried to promote change by advocating the use of lime, planting of clover, and reclamation of salt marshes, but such advocates got little attention from ordinary farmers.

As with crops, so with livestock. Animals were poorly housed and fed, partly because that had been English practice and partly because the early settlers, at least, had to pay first attention to their own survival. Yet Connecticut towns paid some attention to selection of the best sires for cattle and sheep, and the legislature required that undersized horses be gelded. Surviving cattle tended to be hardy though smaller than English cattle, but hogs ran larger because of the natural abundance of food for which they could forage. Connecticut early encouraged the raising of sheep for wool, and although the sheep never attained the quality of English animals, Connecticut was notable in the colonies for its flocks. The legislature even authorized meetings of sheep owners, who could choose a clerk and make regulations for managing their animals. Still, the eighteenth century did not see much improvement over the seventeenth in general livestock management. Owners of animals did not pay enough attention to winter feed and to selective breeding. Some regional specialization developed, however, Windham and Litchfield counties becoming notable for stock raising and dairy products, for example.

*   *   *

Even in the seventeenth century Connecticut produced some surpluses of grain and livestock, which it exported in the form of biscuit, flour, barreled beef and pork, and live sheep and horses to neighboring colonies and to Newfoundland and the West Indies. In the next century this trade increased greatly, enabling the colony to earn the means to import British manufactured goods from Boston and New York. Despite subsidies and other methods of encouragement, Connecticut never succeeded in developing any significant volume of direct trade with Great Britain. Individual merchants, like Jonathan Trumbull, tried to open up direct trade, using whale oil as the means, but with little success. More typically, Trumbull collected cattle and hired drovers to take them to Boston, or barreled beef and pork and sent it to the same market. The

English goods he received in return he sold from his store in Lebanon, either to other storekeepers in the vicinity or directly to his own customers.

Goods from abroad were also warehoused in towns like New London and Norwich and distributed to interior towns by owners of general stores and to isolated farmhouses by peddlers. Shortage of cash often meant that the storeowner had to be satisfied with barter, so that he was as much a trader as a retailer. He obtained his British goods by the wagonload and sent out corn, cider, pelts, and other local products to a market where they could be disposed of. He complained of the competition from the peddler, who shouldered a pack or loaded a horse and delighted the eyes of housewives and husbandmen with pins, buttons, cloth, pots, knives, and the like.

Some of Connecticut's trade was triangular in nature, but its volume was probably not great compared to direct trade between Connecticut ports and Boston, New York, or West Indian ports. The destruction by fire of the port records of New London, which was the main port of entry, makes a statistical analysis impossible; yet we do know of some triangular routes. In the seventeenth century New London merchants sent beef and provisions to Newfoundland in exchange for fish, which was sold in the West Indies for sugar and molasses. In the eighteenth century ships from New London traded flour and lumber in Spanish ports on the Mediterranean Sea for mules, which were exchanged for West Indian products that were wanted in Connecticut.

From time to time charges were made that Connecticut merchants engaged in illegal trade in violation of the Acts of Trade and Navigation. Such accusations were most often aired when Britain was seeking to curb the too great autonomy Connecticut enjoyed. Thus in 1707 the surveyor-general, Robert Quarry, reported gross violations of the acts, citing specifically clandestine trade with the Dutch in Surinam and Curaçao and trade in Virginia tobacco for which the duties had been falsely entered as paid. Quarry may have been seeking the replacement of customs collector Daniel Wetherall. The historian William Douglass, with no axe to grind, claimed, however, that 40 percent of Connecticut's shipping returned from the West Indies guilty of violations, most probably smuggling foreign molasses into the colony. Even during war Connecticut and other merchants resorted to smuggling. Lieutenant Governor Cadwallader Colden of New York wrote to William Pitt in 1760 that badly needed provisions had been exported to the French chiefly from New Haven, New London, and Rhode Island, the smugglers returning with French sugar, which was either labeled as British or entered as "prizes" captured in privateering operations. After the Sugar Act of 1764 tightened controls, Connecticut collectors obtained £1,225 sterling from imported molasses in the first year under the new law. By contrast, for the first seventeen years under the Molasses Act of 1733, revenues had amounted to only £99.*

In its occasional reports to the Board of Trade in 1730, 1749, 1756, 1761, and 1774, which were required of all colonies, Connecticut showed a steady growth in external trade. Mention is made of exporting fish to the Mediterranean in return for bills of exchange used in buying British goods; ships are reported as going to the coast of Guinea; pot and pearl ashes, tobacco, and rum are listed in addition to the usual commodities. In the third quarter of the century, flaxseed was sent in considerable amounts in response to sharply increased Irish demand. The government sought to protect these distant markets by laying down quality controls for the packing of meat, tobacco, and other goods. The number of Connecticut ships and sailors as reported to the Board of Trade steadily increased in the eighteenth century. The 42 ships of 1730 ranging in size from 10 to 80 tons capacity had grown by 1774 to 180 with a total of 10,317 tons. The total value of imports grew from £50,000 in 1756, the first year for which totals were reported, to £200,000 in 1774, and of exports from £130,000 to £200,000. A comparison of Connecticut's annual commodity exports between 1768 and 1772 with those of other colonies throws light on its relative trade position. Connecticut's per capita figure was £0.5; New Hampshire's, £0.7; Massachusetts's, £1.0; Rhode Island's, £1.4. Southern colonies far surpassed these figures: for example, South Carolina, £3.7; Georgia, £3.2.†

The growth of Connecticut's trade exhibited familiar cyclical patterns. The outbreak of wars with the French was a stimulus for those who could obtain contracts to supply British troops with provisions, but the

---

* These figures are taken from Parker Bradley Nutting, "Charter and Crown: Relations of Connecticut with the British Government, 1662–1776," (unpublished Ph.D. dissertation, University of North Carolina, 1972), pp. 139–40, 187.

† James F. Shepherd and Gary M. Walton, "Trade, Distribution, and Economic Growth in Colonial America," *Journal of Economic History* 32 (March 1972): 133.

end of a war usually brought a trade depression. In Connecticut and elsewhere the early 1750s were years of depression, as were those of the early 1760s, after the French and Indian War. Loss of trade depressed land values as well: land that a decade before had sold for £30 "old tenor" per acre declined to £19 in 1762. The 1770s saw a sudden increase in the number of tax collectors who were in arrears, the excuse being the number of poor who could not pay or the number who were moving from the colony without paying their taxes. These conditions, of course, only exacerbated relations with Great Britain during the period when Parliament was resorting to direct taxation of the colonies.

Periodically shortages of export products developed, and the government stepped in with embargoes to preserve dwindling supplies for Connecticut consumption. Scarcities in grain and flour appeared in 1737, 1741, 1772, and 1775. The assembly usually granted exemptions for those who could make a case, however. Sometimes export controls were designed to regulate rather than forbid trade. In 1747, lumber products for a time could not be shipped to other New England colonies in order to protect Connecticut's West Indian trade and its own shipbuilding industry. From almost the beginning of the colony, Connecticut had sought to preserve its leather supply by establishing quality controls and forbidding the export of tanned or even untanned hides. And various measures were adopted to put noncitizens of Connecticut at a disadvantage in trade within the colony either by outright prohibition or by discriminatory import duties favoring local producers; but such laws were repealed in 1770 as "prejudiceal to commerce," although the real reason was that Connecticut feared trouble with England, whose merchants disliked this kind of favoritism.

Connecticut was not content to allow commerce to be regulated by market conditions but rather sought to stimulate production of farm products for export by various means. The colony kept an eye on supplies and their channels of distribution, set quality controls, sought to regulate trade in the interest of its own citizens, and tried to free itself of too great dependence upon Boston and New York as sources of overseas goods.

Another area of regulation was the control of prices and wages. Connecticut magistrates shared the common Puritan fear in the seventeenth century that workers and merchants might take unfair advantage of market conditions and drive wages and prices up. Thus in 1641, the General

Court drew up wage scales for summer and winter work. For carpenters, plowrights, wheelwrights, masons, joiners, smiths, coopers, and mowers, the wage for an eleven-hour day in the summer was to be twenty pence and for a nine-hour day in the winter, eighteen pence. Lesser artisans and laborers were to receive seventeen and fourteen pence, respectively. In 1645, the court decreed that contracts specifying payment in grain should be interpreted to mean wheat at four shillings per bushel, rye and peas at three, and corn at two and six pence. This regulation lasted for five years; but it long remained customary for the government in accepting produce for taxes to set such figures, an action that must have affected market prices.

In the eighteenth century the General Assembly did not spell out daily wages for all workers, but it did set by law the amounts a miller could keep for grinding and bolting the farmer's grain. The printed laws of 1715 and 1750 defined oppression as a "mischievous evil," by which was meant excessive wages for work and unreasonable prices for merchandise. The legislation of 1750 made it a criminal act to demand excessive wages or unreasonable prices, although no definition of these terms was included. The same laws set interest rates at 6 percent for the loan of money or merchandise "and so after that Rate for a Greater, or Lesser Sum, or for a Longer, or Shorter Time." Notable gains in population, the economic opportunities afforded by the offering of new lands for sale, and the increased supply of currency probably diluted the effect of legislation that attempted for largely moral reasons to regulate wages and prices. Conditions were changing too rapidly to permit such laws to deter those seeking their own betterment.

*   *   *

As one would expect, the Connecticut government played a role in stimulating and encouraging industry, although manufacturing and mining never rivaled commerce in agricultural and forest products. As early as 1656, John Winthrop, Jr., had promoted the erection of an iron furnace in New Haven, not yet a part of Connecticut, but it never approached the production of the better known works in Saugus, Massachusetts. Earlier the General Court had given Winthrop mining rights in Connecticut proper on generous terms. He was to enjoy forever rights to any deposits of lead, copper, tin, antimony, or other minerals he might discover, as well as timber and water rights needed to develop them. The big discoveries, however, came not in Winthrop's time but in the eighteenth century. Copper mines were found in Simsbury and Wallingford about 1707 and large iron ore deposits in Kent and Salisbury in the 1730s.

By the 1750s two thousand tons of iron ore were being taken annually from the Salisbury bed, two to two-and-one-half tons yielding one ton of pig iron. Furnaces were built near the deposits, and the legislature encouraged at least one enterprise by lending £1,200 for capital development. Before the Revolution, Connecticut had not only a number of pig-iron furnaces but also eight forges with tilt hammers operating in the eastern part of the colony. The best known of the early ironmasters was Samuel Forbes, who set up a furnace at Lakeville and began production of pots and other kitchen utensils of good quality. During the Revolution Salisbury became a producer of cannons, swivel guns, cannonballs, grenades, grapeshot, and other weapons. It is estimated that one thousand cannons, ranging in size from three to thirty-two pounders, were cast in Salisbury ironworks. Guns were tested locally before being sent to the armies and ships.

The copper mines of Simsbury underwent several reorganizations with the blessing of the General Assembly, but in the long run they proved unprofitable. Works were set up clandestinely to refine the ore, contrary to English law, but secrecy only helped to swell the losses. Unrefined ore was also shipped to England. For a time a petitioner named John Read urged the assembly to permit the making of copper coinage for all New England's benefit, but it refused, probably because it feared the king's displeasure, the coining of money being a royal prerogative. By mid-century the Simsbury mines were deemed of so little economic value that they were readily converted to a prison for the worst type of criminals and for Tories during the Revolution.

Encouragement of industry was fraught with some danger, for England did not like to see the colonies become competitors and lessen their dependence upon the mother country for manufactured goods. In 1731, Connecticut assured the Board of Trade that it had given no premiums to stimulate manufacturing, but three years later it was offering premiums to encourage the manufacture of sewing silk, silk stockings, and silk cloth and the making of water-rotted hemp, canvas, and fine linen. In 1769, the legislature offered a grant to a petitioner who claimed to be able to make type fonts and promised a bounty on each quire of paper produced by a paper mill in Norwich. In 1772, it offered an interest-free loan of £500 to a steelmaker in Killingworth.

The easiest and, perhaps occasionally, the most wildly optimistic kind of help the assembly gave was the grant of a monopoly for a given period of years, provided production met stated standards. One man in 1717 got a ten-year monopoly on making molasses from corn stalks, and in 1774 another was given a monopoly on grinding grain by harnessing the action of the tides. More sensible, perhaps, were monopolies granted for slitting mills and making steel, potash, salt, and glass.

While the government sought in various ways to encourage the manufacture of products deemed basic to the economy, individual craftsmen in clockmaking and tinware were laying the foundations for industries that would earn Connecticut a national reputation by the early nineteenth century. Clockmaking as a sideline of gunsmithing began in the colony in the seventeenth century, but it was of no commercial significance until the 1720s. By then many of the larger towns had craftsmen who produced striking, eight-day clocks with brass works at lower cost than those imported from abroad. It is not possible now to trace in detail how these skills were passed from worker to worker, but native ingenuity was an important factor, for craftsmen, lacking resources enough to import tools and parts, had to rely on their own inventiveness. They used wood as well as brass for the gearing, and by 1745, tall clocks with wooden works that ran for thirty hours by means of cords and weights were being sold in other than local markets. The best known clockmaker working with wood was Benjamin Cheney of East Hartford, where clockmaking centered for a number of years. The talent that accumulated over the decades made possible the mass production of clocks that Eli Terry, using interchangeable parts, introduced early in the next century.

In 1740 two Irish tinsmiths, William and Edward Pattison, bringing with them a supply of tinned sheet iron, opened a shop outside Berlin, where they produced plates, cups and saucers, lanterns, candlesticks, and other useful and attractive household items. These shiny products, light in weight, easy to clean, drew into the Pattisons' shop women tired of woodenware and desirous of something less expensive than pewter and plate. At first the Pattisons sold their wares only in the local area, but as that market became saturated, they traveled as peddlers. As the popularity of tinware grew, they increased their imports of tinned sheet iron and taught apprentices the skills of shaping and soldering. War with Great Britain temporarily cut off supplies of their raw material, but the Pattisons kept in business by peddling other goods. When peace came, manufacture of tinware on a large scale became possible, and Connecticut tinware found its way all over the United States.

Other industries in colonial Connecticut were shipbuilding—the colony made more ships than it used for itself—rum distilling, and cloth fulling. One of the earliest centers of shipbuilding was New London, which began with small ships and gradually increased the size of the vessels that it turned out. Norwich and Saybrook also became shipbuilding centers. In 1769, Connecticut built fifty ships, ranking below only Massachusetts Bay among the colonies. Although Connecticut in 1654 forbade the importation of rum, or "kill devil," the government eased up a bit within a few years and probably by 1659 was taxing it. In 1699, the General Assembly set the price of rum by the drink along with that of other beverages. Briefly in 1727 Connecticut tried to prevent the distillation of rum because molasses was scarce and "the spirits drawn off therefrom" were "very unwholesome," but because other colonies did not follow Connecticut's lead, the law was repealed. By 1735, rum distilled in the colony was taxed at twelvepence, that imported in Connecticut ships at only eightpence per barrel. Fulling mills for the treatment of cloth were established in Connecticut at least as early as 1693, and mention of a number of such mills is made in the early eighteenth century. But Connecticut lacked the capital, labor, and the agricultural surpluses that would have permitted the growth of major manufactures. Most farmers still had to supply many of their own wants. Home manufacturing and the artisan's shop were more typical than ironworks and shipyards.

*   *   *

Like all the colonies, Connecticut suffered from a chronic shortage of currency, the reasons being the unfavorable balance of trade with England, newcomers' bringing with them goods rather than money, and the laws of Parliament, which forbade both export of coin to the colonies and coinage of money there. In the early days corn and wampum were made legal tender, and for many years colony taxes were payable in commodities at fixed prices. Wampum was valued according to the color of the beads; three black or blue beads or six white ones were worth one penny. Connecticut first resorted to paper money, or bills of credit, in 1709, when, because of the expense of the expedition to Canada, it issued £8,000 worth of bills to be redeemed by a tax of tenpence on the pound, payable in May 1710 and 1711. Between 1709 and 1737 the colony regularly emitted bills, never fully retiring previous issues, so that new emissions were always added to bills outstanding. In this period the largest amount issued in any one year was £18,941 in 1710, the smallest, £789 (£23,681 were then outstanding). The largest amount retired by taxation in any one year was £6,400, the smallest, £2,301. In addition to these emissions, the colony loaned to private persons in 1733 nearly £50,000 in bills, of which £33,594 were still outstanding in 1740. Apart from the loan bills, the colony expected to have all its bills retired in 1739, an expectation that was not fulfilled.

Originally the bills of credit were made usable for the payment of taxes, but in 1718 the General Assembly made the bills legal tender for all private contracts dated after July 12, 1709, unless a contract specified otherwise. By renewal of this law, this provision remained in force until July 1735. In 1740, in response to the financial demands of King George's War, Connecticut began again to issue bills of credit in large amounts. These new bills were called "new tenor," the old ones, "old tenor." Benjamin Trumbull estimates that during this war Connecticut issued a total of £80,000 of bills.

Richard Bushman has pointed out in interesting detail that pressure for currency emissions arose not only from the demands of war but also from the needs of rising businessmen who lacked the capital they required and who resented the unwillingness of well-established merchants to see the government expand the money supply. Paper money, then, became a divisive issue pitting comfortably well-off merchants against newcomers, who saw opportunity beckon if only they could get their hands on money. Division, moreover, tended to be along territorial lines. In the first half of the eighteenth century the area east of the Connecticut River was the fastest growing section of the colony, and here the demands for currency expansion were sharpest, as businessmen sought to finance new ventures. A rising money supply made it easier for them to pay off debts if things went sour. More conservative merchants preferred to lend their surplus cash at high interest rates and looked upon currency expansion with self-righteous distaste.

Obviously the issuance of quantities of paper money without prompt redemption in full through taxation caused depreciation of the bills. In

1735, the colony's agent was already mentioning "the very great fall of your Currency," and in 1740 when new tenor bills appeared, they were designated at 2.5 times the value of old tenor notes of the same denomination. Four years later old tenor notes had sunk to one-fourth the value of the new. Later the relationship between the two was stabilized at 3.5 to 1. In 1749, when the assembly decided to establish all fees in the laws in terms of proclamation money, defined in Queen Anne's time as 6s.8d. per troy ounce of silver, old tenor was described as one-eighth of the value of proclamation money. Meanwhile new tenor bills had depreciated as well. In 1752, £50 proclamation money was held to be equivalent to £114.5.9 in new tenor bills, roughly 2.25 to 1, although originally the ratio of new tenor amounts to proclamation money was 4 to 3.3. In 1751 Parliament enacted a statute applying only to New England that forbade making paper currency legal tender for private transactions. The law also put limits on the amount that could circulate, but these provisions seem to have had little effect in Connecticut. The colony was itself concerned about excessive amounts in circulation and the resulting depreciation of the bills.

Connecticut was not unique, of course, in having its paper money depreciate. Depreciation occurred in Massachusetts Bay, Rhode Island, and New Hampshire as well. Consequently from time to time Connecticut sought to protect its own bills by restrictive policies. In 1747, it declared the bills of neighboring colonies unacceptable; in 1752 it outlawed Rhode Island bills for payment of any kind except for contracts in which they were specified; in 1755 it forbade the circulation of both Rhode Island and New Hampshire bills. Connecticut had to guard against bills of credit issued by private citizens as well. In 1733, the assembly had dissolved the New London Society United for Trade and Commerce, established to encourage trade with Great Britain and elsewhere, for issuing bills of credit intended to pass as currency; and the assembly made it a crime for anyone or any society to issue such bills.

The issuance of paper money by the government filled a real need in the colony's economy, but control of the money supply was necessarily imperfect. The demands of war caused the amount to burgeon beyond the willingness of taxpayers to redeem it on schedule, with consequent depreciation of its value. But the paper served to finance the various war efforts, its depreciation functioning as a kind of tax. Thus a pattern was established that would be repeated in the Revolution.

Prior to the outbreak of the French and Indian War Connecticut called

CONNECTICUT PAPER MONEY, OBVERSE AND REVERSE. The rather fresh appearance of the currency issued by the New London Society United for Trade and Commerce is probably due to the promptness with which the legislature outlawed issues from private sources. Usually currency had hard usage and the repeated folding of the paper to make it fit into wallets or pockets caused the bills to tear. For a time in the colony, parts of bills called "broken money" continued to pass, their value being fractionally proportionate to the value of the whole bill. The four-shilling note illustrated here was patched together in

our own day. By 1740 Connecticut made parts of bills non-redeemable so that they could no longer pass as currency. An "indented bill" meant one torn from a stub, the edge of the bill being deliberately made uneven so that it could be matched upon redemption. The stub and bill also had identical numbers. The obvious purpose of these measures was to thwart counterfeiters. The term "indented" continued to be used even though the time-consuming matching of stubs with bills was discontinued in actual practice. The New London bill measures approximately 4″ × 6″; the other, 4¾″ × 3¼″. *Courtesy of the Massachusetts Historical Society.*

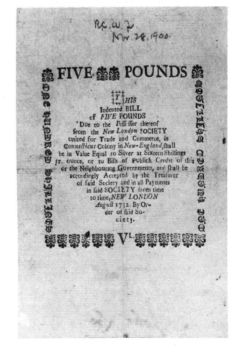

in all old and new tenor bills, which it stood ready to redeem in gold and silver at the depreciated rates of 58s.8d. old tenor per ounce of silver and new tenor valued at 2.5 times the old. But the colony had to turn to bills of credit once again to finance its war effort. The new bills were designated lawful money, and they differed from previous issues in that they bore interest at 5 percent. During the French and Indian War a total of about £340,000 was issued, but always with a tax measure to retire the bills. During and after the war period, authorized taxes payable in a given year rose as high as 20d. in the pound for 1765 and 12d. and 14d. for 1766 and 1767 respectively, although taxpayers did not ultimately have to pay such sums. Despite the large amount of these bills emitted, they did not depreciate as had earlier issues. In fact, even though Connecticut raised taxes not only to retire the bills but also to pay war expenses, it was able to discharge at full face value all but £82,000 in bills by 1763, the year the war concluded. According to an assembly committee report, the bills "remained invariable, permanent, and stable." These bills were not legal tender and could not be redeemed for specie until their maturity, when the face value and interest were paid. Before maturity there was a tendency for the bills to be discounted in ordinary transactions, but this was not the kind of depreciation that afflicted old and new tenor.

What made Connecticut's performance so different during the French and Indian War? Connecticut enjoyed an excellent market for its farm goods in New York, one of the centers of war, and it was able to furnish military supplies locally, for which the British government made repayment. Despite heavy taxes, then, Connecticut people enjoyed prosperity during the war years. But this is only part of the story. Connecticut, like other colonies, received large sums in specie as reimbursement for its expenditures during the war. Moreover, Connecticut in presenting its accounts described them as lawful money sums even through before maturity the bills circulated at well under par. Thus, in getting reimbursement, Connecticut enjoyed a substantial premium. Suppose, for example, Connecticut spent £15,000 for muskets, which would have cost only £10,000 had the bills circulated at par before maturity. In seeking reimbursement, Connecticut would note an expenditure of £15,000 lawful money and expect a sterling equivalent, when, strictly speaking, reimbursement should have been for £10,000. Not only did funds from Britain enable Connecticut to retire most of her bills by the war's end, but the taxpayer also found that the large tax rates authorized for the years after 1763 did not have to be paid. Connecticut was in such good financial shape that bills of credit issued in 1770 bore only 2.5 percent interest, and issues after that date bore no interest at all. The assembly declared that after 1772 bills of credit from any other colony that were not redeemable in gold and silver within two years from the date of issue could not pass in trade. The only exception was New York bills issued before January 1, 1769. Thus, before the Revolution Connecticut's currency was more sound than it had ever been.

Economic growth in Connecticut, in sum, was largely of the extensive kind; that is, more people produced an increasing amount of goods. But students of economic history believe also that in the colonies there was some growth in the modern sense of increased output per capita, not because technology improved, for it did not, but because increased trade made possible the more efficient use of the unemployed and under-employed. Since the colony's trade did increase, the generalization may well apply to Connecticut, but no systematic study has yet been made to sustain this conclusion.

6

RELIGION AND THE CHURCHES

The Puritans who settled Connecticut and the New Haven Colony envisioned ideal Christian communities organized around a Congregational church to which all would adhere in loving harmony. The cost of maintaining a minister and erecting a meetinghouse would be furnished out of voluntary, not compulsory, contributions from the faithful. As believers in Original Sin and Predestination, they realized that only a relatively small number would achieve eternal salvation through the agency of God's mercy, and most in Connecticut thought only such should be full members of the church. But all the inhabitants of the town were required by law to attend services, to listen to the word of God as preached by the minister, to heed his moral instruction, and to try in every way to live as a Christian should regardless of whether salvation would be the reward; indeed, there could be no reward for efforts at righteous living. Salvation was God's free gift to a chosen few. Yet all must strive—ceaselessly. One's assurance of salvation was never a certainty even for those accepted by their fellows as members of the elect; for the others, the health of society demanded unremitting effort to live according to God's laws. Laxity, indifference, could only result in the destruction of society, as God had destroyed Sodom. Every Puritan was expected to watch over not only his own behavior but also the actions of his neighbors as well. In seeking outward prosperity, the community sank or swam together. The Puritan colonists believed literally that natural catastrophes, sickness, Indian raids, were all means employed by God to punish a people for their wicked ways.

Thus a Puritan church was not just a nourisher of individual faith but an important instrument of social control, directly for those in full membership, less directly for those who merely attended. The minister and those who assisted him, like the deacons, were interpreters and upholders of the moral law, the very cement of society. In this, the Puritan church was no different from any other Christian church of the seventeenth or earlier centuries, except that the Puritan effort was more intense, more highly organized, more pervasive. In the American colonies, New England Puritans made greater and more effective use of government over a longer time to institutionalize and enforce religious instruction, morality, and Christian unity than did members of the Church of England in the southern colonies during the seventeenth century. Theoretically, Puritans favored separation of church and state in the sense that they did not want to see the clergy running the state as Richelieu did in France or as the popes had governed the Papal States; yet the arm of the state was ever ready to enforce Puritan conformity and morality. Indeed, the preamble to the Fundamental Orders asserted that Connecticut people associated together to preserve "the liberty and purity of the gospell . . . as also the disciplyne of the Churches," as well as to promote civil affairs.

Still, the emphasis in the beginning was upon voluntarism. Selection of a particular minister to serve a community long remained a matter of local preference, as Congregationalism ideally required. The first ministers in Connecticut either migrated with their flocks, as did Thomas Hooker to Hartford, or John Warham to Windsor, or were chosen shortly after arrival, as Wethersfield settlers chose Henry Smith. Eschewing any direction from above, Congregationalists believed in a free choice, though they were expected to seek the advice of nearby churches. Most commonly they preferred to hear a man several times before they made their selection. Once ordained to serve them, the usual minister expected to spend his life among his congregation. A careful bargain was struck, stating his salary and such perquisites as firewood, rights to land, and provision of a house. In a large community a minister might have an assistant to help him, and always there were designated laymen, elders and deacons, who helped to manage church affairs. But it was to the whole body of the congregation, church members and attenders both, that the minister was ultimately responsible, and they to him.

The minister was greated aided in his task of inculcating religious principles and nourishing faith by the functioning of the family, which the Puritans felt had been the first church. It was the duty of the family's head, the father, to conduct simple religious observances and to catechize his children and servants. Any head of family who neglected this duty could be called before the grand jury, and ministers and town leaders were supposed to check regularly to see that there was no neglect. When the General Assembly expressed concern that young people were slipping too soon from the governance of parents and masters, it ordered selectmen to determine whether boarders and sojourners were staying in suitable homes.

*   *   *

The ideal cohesiveness of the Puritan community, in which the congregation voluntarily supported a minister and all those in the town remained under his spiritual guidance, early began to undergo change. Men being what they are, it was not surprising that adequate financial support failed in some towns. Carving new homes out of the wilderness meant, for most, years of struggle and hand-to-mouth existence; shirking the responsibility of supporting a minister and erecting a meeting-house must have seemed to some an easy way to lighten their burdens. At any rate, as early as 1644 in Connecticut, at the suggestion of the United Colonies, the General Court recommended that the several congregations of the infant colony come separately together to pledge support, each man indicating what he was willing to pay. If any man refused to promise a just proportion of the cost, he was to be taxed for a suitable amount, a tax enforceable through the civil power. Here was voluntarism of a sort backed by governmental force. It was but the beginning of a long list of measures and actions to assure financial support for ministers, meager though it might often be.

By 1658 no persons could "imbody themselves into Church estate without consent of the Generall Court, and approbation of the neighbor Churches," nor could anyone attend any ministry distinct and separate from or in opposition to that publicly observed. In 1697 ecclesiastical societies were required by law to collect taxes for support of a church even when they had no settled minister. The money was to go to the county court, which was to furnish supply ministers; and if the society took too long to settle a minister, the court was authorized to choose one for it.

Obviously such a law indicates that more was amiss in some communities than just the hard struggle to make the land bear. In the last third of the seventeenth century many congregations were wracked by theological disputes. The prized autonomy of the Congregational way and the Puritan emphasis on individual responsibility in religious matters fairly invited otherwise-mindedness. The Half-Way Covenant permitting limited membership to descendants of the elect and adopted by a Massachusetts synod in 1662 became a source of contention in Connecticut, dividing congregations over the merits of their ministers and leading sometimes to splits and the formation of new churches. When in 1708 Connecticut churches adopted the Saybrook Platform, thus moving themselves a long way toward Presbyterianism and away from the local autonomy of Congregationalism, there was again cause for factional dispute. The climax of interchurch and intrachurch quarreling came with the Great Awakening in the 1740s, when men and women became divided over whether the religious revival of that time was truly a work of God, and more specifically, over the nature of conversion and the process that led to it.

Yet it was not just theological differences among Congregationalists that altered the religious ideal with which Connecticut had begun. The very process of growth—the expansion of old towns and the settlement of new ones, the influx of peoples with different religious ideas and their spread in some sections—all had great impact. Gradually Connecticut worked out its ways for dealing with such changes, taking some of its steps reluctantly and holding to a system that achieved a remarkable if suffocating stability called the Standing Order.

As towns grew in population and some settlers established their farms in areas remote from the original center where the meetinghouse stood, it was natural for them to want their own meetinghouse near at hand. The kind of close community that had marked the old center was disrupted in favor of creation of new communities within the town limits. This was the pattern in the oldest towns, but in towns founded late in the seventeenth century and in the eighteenth century, there was often no recognizable center of settlement from the beginning. Two or three groupings of home lots might be made, or later, in towns of speculative interest, the division of lands included the whole township right from the start, so that one church could scarcely serve the whole township as it began to fill up; homes were too widely scattered.

Indeed, the ecclesiastical society did not even have to lie entirely in one township. For example, in 1746 some people living in the southern parts of the first and second societies of Coventry wanted to join with others living in the northern end of the second society of Lebanon and in the northeast part of Hebron; the General Assembly approved their request. Successful petitioners living in southwestern Litchfield had themselves transferred to the parish of Judea in Woodbury. And one could cite other examples of societies that cut across town lines. Such arrangements received recognition in a law providing for the administration of property reserved for the ministry. The General Assembly was usually favorable to those who could demonstrate that convenience made plausible such transfers or the creation of new societies.

The General Assembly went even farther; in numerous instances it authorized small groups that were a hard-traveling distance from the meetinghouse to make use of winter ministers, men who would preach to them during a period of four or five months, say from November or December through March. During this period such groups were exempt from the taxes of their usual church; instead they were authorized to tax themselves to support their winter minister. Petitioners from Wapping parish in East Windsor, claiming that their average distance from the meetinghouse was four and one-half miles, persuaded the General Assembly to extend their winter minister's preaching term beyond the usual five months to eight. During that time they were exempted from taxes for ministerial support in the First Society and also denied the right to vote in that society's affairs.

All ecclesiastical societies were recognized by the General Assembly as taxing agencies for support of the ministry. Such societies annually levied taxes on polls and estates for that purpose, as did towns that had undergone no division into separate parishes. When such societies were getting started, the General Assembly was usually quite willing to authorize special taxes for a period of years on improved and unimproved lands, on residents and nonresidents alike, in order to establish a minister, build him a house, and erect a meetinghouse.

Having authorized such taxes and firmly committed itself to the proposition that public support of religion was essential for doing God's will, as well as for promoting morality and civilized communities, the Connecticut General Assembly stood ready at all times to support the system. When the Reverend George Griswould of Lyme, minister there since 1722, complained in 1750 that he had received no pay since 1748, the assembly ordered payment and named a collector to make assessments on the proper listing of estates. Griswould returned with the same complaint in 1752, and the assembly acted as before. When the Reverend Samuel Dorrance of Voluntown asserted that his congregation had kept his salary at £100 old tenor without regard for depreciation of the currency, the assembly ordered that he be paid £200 old tenor. Dorrance, like Griswould, made additional pleas in subsequent years, the assembly promptly issuing its orders to a town apparently not at all overawed by Connecticut authority. Yet obligation did not run in only one direction. When Newington sought relief because its minister, the Reverend Simon Backus, had died in the siege of Louisbourg, the assembly awarded the town £150 old tenor as some compensation for its loss and as an aid in securing a replacement.

The concern of the General Assembly extended to matters other than payment of the minister's salary. Even in the seventeenth century before the adoption of the presbyterial Saybrook Platform, the assembly's authority in the form of recommendations or outright orders impinged in numerous ways upon the local autonomy that was the Congregational ideal. The statement in the Code of 1650 is unequivocal: "the Civill Authority heere established hath both power and Libberty to see the peace, ordinances and rules of Christe bee observed in every Church according to his word."

In Wethersfield in 1643, when many threatened to remove from the town because of their dissatisfaction with the Reverend Henry Smith, the legislature urged Smith to "lay downe his place, if it may be done according to God." In the 1650s and 1660s when both the Wethersfield and Hartford churches were torn by internal dissension, caused partly by the clash of personalities and partly by differences over admission to church membership and the right to vote in selecting a pastor, the General Court repeatedly urged the calling of church councils within Connecticut and even prevailed upon Massachusetts churches to send representatives to help resolve the disputes. In March 1659, the General Court itself set up a council for such purpose. When efforts at conciliation failed, the court ordered the Hartford church not to discipline the disaffected and forbade the dissidents to withdraw and join another church. In 1660, when Middletown people manifested great dissatisfaction with the Reverend Nathaniel Stow, the General Court authorized his replacement by another who had to meet the approval of a committee appointed by the court. Meanwhile Stow's pay was to continue, and his parish was to furnish him with testimonial letters. One final example will illustrate early exercise of the legislature's authority. In 1659, when Lt. John Hollister, excommunicated from the Wethersfield church, complained because he had been given no statement of charges, the General Court held he was entitled to one and named two men to receive it from the town's minister.

In the eighteenth century the legislature regularized by law some of the procedures of the congregations. In 1708 the General Assembly stipulated that a legal call to a minister could go out from the majority of inhabitants of a town or a society who were either qualified by law to vote in town affairs or accepted as members in full communion of the particular church, and who were present at a legally announced meeting. Such majority vote was to be binding on others in the town or society. There are two noteworthy aspects of this law: first, a person did not have to be a member of the church in full standing to participate in the choice of a pastor; second, if one was a full-fledged member, one did not have to meet the requirements for voting in town affairs. After Connecticut had given some legal recognition to groups dissenting from Congregationalism, the assembly decreed that those exempt from taxes for religious purposes could not vote on church matters within the town or society. Presumably a minister could be dismissed by majority vote also; but when in 1748 the second society of Norwich dismissed Henry Wills by a narrow vote, the legislature, memorialized by Wills's supporters, set the vote aside and ordered a new meeting under the direction of Jonathan Trumbull, at that time a member of the upper house. Eventually Wills resigned. On at least one occasion when no majority could agree on a choice, the assembly allowed a minority to call and settle a minister and tax themselves.

Another source of local disputes was the location of the meetinghouse, for a site would be more convenient for some than for others. An apparently exasperated assembly, impatient with the many quarrels over location, in 1731 ordered that a two-thirds vote be required to proceed with construction of a meetinghouse and that application be made to the assembly to fix the spot. Once that was chosen, the society could proceed to levy the necessary tax; if it failed to do so, the assembly would levy the tax to assure erection of the building. The important thing was to go forward. When the Second Society of Coventry in 1742 despaired of getting a two-thirds vote and asked for relief, the assembly authorized it to proceed without the required vote. In 1753, the assembly permitted the First Society of New Haven to go ahead with merely voluntary contributions because no two-thirds vote could be secured. The assembly agreed to choose the site on the condition that no one was to be taxed for the building. This action was the more unusual because in 1748, the assembly had turned site approval over to the county courts, which were entitled to exact a fee from societies. Even so, the assembly accepted an occasional appeal to review and set aside court decisions.

In many ways the General Assembly exhibited a more general concern for the soundness of Connecticut's religious life and sought actively to encourage walking in the right way. By 1680, it was urging ministers to undertake catechizing young people, since leaving that duty solely to families seemed insufficient. In 1694, it authorized ministers to perform marriages for those conscientiously desirous of such ceremony, although traditionally Puritans had held marriage to be but a civil contract. The first volume of Connecticut's printed public records is replete with calls by the General Court for days of fasting and humiliation or the giving of thanks to a merciful God, a practice that continued into the next century. Indeed, as late as 1770, the General Assembly ordered punishment for those in Fairfield County ignoring a proclaimed fast day. By that date, however, political as well as religious motives entered into consideration, for Fairfield County was a center of pro-British sentiment; ignoring the fast day was deemed an act of political defiance.

Repeatedly the legislature enacted laws to guard the sanctity of the Sabbath, in 1676 decreeing that there should be no sporting in the streets even after sunset on Sunday. It assessed fines for nonattendance at some congregation authorized by law and for unnecessary travel on the Lord's Day. In 1706, it added to the long-standing exemption of the persons of clergymen from taxation the exemption of their families and estates. There is even an instance of a retired minister's being freed of taxation, the General Assembly ordering his parish to repay taxes improperly collected. Despite its care, the assembly after Queen Anne's War saw "evident tokens that the glory is departed from us" and called for an inquiry into the state of religion. When ministers reported that religious concerns were much neglected, the assembly called on justices of the peace, grand juries, and selectmen to take action. Every family was to have a Bible, and the long list of laws against Sabbath-breaking, swearing, lying, and other offenses was reiterated for the edification of lax

FARMINGTON CHURCH. The foundation of this meetinghouse was laid in 1771, constructed by Captain Judah Woodruff, one of the best builders of his day. The original Puritans worshipped in plain rectangular or square buildings, unadorned inside and out; but in the eighteenth century, Congregationalists followed the lead of English architect Christopher Wren, and added spires to their meetinghouses. The Farmington church surely has one of the handsomest of this period. The main door on the west side was provided with a porch at a later period, when architectural style was under the influence of the Greek revival that swept the country. Today, these windows have been replaced with those of forty panes each, as had existed in the original structure.

constables. In short, the assembly did not confine itself to settling complaints that came before it; it saw itself as duty-bound to promote the word of God, in the eighteenth as much as in the seventeenth century.

But the assembly was a political body after all, used to the ways of compromise and preferring settled and orderly ways of proceeding. If absolute uniformity and purity in the church proved unobtainable, then some sort of alternative had to be found. Events in Connecticut after Massachusetts Bay's adoption of the Half-Way Covenant in 1662 illustrate the point.

It should be recalled that Massachusetts Bay, from which the Connecticut settlers came, had early adopted the principle of admitting to full membership in its churches only those who could narrate a convincing account of their experience of salvation. Congregations by vote admitted to communion only those who were of the elect; and only such persons were entitled to have their children baptized. In practice, this meant that the children of mere church attenders, no matter how godly, were denied the sacrament. Even parents who were themselves baptized (*their* parents having been of the elect) but had never undergone a conversion experience to become full church members saw baptism denied to their children. With the passage of time and the failure of many grown-up baptized children to experience conversion, pressure grew to make modifications in membership requirements. The outcome was the synod of 1662, which made half-way members of adults baptized as children provided they owned the covenant and led decent lives. Such half-way members could have their own children baptized and subjected to the watch and care of the church. Since Connecticut churches had not sent representatives to the synod of 1662, the decision reached had no immediate effect in Connecticut, but that colony could not escape the problem that Massachusetts Bay had faced. Indeed, in Connecticut the problem took on an added dimension, for pressures existed there to make membership much broader.

In response to a petition from William Pitkin and others, deploring the exclusion of their children from baptism, the General Assembly in 1664 raised the question of whether church membership should be open to all those who were of honest conversation, knowledgeable in the principles of religion, and desirous of owning the covenant. Such persons might have their children baptized, and the church would watch over them. What the assembly was proposing went far beyond the synod of

1662, and the proposal drew some adverse reaction; but while the assembly pursued the question no further, neither did it formally withdraw its suggestion. Several churches, however, became battlegrounds over admission policies.

The refusal of John Warham of Windsor, an early advocate of lenient membership requirements and of the half-way principle, to admit half-way members after 1664 or to broaden membership in the way the assembly had suggested caused some inhabitants to leave the town and to establish a more liberal parish in the new town of Simsbury; a few years later dissidents formed a second church in Windsor. In Stratford the new minister, Israel Chauncy, refused to accede to the freemen's demand for a more inclusive church membership, with the result that the minority opposition called a minister of its own, Zechariah Walker; thus, the town for a time had two ministers and two congregations using one church. Similar trouble broke out in Hartford.

These troubles stirred the assembly once more to take a hand. In 1669, after the failure of councils to resolve church disputes, the assembly decided that until "better light in an orderly way doth appear" those with different views about membership should be permitted to continue in their beliefs so long as they were orthodox in the fundamentals. More than in Massachusetts Bay the issue of baptism was but the surface cause of strife, for the deeper issue was whether to permit far less strict requirements for membership. These embroilments revealed another development as well: the increasing tendency of ministers to make decisions about membership and other matters rather than leave such decisions to the congregations, where final authority traditionally was supposed to lie.

By the 1670s most Congregationalists had accepted the Half-Way Covenant or were at least willing to have others do so. Even in New Haven, which had been a stronghold of strictness under John Davenport and his successors, the Half-Way Covenant had triumphed by 1685, according to Robert G. Pope. By the end of the century it was possible to distinguish four responses in Connecticut to the years of turmoil over membership questions. There were still some strict Congregationalists who held to the old belief of reserving membership for the elect or visible saints, as, for example, in the Farmington and, perhaps, Branford churches. Then there were churches like those in Norwich, Middletown, and New Haven, which accepted the Half-Way Covenant as originally intended by the synod of 1662. A third group of churches went beyond the second in offering baptism to adults and their children who had never been members of the church in any sense; these churches still denied the sacrament of communion to all but the elect, however. The first church of Hartford, the second of Windsor, and the church in New London fell into this category. Finally, churches in Killingworth and Wethersfield, and, after 1690, those in Woodbury and Stonington, threw membership open to all men and women who led decent, godly lives. Thus the principle laid down by the assembly in 1669 that different views on membership were acceptable had triumphed. In 1699, the assembly, recognizing differences among the churches in defining membership, allowed choice of a minister by a majority of householders in an accepted ecclesiastical society.

But it would be a mistake to think that the assembly was willing to give up all effort at uniformity; its duty to oversee the discipline of the churches had been clear from the earliest days. Among Puritans, the fear that churches, if too autonomous, would be likely to veer from the true path was never stilled. Both Massachusetts Bay and Connecticut saw efforts to regularize and bring under greater control the separate Congregational churches. In Massachusetts the effort finally failed, one of its fruits being the influential defense of Congregationalism written by John Wise. In Connecticut, near-presbyterian principles won out with the writing and establishment of the Saybrook Platform of 1708.

The origins of the platform have been traced to men interested in establishing what became Yale College, men who had connections in eastern Massachusetts Bay and were aware of the move there for closer control led by the Mathers. As early as 1703 these Connecticut men sent out a letter seeking opinion on a united confession of faith. A powerful stimulus to the movement came when the Reverend Gurdon Saltonstall became Connecticut's governor in 1707,* for Saltonstall had long advocated greater control over the churches. At length the legislature proposed a series of meetings in county towns, where ministers would meet with lay delegates from a county's churches. These county groups were to send delegates to Saybrook, where "a form of ecclesiastical discipline" would be drafted and be presented to the General Assembly.

---

* Saltonstall was the only Connecticut minister to achieve high office in the colonial government.

Aside from accepting the doctrine of the Savoy Synod of 1658, as it had been adopted in substance by Massachusetts Bay in 1680, and which made very few modifications in the Westminster Confession,* the platform established machinery for the settlement of disputes and for the supervision of pastors and churches. Churches within a county were to form one or more consociations, made up of pastors and messengers from the appropriate churches, which were to meet in council at least once a year and on other occasions if disputes were brought before them. In disputes, the determination of a consociation was to be final and could be ignored only at the peril of excommunication. Within a consociation acting as a council, the vote of the majority of pastors present was to be determining in all cases, even if messengers failed to appear from the consociated churches. The platform also formally recognized the associations of pastors that had long been meeting in Connecticut (as well as in Massachusetts Bay) and delegated to them within their respective counties the power to initiate council action if any pastor was accused of scandal and to give approval to new ministers whom churches proposed to call. The meaning of all this machinery was that pastors would exert greater control than ever before over the individual churches and that those aggrieved would have fewer opportunities to stir up trouble by repeated appeals or by personally selecting councils favorable to their cause. Within a month the General Assembly approved the work of the Saybrook meeting.

This platform, like any such document, was open to varying interpretations. Some chose to regard council rulings as decisive; others saw only a necessity to justify carefully their continued difference from a council ruling if they remained unpersuaded. The tendency of clerical and political leaders in enforcing conformity was to move slowly; the platform itself mentioned application of severe discipline only after "due patience." Even so, some Connecticut churches rejected the Saybrook Platform either from the start or later, claiming adherence to the Cambridge Platform of 1648 as the true basis of Congregationalism. Derby, Woodstock, Lisbon parish in Norwich, and eventually the first societies in Norwich and East Windsor were examples.

The patience urged in the platform was, however, "due" not limitless,

---

* The Savoy Conference, meeting in Savoy Chapel in London at a time when radical sects were springing up, had put emphasis on Congregational polity.

and there were those who suffered from the weight of consociation or association rulings. When the Reverend Blossom of Pomfret, called before the association to account for his religious doctrines, refused to attend, he was tried in absentia. An additional charge of plagiarism caused the association to order him to stop preaching and his parishioners to cease attending any services he might conduct. In 1738 the consociation of New Haven County ordained Samuel Whittelsey minister in Milford against the wishes of a large minority, who said that his preaching lacked warmth and that he put too much emphasis on good works as a way to salvation. When the minority withdrew to form a separate church, its members were directed to continue paying taxes to support Whittelsey. Despite the minority character of the opposition to the consociation's choice, the handling of the affair suggested steamroller tactics rather than Christian charity. In 1744, the consociation of Windham County ordained James Cogswell at Canterbury, allegedly against the wishes of a majority in the town; separation followed here, too. Ministers dismissed on the insistence of associations include Timothy Allen of West Haven, for denying that Bible reading would help in conversion; Jonathan Parsons of Lyme, for itinerant preaching; and Philemon Robbins of Branford for preaching to Separates and Baptists in a parish controlled by establishment Congregationalists. Most of these incidents occurred during the period of the Great Awakening, when those opposed to change found the machinery of the Saybrook Platform most useful for attacking those supporting the revival.

*   *   *

Handling dissent from the decisions of the Standing Order was too important to be left solely to church leaders, however; here, as in so many other matters, the General Assembly played a key role. The seventeenth-century assumption that there was only one truth in religion died hard in Connecticut. The eighteenth century saw grudging concessions to non-Congregationalists and eventually even token concessions to Congregationalists who opposed the Standing Order; but genuine freedom of conscience was not achieved till well after the American Revolution.

Perhaps part of the reason was that Connecticut leaders chose not to understand what freedom of conscience was. In 1665, the royal commission mentioned in earlier chapters presented to the General Assembly for its consideration a proposition asserting that "all persons of civill lives may freely injoy the liberty of their consciences, and the worship of God in that way which they think best, provided that this liberty tend not to the disturbance of the publique. . . ." The answer of the assembly was that "we know not of anyone that hath bin troubled by us for attending his conscience, provided he hath not disturbed the publique." The critical clause was the last one, of course, which was open to interpretation. In 1656, at the instigation of Massachusetts Bay and the United Colonies, Connecticut had forbidden any town to entertain any "Quakers, Ranters, Adamites, or such like notorious heritiques." The next year fines were imposed on those who even spoke to Quakers, unless they were elders who sought information in order to suppress them. A few months later the assembly forbade anyone but elders to possess any Quaker writings. One should recall here the law of 1658 that required the approval of the assembly and neighboring churches to start a church and forbade attendance at unauthorized services. In New Haven, Quakers suffered whipping and branding.

The earliest concession to religious freedom in Connecticut was the assembly's willingness, already mentioned, to allow Congregational churches opposing and favoring the Half-Way Covenant to exist side by side. In 1675, the assembly suspended its law penalizing Quakers for not attending authorized church services on condition that they not hold meetings of their own in the colony; they had to journey to Rhode Island if they wanted to meet without harassment. When the laws were printed in 1702, nonetheless, the laws against Quakers were included. Their permanent repeal came in 1706 after English Quakers made representations to the Board of Trade, on whose recommendation the queen disallowed the Connecticut laws, one of the first instances of royal disallowance of Connecticut enactments. The repeal by the legislature followed.

Although the Quakers were the earliest dissenting group to feel the weight of the legislative hand, they were not the only ones; the struggle of dissenters to win concessions was a long one. Unique to Connecticut were the Rogerenes, a sect named for its founders, John and James Rogers of New London. Beginning as Seventh Day Baptists, the Rogers brothers, members of a respected and affluent family, gathered a congregation of moderate size between 1674, when they were baptized, and 1677, when John, who acted as minister, introduced innovations borrowed from Quaker beliefs. Rejecting oaths and a paid ministry and advocating pacificism, this congregation found itself cut off from fellowship with other Baptists. From 1677 to the Revolution, when they lost their identity, the Rogerenes remained a small separate sect, which never shirked its perceived duty to give public testimony to its beliefs. Particularly insulting to the Standing Order was the Rogerenes' dramatic refusal to obey the laws regulating conduct on Sunday. Although the group never had more than a hundred or so adherents, its willful disobedience of law gave it importance far beyond its size, for the retaliation that the assembly inflicted through repressive laws threatened other dissenting but less obstreperous groups. The Rogerenes never won any concessions from the government.

By the end of the seventeenth century no Baptist churches yet existed in Connecticut, although one did in Boston and several in Plymouth and Rhode Island. The first organized Baptist church in Connecticut, in that part of New London later known as Groton, sought recognition in 1704 as a dissenting church under the English Toleration Act of 1689 and Connecticut's own laws, which required permission of the assembly to establish a church. Although the Baptists were refused by the assembly, they learned, when brought into court for holding church contrary to law, that they could escape fines if they took steps to qualify under the Toleration Act. Meanwhile they went through a prolonged court battle to establish that their minister, who came from Rhode Island, would not be a public charge. The Baptists of Groton did not win legal recognition until 1709, partly because of their delay in qualifying under the English statute, which required certain oaths before a justice of the peace. By that time the Connecticut legislature had passed its law for the relief of "sober dissenters." Professor William McLoughlin is of the opinion that the loss of the charter in Massachusetts Bay, where the struggle for toleration had been bitter, and the Toleration Act both made the way easier in Connecticut for those willing to confine their dissent to orderly paths. Unbudging resistance to religious dissent could only jeopardize the Connecticut charter.

Connecticut's law of 1708 affording relief to sober dissenters simply stipulated that if dissenters qualified under the English law in the court of the county where they resided, they could worship without hindrance, provided always that there be no prejudice to the privileges accorded churches established by law. The last condition, of course, meant that dissenters would be expected to continue to pay taxes to support the establishment. The law of 1708 gave relief to very few. Obviously, since it was based on the Toleration Act, it did nothing for the members of the Church of England, which was the established one in the mother country and from which the English law permitted dissent. Although no organized Anglican parish was established in Connecticut until 1718, a Church of England missionary had baptized about two dozen people in Stratford in 1706. Nor might the Connecticut law have helped Quakers, even though the English Toleration Act made room for dissenters who objected to oaths.* Still, the act of 1708 was a beginning.

But this law did require specific procedures for dissenters to achieve legal status; and when the General Assembly found that some, like the Rogerenes, for example, were ignoring the procedures, it passed a law in 1723 that forbade worship services in private homes under the leadership of men who were not lawful ministers but who nonetheless presumed to administer the sacraments. This law followed two that had been passed in 1721, which were designed to guard more carefully against profanation of the Sabbath. Religious toleration in Connecticut, in brief, was sharply circumscribed. Obviously there was no room for seventh-day believers who ignored the traditional Sabbath nor for preachers not regularly ordained. Even a protest from Stratford in 1710 that Anglicans should not have to pay for the support of Congregational ministers went unheeded, although the Stratford memorialists asserted that such taxation contravened English law and was therefore illegal under Connecticut's charter.

In 1727, however, the same year in which Massachusetts Bay acted, Connecticut granted tax exemption for members of the Church of England in response to a petition from Fairfield; but the Connecticut, in contrast to the Massachusetts, law was permanent, not temporary. The only condition was that there be a settled minister ordained by the canons of the church near enough for adherents to attend his service conveniently. Connecticut rate collectors were supposed to turn over to such ministers taxes for religious purposes taken from church people; the

---

* William G. McLoughlin is the authority for this statement about Quakers, but he implies that the English Toleration Act did not allow for affirmation, although it clearly does. See *New England Dissent, 1630–1833,* 2 vols. (Cambridge, Mass.: Harvard University Press, 1971), vol. 1, pp. 263–64.

Fairfield petition had requested that, by law, members of the Church of England be required to support their ministers. The legislature gave the Anglicans power, too, to raise additional taxes among themselves if the regular rates were insufficient. Connecticut may have been prompted to make this concession to the Anglicans because about this time John Winthrop IV was threatening to test the colony's intestacy law before the Privy Council. One public difficulty with the home government may have been enough. The Bishop of London had already made a pointed request in 1725 that Anglicans not be forced to contribute to the support of dissenting ministers. Governor Talcott had replied that in the only Anglican parish in Connecticut, that ministered to by Samuel Johnson, churchmen did not have to pay such taxes, although the governor did not explain how they got around the law. And he added that Churchmen who did not live near an Anglican church had to continue to pay taxes to support Congregational ministers.

Two years later came tax exemption for Quakers and Baptists, a logical extension. In order to be freed of taxes for support of the Congregational minister and for erecting meetinghouses, such people had to present certificates to show that they did indeed belong to their own societies and attended worship. Quakers and Baptists were left to their own devices to find the financial support they needed, for neither group believed in a religious establishment. Nor did Connecticut law require any proof of the fitness of a Baptist minister, as Massachusetts Bay was to do.

In the colonial period the Baptists, members of the Church of England, and Quakers were the chief non-Congregational religious groups in Connecticut.* The Quakers remained relatively few in number. At the time they were freed from taxation they had no meetings of their own in Connecticut but crossed into Rhode Island for worship, which practice the law explicitly allowed. From the 1720s on the Church of England grew steadily in numbers, its chief stronghold being the southwestern part of Connecticut, although there were very active parishes in such eastern towns as Pomfret, Norwich, and Groton.

---

* For a brief period in the 1740s Moravian missionaries worked among the Indians in Sharon and Kent and apparently persuaded some to migrate to Bethlehem, Pennsylvania. The story that came to the authorities was that the Moravians were stirring up the Indians, and orders went out for interrogation of the missionaries. They made no permanent settlements in Connecticut.

Anglicanism received encouragement from the announced conversion in 1722 of several ordained Congregational ministers and graduates of Yale. That three of these were Timothy Cutler, rector of the College, Samuel Johnson, tutor as recently as three years before, and Daniel Brown, tutor at the time, shocked the Standing Order. Their announcement at Commencement sent a shiver through their audience and led to prompt demands for resignations. Yet their apostasy did nothing for true religious liberty, for adherents to the Church of England believed in an establishment. Once their own exemption from taxes raised for Congregationalists had been won, they sought to obtain a bishop and by aggressive missionary efforts to bring Connecticut people under the establishment of the mother country. In Connecticut it was the Baptists and, later, the Congregationalists who, by breaking with the Standing Order, promoted religious liberty.

Despite gains made by legislation, local practice based upon interpretation of the law often nullified what opponents of the Standing Order thought they had won. For example, Wallingford Baptists, technically members of a Baptist church in New London, met for worship in a private home in the 1730s and thus ran afoul of the law against private meetings. In their own eyes, since they were members of a recognized Baptist church, their meetings were legal, and they should have been tax exempt. In their petition to the assembly they complained that the county court had refused to license them under the Toleration Act, a refusal probably based upon their small numbers and the absence of a settled minister. Although the assembly did not act upon their petition, ways were found informally to persuade the Wallingford authorities not to tax these Baptists. Connecticut laws were not designed readily to accommodate all dissenters to the Standing Order, lest the stability prized by Puritans be undermined; exceptions were made from political necessity, not commitment to an abstract principle. Connecticut leaders were always fearful that an appeal carried to England might threaten the colony's charter. And sometimes local people had less awareness of or concern for political considerations than the assembly. In 1757, Baptists in Enfield complained that though they had long been "embodied into church estate" and had a settled minister, they were still taxed to support the Congregational ministry. The assembly granted relief.

Because many of the early Connecticut Baptists were essentially Calvinist in their doctrine and because the more urbane among them sought good relations with the leaders of the Standing Order, they perhaps clashed less with local Congregationalists than did Church of England members at a similar stage of development in Connecticut.

In New England the growth of the Church of England was encouraged by the founding in 1701 of the Society for the Propagation of the Gospel in Foreign Parts. Church of England ministers were missionaries, many of them born in the colonies, sent by the society to win converts among those regarded as dissenters—Congregationalists, Presbyterians, Baptists, and others—and also among the Indians, although few Indians were converted in Connecticut. As active missionaries, they were resented, of course, by those who saw the Congregational way as the road not only to salvation but also to peace and good order in the community.

The lot of Connecticut missionaries was hard; their annual reports to the society lament the meagerness of their salaries and the excessive size of the area they were expected to serve within the colony. Not only did they have to ride great distances, but their inability to preach regularly in remote places also discouraged growth of the Church of England. Surviving reports indicate that by 1760 and until the Revolution Connecticut had about twenty-six missionaries serving at least double that number of parishes. The total number of those adhering to the church by 1774 has been estimated by Bruce Steiner at about 17,200 or 9 percent of the white population. Since an American had to travel to England to obtain holy orders because there was no bishop in the colonies, it was not an easy matter to increase the number of missionaries. Personal expenses ran as much as £100 sterling, putting most aspirants in debt at the beginning of their careers.

Overworked and burdened as he felt himself to be, the typical Anglican missionary was quick to resent local harassment and to complain about it at length in reports to the Venerable Society. Solomon Palmer of New Haven declared, "We are narrowly watched . . . as a Cat watches a Mouse; and every peccadillo is taken notice of, and made a great crime."* Undoubtedly arrogance on both sides exacerbated many situations. For the missionaries it was particularly galling that in Connecticut the church

---

* Solomon Palmer to the SPG, May 5, 1764, Letter Series B, vol. 23, p. 309, Records of the SPG, London. These records are copyrighted by the United Society for the Propagation of the Gospel, London, and all quotations from them are used by permission of the archivist.

was deemed nonconforming even though it was the state religion of the mother country.

The law of 1727 directing that taxes for religious purposes paid by members of the Church of England should go to the support of their own settled minister and their church was open to local interpretation. How near was a conveniently located church? How frequently did one have to go to claim attendance? How could one determine who was truly a professor of Church of England principles? Local authorities settled these matters to suit local prejudices. In 1728 it was alleged that one had to be no further than one mile from a Church of England minister to qualify under the law. Even where interpretations were not that unreasonable, Congregational tax collectors might persistently neglect to turn over money due the missionary or not collect his rates at all. The missionary was then left to go to the law, a step that only bred expense and bad blood. Judges and juries were said to be partisan; Richard Mansfield claimed in 1755 that judges even removed jurors who were churchmen in order to all but guarantee a hostile verdict.

Churchmen in Derby, where Mansfield preached, demanded their share of the proceeds of ministerial lands set aside originally in 1692 and sold by the town in 1754. Although the town had never intended the lands to benefit a minister of the Church of England, neither, Anglican spokesmen claimed, had it meant the lands to benefit a Presbyterian, which the Saybrook Platform presumably had made of ministers of the Connecticut established church. The tendentious reasoning here is less interesting than the response it evoked in town meeting. A principal citizen thundered that churchmen "had Forfeited [their] Right to the Land as much as a Traitor had to his on the Morning in which he was to have his head cut off."*

Congregationalists were not above using violence in dealing with churchmen. In 1738, when a missionary armed with a deed to land bordering on New Haven Green near Yale College sought to prepare the land for building a church and parsonage, he and a helper were driven off by a crowd led by Yale students and threatened with death if they persisted. This was more than student highjinks. The rector of Yale and other prominent persons were implicated.

---

* Richard Mansfield and others to the SPG, January 23, 1755, Letter Series C/AM, box 3, item 11, Records of the SPG, London.

Yet among the complaints sent by missionaries to the Venerable Society one finds mention of cordial relationships with the Congregationalists as well. Missionaries made some conversions, which they attributed to the desire of converts to escape from the endless quarreling among Congregationalists and to achieve easier salvation. And missionaries did preach to nonchurchmen on occasion. Samuel Peters of Hebron told how Congregationalists contributed to furnishing the missionary church and how in September 1763 he read from the prayerbook and preached in the meetinghouse at the time of election of representatives. Such friendly relationships were doomed with the advent of the revolutionary crisis.*

The granting of tax exemption to Church of England adherents, Quakers, and Baptists caused Congregationalists to complain to the legislature that the task of raising money for the established churches was made harder because of the narrowed tax base and because the irreligious were quick to see the advantage of claiming to be dissenters. Joining the Baptists seemed to be a way of dodging compulsory taxes. Petitions in the 1730s from the North Parish of New London, from the parish of North Lyme, and from Reading, Northberry, and New Concord all made the same point—that Congregationalists were having to assume a greater burden.

In 1730, the General Assembly sought to plug one possible loophole by issuing an interpretation of the law for sober dissenters of 1708, stating that Congregationalists and Presbyterians could not come within the meaning of the act. The year before, the county court had licensed a minority in Guilford that had left the recognized church and had abandoned the Saybrook Platform, dissatisfied with the spiritual state of the pastor. The legislature held that such separating groups were not true dissenters and could not, by rejecting the platform, achieve such status. Although the law of 1708 did not affect tax collection, allowing every objecting group to break away would reduce the Standing Order to a shambles. Moreover, groups that broke away could easily drift into the

---

* A recent study has demonstrated that many more Anglicans than some scholars have realized held public office in eighteenth-century Connecticut right up to 1775. But the greatest number of them converted from Congregationalism to Anglicanism as adults. See Bruce E. Steiner, "Anglican Officeholding in Pre-Revolutionary Connecticut: The Parameters of New England Community," *William and Mary Quarterly* 31 (July 1974): 369–406.

camp of the Baptists, as many were to do in the aftermath of the Great Awakening. Actually, the Guilford group did petition the assembly for tax exemption, holding that English law gave them that right as much as it did Quakers or Baptists. The assembly released the signers of the petition from taxes, but local authorities interpreted the release to cover only signers, not those on whose behalf the petitioners had acted. The separatists of Guilford were not recognized as a society, however, until 1733, after the assembly had initiated several attempts at reconciliation through councils.

Despite the position taken by the General Assembly, some county courts continued to license separating Congregationalists as dissenters. There were two such instances in 1742. In 1743 the legislature removed such cases from the courts' jurisdiction by repealing the law of 1708 and instructing dissenting groups that could be distinguished from Congregationalists and Presbyterians to apply to the General Assembly for relief. If they took the necessary steps to qualify under the Toleration Act, they could expect a favorable decision. The form of relief granted, however, still permitted harassment of dissenters by local tax collectors. The assembly always particularly named the members of the society recognized as a lawful dissenting group, so that as the society grew, newcomers were not covered; a special act of the assembly was needed to afford them tax exemption. Until they were so named—and the bother of getting special legislation was great—newcomers were fair game for local collectors.

This law of 1743 came when the Great Awakening had passed its peak, and its meaning for those Congregationalists who found the Standing Churches intolerable was that they could not legally hold separate services, for they would be running afoul of the law that required attendance for worship at duly recognized churches. Their separate meetings would be Sabbath-breaking and disturbing to the peace. After a time in Connecticut the Separates became the spearhead of the movement for greater religious freedom within the Calvinistic tradition and, more important, for freedom from religious taxation when they found themselves outside the legal system.

One tiny sect appearing in prerevolutionary Connecticut deserves passing mention—the Sandemanians. Beginning in Scotland under the influence of John Glas and further molded by Robert Sandeman, the sect attracted a few adherents in western Connecticut, notably in Danbury, where Sandeman came to live in 1766 after some two years of proselytizing in Portsmouth, Boston, Newport, and elsewhere in New England.

The cardinal belief of the Sandemanians, as they were called in America, was that faith was essentially an intellectual acceptance of the truth preached by the Apostles. One who believed the truth would be saved, but any suggestion of striving toward or doing anything to win God's acceptance was sinful. Merit had no place in the scheme of salvation; belief in the literal truth of the message of the Gospels was what counted. This conception caused Sandeman and others of his persuasion to reject all the popular divines of the day who spun out theological treatises or sought to stir the emotions of their audiences. The effort of the Sandemanians to imitate the simplicities of the early church led them to reject the accumulation of wealth, to promote love feasts, to rely upon the most artless forms of church organization and ordination, and to demand unanimity among members, with excommunication for those persisting in dissent. Within their own group they practiced charity to the point of trying to keep every member independent of public support, but they condemned charity outside the group.

In Connecticut, Sandemanian influence was felt particularly in Danbury, New Haven, Newtown, and New Fairfield, churches being founded only in the first two places. Ministers who were attracted to Sandemanian principles felt the heavy hand of ecclesiastical discipline through their consociations. And more general opposition arose because of the loyalism of Sandemanians, for they taught that obedience to the king was a Christian duty. During the Revolution a number of Sandemanians were arrested as Tories, but the sect survived and continued well into the nineteenth century with a bare handful of adherents.

* * *

Dissent from legally recognized churches greatly increased during and after the Great Awakening, which affected all the colonies and was contemporaneous with a revival of religious feeling in Western Europe as well. In New England the awakening was in part an attempt to resurrect some of the ancient ideals of American Calvinism. It was a reemphasis on grace as the free gift of God, on voluntarism, on the autonomy of the Congregational churches, and most important, on fervor in religion and man's utter helplessness and dependence upon God. For some, it was a rejection of a degree of civil control over religion and a too great emphasis on education and rationality in religion.

New Englanders had believed for a long time that religion was declining. The days of John Cotton and Thomas Hooker seemed in retrospect a golden age; their own day appeared one loaded with evils, which ministers enumerated in their frequent jeremiads. In dress, in everyday morality, in business, and in attitudes toward churchgoing, New Englanders seemed to have fallen far from the standards set in the beginning. The decline paradoxically was underscored by the very economic success New Englanders had achieved. Subduing the wilderness and exploiting surrounding waters had turned the minds of many to schemes for wealth; economic opportunity rather than salvation seemed the concern of most. In consequence, a profound sense of guilt gnawed at the New England mind, for which the established churches offered little comfort. The typical Congregational minister in the eighteenth century showed little fire or zeal. Trained to shun enthusiasm and affected by the rationalistic currents of the Enlightenment, he emphasized decent Christian living to a congregation admitted to the sacraments on the basis of owning the covenant and proper conduct. The minister sought to reach his hearers through appeals to their minds; and in practice, if not in theory, he taught that the way to salvation was through doing good.

Well before the outbreak of the Great Awakening in 1740 there had been stirrings in New England and elsewhere among ministers and people seeking something else—an experimental religion, religion experienced through the heart and emotions. The Quakers, the Rogerenes, and the Baptists had all criticized the Standing ministers for their lack of piety, of emotional commitment, and their inability to stir their parishioners. In western Massachusetts, Solomon Stoddard had had periodic harvestings of souls and had written about the need for ministers to undergo conversion in order truly to reach their congregations with inspired zeal. His grandson, Jonathan Edwards, had presided over a revival in Northampton in 1735. In Connecticut, there had been a revival in 1721 in Windham, where Samuel Whiting had secured eighty conversions in six months. The example of Edwards in Northampton, who was visited by Benjamin Lord of Norwich and John Owen of Groton, served to arouse ministers and people not only in those towns but also in East Windsor, Coventry, Lebanon, Durham, Mansfield, Bolton, Hebron, New Haven, Stratford, and elsewhere. But the coming of George Whitefield to New England in the fall in 1740 really ushered in the Great Awakening.

Arriving in Newport in September, Whitefield made his way to Boston, to the western part of Massachusetts, and then into Connecticut, where he preached at Suffield, Windsor, Hartford, Wethersfield, Middletown, Wallingford, New Haven, Milford, Stratford, Fairfield, Norwalk, and Stamford. The message he brought was everywhere the same —the terrible sinfulness of man and his utter dependence for salvation on the mercy of God. One needed to prepare oneself for grace should it be offered, and the first step in preparation was conviction of sin. Whitefield played upon the emotions of his audience as upon an instrument, bringing forth a cacophony of groaning, weeping, and wailing, followed by the exultation of those who underwent conversion. A magnificent speaker, he enthralled audiences so large no church could hold them. Without electronic aids, his voice penetrated to the very fringes of crowds of five thousand and more.

On hearing that Whitefield was coming to Middletown to preach, Nathan Cole ran from his field work and hurried his wife to horse so they might hear the great preacher, fearful all the time that they might arrive too late.

I saw before me a Cloud or fog rising, I first thought, off from the great river, but as it came nearer the road I heard a noise something like a low rumbling thunder and I presently found it was the rumbling of horses feet coming down the road and this Cloud was a Cloud of dust made by the running of horses feet. It arose some rods into the air over the tops of the hills and trees and when I came within about twenty rods of the road I could see men and horses Sliping along in the Cloud like shadows and when I came nearer it was like a stedy streem of horses and their riders, scarcely a horse more then his length behind another all of a lather and fome with swet, ther breath rooling out of their noistrels . . . every hors seemed to go with all his might to carry his rider to hear the news from heaven for the saving of their Souls. It made me trembel to see the Sight how the world was in a strugle.*

---

* Quoted by George Leon Walker, *Some Aspects of the Religious Life of New England* (Boston, 1897), pp. 89–92.

At first, established ministers welcomed the efforts of Whitefield, hailing the rejuvenation of those who flocked to their churches; but their approval was short-lived, for Whitefield urged his hearers to inquire into the spiritual state of their ministers. His cry was that those who had not experienced conversion themselves could hardly prepare the way for others. Standing ministers had reservations, too, about the unrestrained emotional outpourings of the crowds, and they were offended by the claims of the converted, who were numbered in the hundreds, that they were certain of their new state. A mark of New England Calvinism had been uncertainty about one's condition even after the experience of conversion. The road to conversion itself had usually been a long one involving much self-examination and prayer; self-probing for the typical Puritan, moreover, ended only with his death. The instant conversions of the 1740s were suspect, and the arrogance of the converted was galling.

All of these annoying characteristics of the revival were only intensified with the appearance on the scene of itinerant preachers and lay exhorters. In 1741, Gilbert Tennent of New Jersey visited New England, stopping in such Connecticut towns as New London, Lyme, Guilford, and New Haven. In that year also, James Davenport of Long Island visited Connecticut towns, where he claimed to know at once who was converted and who was not and railed against established ministers as pharisees. Davenport was put on trial and expelled from Connecticut, the General Assembly claiming that he was out of his mind. The greatest of the itinerants was Jonathan Edwards, of Northampton, Massachusetts, who in 1741 preached at Enfield, Connecticut, the most famous of Great Awakening sermons, "Sinners in the Hands of an Angry God." His whole effort was to make his listeners feel their wickedness and their helplessness, that only an angry God could save them at His mere pleasure:

> O sinner! consider the fearful danger you are in: it is a great furnace of wrath, a wide and bottomless pit, full of the fire of wrath, that you are held over in the hand of God, whose wrath is provoked and incensed as much against you, as against many of the damned in hell. You hang by a slender thread, with the flames of divine wrath flashing about it, and ready every moment to singe it, and burn it asunder; and you have no interest in any Mediator, and nothing to lay hold of to save yourself, noth-

ing to keep off the flames of wrath, nothing of your own, nothing that you have ever done, nothing that you can do, to induce God to spare you one moment.*

These men were ministers, but others came who were unordained, heeding merely a call from God, and often heaping abuse on ministers who stressed the importance of collegiate training and doctrinal study. Naturally the Standing Order struck back. Thomas Clap, rector of Yale College, who had earlier welcomed Whitefield but became disillusioned by Tennent and Davenport, was instrumental in persuading the General Assembly to issue a call for a general consociation to meet in Guilford in November 1741. This meeting, dominated by opponents of the revival, drafted a set of resolves reminding everyone that only properly licensed ministers were legal in Connecticut, that it was unlawful for congregations to censure or remove ministers and to institute reforms, that the procedures of the Saybrook Platform should be followed in dealing with separations from lawful churches, and that a minister could not enter the parish of another to preach without prior consent. When these resolves were presented to the assembly, it responded in 1742 with a harsh law against itineracy, not repealed until 1750.

First, the assembly made it unlawful for any licensed minister to enter another parish unless invited by the minister and a majority of the congregation, on pain of losing all financial support. Laymen who sought to preach uninvited were to be bound for their future good behavior by £100 bonds. Noncitizens of Connecticut, whether ordained or not, who came into a parish to preach without proper invitation were to be treated as vagrants and expelled from the colony. Benjamin Pomeroy of Hebron preached in a grove in Colchester in 1742 when the local minister denied him the use of the meetinghouse; for his pains he was denied public support until 1748. When Pomeroy presumed to condemn the law against itineracy, he had to post a £50 bond and pay court costs of over £32 old tenor. The Reverend Jedidiah Mills of Ripton Parish in Stratford was also denied his rates in 1742, and they were not restored until 1749.

Thus Connecticut people became bitterly divided over the legitimacy

---

* Quoted in Russel B. Nye and Norman S. Grabo, eds., *American Thought and Writing*, 2 vols. (Boston: Houghton Mifflin, 1965), vol. 2, pp. 399–400.

of the Great Awakening. Those who opposed it because they feared its excesses and its threat to established order came to be called Old Lights, and those who saw in the awakening the marvelous hand of God were known as New Lights. The latter varied in the intensity of their support for the revival and in the steps they were willing to take to bring about change. Moderate New Lights were satisfied with reforms in the churches that served them. They demanded that their preachers be able not only to demonstrate their own conversion but also to move their hearers to a conviction of sin, thereby opening to them the possibility of salvation by God's free gift of grace. Ultimately some called for limiting membership to those truly converted. Where New Lights could not get the kind of preachers and preaching they wanted, they might break away from the established church, only to return when reforms were effected. When they did break away, because they could not cope with associations dominated by Old Lights, they often retained fellowship with non-separating New Light pastors, who helped them ordain their ministers. Some moderate New Lights condemned separation in principle, however; and most moderates were willing to operate within the Saybrook Platform provided they could control their associations and consociations. Where they could not, they condemned the platform and announced their return to Cambridge-Platform principles, particularly that of autonomy for individual churches. If such New Lights were comfortable within the system, they had no objection to tax support, of course. Moderate New Light churches were organized in towns like Hartford, Wethersfield, Coventry, Lebanon, Groton, Branford, Milford, Woodbury, and Canaan.

Such moderates, even those who separated for a time, must be distinguished from the radical pietists, or Separates, who wanted nothing to do with established eccelesiastical authority. They rejected outright and in principle the Saybrook Platform and reasserted congregational autonomy. They particularly condemned the veto power that ministers had in consociations over the laymen messengers; it was not right for ministers to exalt themselves above the truly converted. The Separates rejected, too, the Half-Way Covenant, demanding that each applicant for church membership be able to describe his own conversion, God's proffer of grace to him. In separating and thus cutting themselves off from other New Lights, the Separates were forced to choose lay leaders as ministers and thus pay less attention to learning and more to pietistic spirit. The first separations began in 1744, and ultimately over one hundred Separate churches were organized in Connecticut. Separatism flourished mainly in eastern Connecticut, in New London and Windham counties, in towns like Norwich, Windham, Stonington, Lyme, New London, and Groton, although separations also occurred in Middletown, Windsor, Suffield, and elsewhere. Richard Bushman, with considerable insight, has tied these separations in the area east of the Connecticut River to the turmoil there arising from conflict over land titles, currency, and other economic issues. The loosening of ties and the repudiation of traditional leadership made the area ripe for radical pietism with its exaltation of individual experience over institutionalized controls.

While most nonseparating New Lights did not object to taxation for religious purposes, the Separates came finally to the view that such taxation was intolerable. Had they been able to choose, they would have accepted the position enjoyed by the Church of England in Connecticut, to which state-collected taxes were distributed. But the Separates were outside the pale. The law of 1743, already mentioned, did not include Congregationalists within the meaning of sober dissenters. Thus by 1750 some Separates were staunch advocates of voluntarism. They saw no reason why the colony could not accommodate more than one version of Congregationalism, and they objected to paying taxes for a church they did not attend. Yet rejection of taxation was not a repudiation of all civil authority in religious matters. In fact, as William McLoughlin has demonstrated, Separates came to be opposed to compulsory taxation for the support of religion only after it became clear that they would not be included in the system. Separates did not want to discard laws against blasphemy, those regulating conduct on the Sabbath, or those requiring church attendance. Nor did they want Roman Catholics, non-Christians, or atheists to enjoy toleration.

Not until 1755 did a Separate Church win tax exemption, and after that there were only scattered such instances. By treating the Separates as uncompromisingly as it did the Rogerenes, the General Assembly sought to wear out their resistance. Many Congregationalists were imprisoned for nonpayment of taxes. By 1765, Connecticut Separate churches numbered no more than fifteen or sixteen, although earlier their total had run over one hundred. In 1770, the General Assembly gave blanket permission to all Protestants who rejected the established churches to hold separate worship without penalties, but the end of compulsory taxation for religion did not come until 1818, when Connecticut adopted a new constitution. The concession made in 1770 may have come because the Separates were by then seeing their cause as bound up with the more general struggle for liberty that marked the pre-revolutionary years. It was embarrassing to have Separates claim a parallel between their own struggle for freedom and that of Connecticut people as a whole during the Stamp Act and other such crises.

For Separates, the easiest route to tax exemption was to go over to Baptist principles, and many of them did after first trying to have both opponents and advocates of infant baptism in the same congregation. Ultimately the Baptists were the principal gainers from the Great Awakening in New England; and there is some irony in this, for the Baptists had initially opposed the revival. Those urbane Baptists who had sought reconciliation with Congregationalists before the revival could only regard the outburst of fanaticism with distaste. Rural, pietistic Baptists at first saw the revival as likely only to reinvigorate Congregationalism and thus not in their interest. One estimate is that as many as half of the Separates in New England ultimately became Baptists, particularly after 1750. In Connecticut, the number of Baptist churches rose from three on the eve of the Great Awakening to ten by 1760 and nearly twenty by the outbreak of the Revolution. But going over to Baptist principles was not without its difficulties for the Separates. In particular, they did not at once make a clear-cut decision against infant baptism and refused to undergo rebaptism by immersion (repudiation of their original baptism—a sacred act—was deemed blasphemy); thus, Separate churches aroused the suspicions of the General Assembly, which needed firm assurance through investigation that they were truly Baptist if they were to enjoy tax exemption. Repeated investigation and more than one petition might be necessary before Baptist status was achieved.

Baptists were not the only gainers; many conservatives, tired of the endless disputes, moved into the Church of England, although such increases should not be exaggerated. In eastern Connecticut evidence suggests that the Awakening hurt as much as it helped the church, for the charge of Arminianism was sounded with great vigor against churchmen. There was no great surge of membership in the 1740s; growth was steady in this period, increasing more rapidly some ten years after the Awakening. The Church of England was attractive not just because it was uninvolved in the disputes tearing at Congregationalists, but because, as always, it freely offered the sacraments without public confession of conversion.

Apart from denominational gains, what was the meaning of the Great Awakening for Connecticut? For many, religion was revitalized because of the new emphasis on fervent preaching to produce a conviction of sin; yet those who suffered under that conviction would look to the mercy of God to lift the burden of guilt and more. Richard Bushman feels that the "deepest meaning" of the Great Awakening lay in the recognition that "God's infinite power overruled the older authority that had stood over every Puritan conscience."* God's power took precedence over the law. Converts experienced a sense of relief; they were less amenable to law and authority and ready to construct a different society, one less concerned with institutional order. Churches whose membership consisted wholly of those who had undergone conversion reasserted the autonomy of each congregation, defying consociations established by law.

When nonseparating New Lights managed gradually to gain control in county associations and consociations, they put less emphasis on ministerial control of the lay messengers, but they kept careful watch over the ordinations. Their growing power forced Old Lights into the position of defending the liberties of congregations, making their position hardly different from that of the Separates. This reversal of roles of Old Lights and New Lights in addition to the defiance of Separates had a liberating effect in Connecticut society that bore fruit as the Revolution approached.

New Light opposition to antirevival laws passed by the General Assembly, such as the itineracy law, caused definable factions to arise for the first time in Connecticut politics. Old Light domination of the assembly caused the New Light Elisha Williams to lose his place on the Superior Court in 1743, and lesser men failed to obtain renewal appointments as justices of the peace if they were too friendly to the revival. By the end of the 1740s, however, New Lights had made enough gains to win election to the assembly and to exert their influence there for eliminating the law against itineracy in 1750. Perhaps the most dramatic example of the rise of political power among New Lights is the conversion of Thomas Clap, president of Yale, to their side in 1755, even though he had been a foe of

---

* Richard L. Bushman, *From Puritan to Yankee: Character and the Social Order in Connecticut, 1690–1765* (Cambridge, Mass.: Harvard University Press, 1967), p. 194.

the revival and had expelled New Light students from the college. Having fallen out of favor with the Old Light faction, Clap was astute enough to see that alliance with the New Light faction, which was growing in power, could be a means of restoring government support to the college. Obviously, *Old Light* and *New Light* had become political terms.

The one theme that runs through the development of religion in Connecticut is the wish to impose order on the individual churches. The desire of the government was to have as nearly an all-encompassing church as possible, free of troublesome dissent, policed by county-wide institutional controls, supported by compulsory taxation, and dedicated to the promotion of morality and good order in the community. What clerical leaders sought was an imposed orthodoxy that would guard men and women from the mortal dangers of error in belief. The very nature of Congregationalism with its original emphasis on the individual responsibility of the believer and the autonomy of the congregation militated against these wishes. Exceptions and grudging compromises had to follow. Gradually Connecticut was pushed toward greater religious freedom for Protestants, and the two largest religious factions became politicized, thus further destroying the sense of community with which the Puritans had begun.

7

SOCIAL SERVICES AND GOOD ORDER

The sense of community for which Connecticut people strove was reinforced by the colonial government's insistence upon local responsibility for educating the young and the ignorant, caring for the poor and the ill, and enforcing the manifold regulations affecting daily living. From the beginning, Connecticut life was close-knit and carefully superintended by a legislature that clearly distinguished local from colony-wide responsibilities down to the last few pence. Ready to punish lapses from good order, it was yet willing to make exceptions upon proper appeal from towns or individuals; but in the long run communities could not escape their duties. Only toward the end of the colonial period, when the records reveal growing numbers of tax collectors in arrears, businessmen unable to meet their debts, and large numbers moving out of the colony, does one get a sense of the weakening of local effort.

*   *   *

One of the meanings of the Protestant Reformation was that each person was expected to seek God through the Scriptures rather than merely through church tradition and the mediation of priests. This change put a heavy burden of responsibility on each man and woman, and reformers early recognized the need for education at least in the vernacular so that the Scriptures would be accessible. In England the sixteenth and seventeenth centuries saw a tremendous increase in the number of schools as a result. Since the Puritans were among the most radical of the religious reformers, it is not surprising that they put strong emphasis on the need for learning so that each person, child and adult, could learn God's laws and the laws of men designed to enforce them.

The education of children, obviously, had to be ultimately the responsibility of their parents, and the Puritans who migrated to the New World rather early spelled out this responsibility. As is well known, Massachusetts Bay in 1642 required parents and masters to see to it that children in their care learned to read well enough to understand the principles of religion and the capital laws of the colony, based as they were upon the Mosaic code. For its children, Connecticut laid down a similar injunction in its Code of 1650. To the requirement that children and apprentices be taught to read, Connecticut added the stipulation that heads of families catechize their children and servants once a week. Like Massachusetts Bay, Connecticut also required children to be trained in an honest calling so that they might contribute to the commonwealth as well as to their own well-being.

This last provision made it apparent that education was not necessarily confined to formal schooling. Then, as now, education took place in dozens of ways, at the hands of an artisan, shopkeeper, or professional man, under the tutelage of clergymen, and, of course, in the family. In fact, the Massachusetts law of 1642 made no mention of schools; and even when Massachusetts Bay made formal provision for schools in 1647 in its famous Old Deluder Satan act, it did not require children to go to school. Parents could teach their own children to read and write if they preferred. Family education, unfortunately, was unlikely for either enslaved blacks or for Indians who chose to leave their tribes and live among whites; but for Puritan whites it was central to child nurture. Connecticut copied into its code of 1650 the 1647 school law of Massachusetts Bay verbatim, and this is the first mention of formal education in its records.

This first law on schools mentioned two kinds: those providing training in reading and writing and those offering instruction in subjects suitable for entrance into the university. Here the Puritan colonies were following the example of England, where a distinction was made between petty and grammar schooling. Massachusetts Bay and Connecticut, by requiring towns with fifty households to establish a school for reading and writing and those with one hundred families to add a grammar school to prepare boys for college, sought to maintain a pattern with which they were familiar; but in practice the distinction broke down, for the expense and the numbers of children involved made such division an impractical burden. In New England, grammar schools taught petty scholars, as well as those beginning Latin and Greek, the two languages necessary for college work. Nothing else could be justified economically.

Maintaining schools in the seventeenth and even in the eighteenth century was a hardship, for it meant a commitment of from one-fifth to one-third of the total public funds available to towns. Even then parents were expected to furnish their children with pens, paper, and books, and in the winter months as much as a cord of firewood per child. Besides a building or a room, the town furnished only a Bible for the schoolmaster. Public funds went mainly for the master's salary, which varied with place and period but was not so low as some have imagined, running from a yearly average of thirty pounds in 1700 to seventy-five pounds on the eve of the Revolution.* Schoolmasters generally received less than ministers but more than many persons who were gainfully employed. Since most were young bachelors, they could live in relative comfort until they found their real life's work. Teaching school was commonly the occupation of a graduate fresh from Harvard or Yale who expected ultimately to go into the ministry, law, or business.

The burden of maintaining schools was lightened in some New England communities by private philanthropy. In Connecticut there was the well-known bequest of Governor Edward Hopkins, who left £400 to Hartford and to New Haven toward the maintenance of a grammar school in each place. The income from the bequest seems to have been handled better in New Haven than in Hartford during the colonial period, but in any case the funds were a notable addition to local resources. The earliest recorded bequest from a private person to support Connecticut schools was from William Gibbons of Hartford, who died in the 1650s. Robert Bartlet of New London and other persons left similar legacies, but these, which the General Court made tax free in 1684, were not enough, in addition to town funds, to put public schooling on a secure financial foundation. Aid had to come from the colony itself, and Connecticut proved more consistent than Massachusetts Bay in offering such assistance.

The colony of Connecticut did not at first recognize this need of the towns for help, and when it did, it took the easy way out. In 1672, in an often-cited law, Connecticut granted 600 acres each to the four county

---

* Figures on the cost of education and teachers' salaries are from Robert Middlekauff, *Ancients and Axioms: Secondary Education in Eighteenth-Century New England* (New Haven: Yale University Press, 1963), pp. 25, 177.

seats of Fairfield, New London, Hartford, and New Haven. The colony made no distinction, although the latter two towns already enjoyed the fruits of the Hopkins bequest. Sometimes overlooked by historians is that these land grants were meaningless at the time, for the legislature did not actually issue orders for the laying out of these tracts until 1702, thirty years later. Even then, actual survey of Fairfield's land did not occur until 1709, and Hartford was still waiting for its survey in 1714. Hartford did not sell its school lands, which were in Stafford, until 1776. Until land was laid out in a particular place, it could bring in no income. Yet the colony expected grammar schools to come into being nevertheless. By 1673, the provision in the Code of 1650 that had required a grammar school in every town with one hundred families had been changed to require one only in every county seat.

In 1677 the legislature provided fines of ten pounds per year for county seats neglecting to establish a grammar school and stipulated that the money would go to any town in the county that would set up such a school. At the same time the General Assembly established fines of five pounds for towns neglecting to keep a petty school at least three months in the year, the money to go to the support of the grammar schools. Money for both types of schools, the assembly declared, could be raised through town rates unless townspeople found another way. The next year the legislators decreed that every town with merely thirty households rather than the fifty of the Code of 1650 had to maintain a school to teach reading and writing.

Some years later the assembly considered once again how it might help towns underwrite the cost of schooling. In 1687, finding "certain sums" to be due the colony, it ordered its committee, after paying the colony's just debts, to assign the surplus, if any, to the counties for their grammar schools, or to ordinary schools in those counties lacking the more advanced ones. The printed records provide no indication of how much money was involved, but in any case here was another one-time casual attempt to bail out the towns. What was needed was a firm and continuous commitment. It finally came in 1690.

In that year the General Assembly declared that there should be "free" schools in Hartford and New Haven teaching reading, writing, arithmetic, Latin, and Greek—in short, grammar schools that made room for petty schooling as well. The major innovation was that half the master's salary of sixty pounds per year in "country pay" (produce at established prices) was to come from the colony treasury, the other half from the two towns themselves and from school revenue arising from private persons, presumably the Hopkins bequest and others. Although an attempt was made to get similar support for grammar schoolmasters in Fairfield and New London in 1691, success did not come until 1699. Even then the General Assembly would contribute only half of a twenty-pound salary for each schoolmaster. In the 1690s, then, came the first real commitment from the colony to support schooling on a regular basis, and once made, it was modified from time to time but never wholly abandoned.

In 1690, too, the General Assembly recognized, so it said, that parents and masters might be under the necessity "to improve their children and servants in labour for a great part of the year" and thus should not have to keep a school for reading and writing for longer than six months in the year, a gesture that was probably made for economic reasons. It certainly did nothing for formal education. Yet paradoxically, the assembly in the same year complained that "many persons [were] unable to read the English tongue" and ordered the grand juries to inspect families to see whether children and servants were getting proper training in reading and other skills. If they were not being taught, the juries were to impose fines of twenty shillings on parents and masters.

The next major legislation came in 1700 and marked in Connecticut both a turning point in school financing and a weakening of the laws requiring schools. Reiterating its stipulation that there be a grammar school in each of the four county seats, the General Assembly now resolved that only those towns with seventy families had to keep a school for reading and writing during the entire year. Towns with fewer families need keep school only half the year. The assembly then added both a carrot and a stick; each local treasurer was to add a 40s. rate to every £1000 in the tax listing, which would go to the support of such schools, but if the town did not keep a school, the money would go into the colony treasury. Neglect of education would now mean paying taxes anyway—hardly a pleasant prospect. If the 40s. rate was insufficient to keep a school going, the town had to pay half the sum lacking and could charge the other half to the children actually attending school. Except for later modifications in the method of assigning and distributing the 40s. rate and apart from temporary changes in the rate itself, the arrangements of the law of 1700 became the basic means of colony-wide support for local schools throughout the colonial period.*

---

* Beginning in 1711 the money produced by the 40s. rate came directly from the

From time to time the central government recognized that its flat rate was insufficient, and it found other means of assistance, not all of them permanent, however. When the colony decided in the 1730s to auction off the rights to seven western townships, it provided that the money obtained go to towns and parishes already in existence for the purpose of supporting their schools. The recipients were to lend the money at interest to create a perpetual source of income. Within the new western towns themselves one full right, that is, one fifty-third of the township, was reserved for perpetual support of schools. Reserving land in new towns for schools was a pattern that Massachusetts Bay had gradually established earlier. In the very year of the auction, 1737, the General Assembly decided, however, that the *auction* money could go for "support of the gospel ministry as by the laws of this Colony established," but in 1740 this stipulation was repealed because of "misunderstandings." Actually, Anglican freemen numbering over six hundred petitioned the assembly to repeal the clause because it was discriminatory; and when the assembly ignored the plea, threats by Samuel Johnson to appeal to the Privy Council moved the assembly to act.

Less certain than these perpetual funds were enactments making available to schools certain excise monies. In 1766, town selectmen were authorized to obtain from collectors unpaid excises on tea, liquor, and the like, the sums to be lent at interest. Excise money already paid into the colony treasury was lost, but interest on it at 5 percent was designated for the schools. In 1774, the colony treasurer was ordered to pay out to the towns for the use of their schools "the principal sums paid in by them [the towns] as excise money together with interest due at the time of payment."

---

colony treasury because the General Assembly found "great backwardness and neglect amongst the people . . . in paying." In 1712 distribution was made directly to parishes that had schools. In 1717 the law of 1700 was rewritten, *parish* or *ecclesiastical society* being substituted for *town*; but in 1728 town selectmen or committees were designated to receive the money for distribution to the parishes. In 1753 the rate was reduced to 10s. and in 1766 it was raised to 20s. In 1767 the full rate of 40s. was restored. The "reduction" in 1753 came from a change in money. In that year 3 farthings lawful silver money was the tax rate per £1. The 40s. rate was in bills of credit. In 1753 lawful money was worth 2.43 times as much as new tenor and 8.5 times as much as old tenor. Of course, between 1700 and 1753 property was evaluated upwards, as well. *Conn. Col. Records*, vol. 5, pp. 213–14, 353; vol. 6, p. 10; vol. 7, p. 178; vol. 10, pp. 157–58; vol. 12, pp. 497, 561. Thus the reduction in the amount of money intended for schools was not so great as it seemed.

How deep was the colony's commitment to public schools? It is true that in the seventeenth century noncomplying towns were fined, and in the next century such towns, if they held back, lost tax monies that went to benefit others; but the General Assembly on occasion did allow towns to use school money in other ways, to the obvious disadvantage of their children. In 1709, Wallingford was permitted for two years to use its forty-shilling rate to support its aged minister, and Windsor successfully petitioned in 1711 for its school money raised on the 1710 listing, even though it had not kept a school as the law required. The printed records do not say what Windsor wanted the money for. And it was possible, as just noted, for money arising from the auctioning of western townships to be used for an approved minister instead of for schools if a town so desired. Still, in 1714 the assembly did order inspection of schools by selectmen four times a year to observe both masters and pupils. When private schools began to appear, the General Assembly in 1742, fearful that they might "train up youth in ill principles and practices, and introduce such disorder as may be of fatal consequence to the public peace and weal of the Colony," ruled that no school, seminary, or college could operate without license from the assembly.

This concern for the public weal reveals something important about Connecticut's conception of education that was in no way unique among colonies committed to public schooling. The immediate cause of the act of 1742 was the appearance of a Separates' school in New London. Although religious societies "allowed by law" could keep schools, the Connecticut establishment at this time did not want to encourage Congregationalists disrupting the unity of the churches because of their impatience with the excessive rationalism of the Old Lights. In short, the prevailing opinion was that education, however important as a means of access to God's Commandments, should promote uniformity. Masters were expected to be orthodox enough for the approval of local ministers, and the morality taught in school was not to challenge the mores of the community. Anglicans were no different. In their schools the educational message was "respect for monarchy, belief in episcopacy, unerring obedience to minister and magistrate, and quiet acceptance of place and station."*

Apart from schools established by religious groups, private schools

---

* Laurence A. Cremin, *American Education: The Colonial Experience, 1607–1783* (New York: Harper and Row, 1970), p. 346.

taught by masters who hoped to make a living from student fees appeared in the eighteenth century. Generally they were of two kinds: those offering the traditional subjects—the classical languages, mathematics, logic, rhetoric—and those offering practical studies in navigation, surveying, shorthand, bookkeeping, and the like. For girls, schools taught sewing and simple arithmetic, as well as reading and writing, and for the sake of gentility a smattering of history and geography, or even French. For the most part, girls were not thought to need more than a knowledge of the home arts and a few social graces.

Schools offering practical subjects appeared only in the larger cities, where sufficient enrollment could be obtained. New Haven had a navigation school, and New London and Hartford, schools teaching bookkeeping, for example. The private schools offering traditional studies were often welcomed in towns that lacked grammar schools, for sons going to college needed classical training. Few questioned the rightness of publicly supporting schools that taught Latin and Greek to a handful of boys bound for college and the professions. A liberal education commanded wide respect for what it would mean in career and social status. Although petty schooling was lumped with study of classics, and on occasion a town might warn that reading and writing should not be neglected by the master who might prefer more time with his Latin scholars, the assumption that study of the classics was the best way to higher advancement went largely unexamined.

Connecticut very early showed its willingness to support higher education. In 1644 on the recommendation of the United Colonies, two men were appointed in each Connecticut town to ask every family what it could give to help support poor scholars at Harvard College in Cambridge. The intention was to make these collections annual. During the seventeenth century Harvard was the only college Connecticut sons could attend. In 1701, the General Assembly established a collegiate school with ten ministers as undertakers or trustees and offered to furnish £120 per year for its support. The trustees' purpose was to promote orthodoxy, for by the standards of some, Harvard had grown too lax in its religious tenets. The initiative for this new institution had come not from the assembly but from three ministers who had first broached the idea in 1698.

For most of the eighteenth century the curriculum at the new college, called Yale from 1718 on, was the classical one that had long been taught in British universities. The difference was that Yale had fewer texts from which to teach, although some changes were made over the years, and the burden of teaching fell upon tutors, who were recent graduates and taught largely what they had learned. They were not advanced scholars, nor did they stay long enough to develop into mature thinkers. A few, like Samuel Johnson, David Brown, and Jonathan Edwards, had through their own efforts gone beyond their undergraduate fare, but they were exceptional.

A common misapprehension is that the colonial college existed solely to train young men for the ministry; actually the aim was broader—to train them for leadership. Those going into the ministry expected to study for three years beyond their undergraduate work, usually as apprentices of a sort to clergymen. Yale men were trained in the arts and sciences. To enter, freshmen had to demonstrate a knowledge of Latin and Greek grammar and an ability to write Latin. Their initial year was largely spent studying Greek and Hebrew grammar and reviewing Latin for the first four days of the week. The main study of the second year was logic; of the third, natural philosophy; and of the fourth, mathematics and metaphysics. Upperclassmen also translated the Old Testament from Hebrew into Greek and the New Testament from English or Latin into Greek. On Fridays and Saturdays all classes studied rhetoric, oratory, ethics, and theology. Besides reciting, all students were expected to participate in disputation and declamation.

Much of this effort was unimaginative and plodding, but between 1767 and 1777 the college became a somewhat more exciting place intellectually through the informal efforts of undergraduates and tutors who wanted to see more emphasis on English and composition. Men like John Trumbull, author of the satirical commentary on the college named the *Progress of Dulness*, Timothy Dwight, and David Humphreys, later called the Connecticut Wits, did manage to encourage in their fellows and charges an appreciation for literature and a desire to improve their speaking and writing ability.

The college day was a long one. Students rose at six o'clock, or at sunrise in the winter, attended morning prayers, breakfasted, and then attended classes until mid-morning. After a break for snacks at the buttery, a store run by the college butler, classes resumed until dinner. After this second meal, students had an hour and a half for recreation, although many activities were forbidden—football in the college yard, for example. More study followed, with evening prayers at four or five o'clock, and then supper. After the meal students were free until nine o'clock, but after that time they had to stay in their rooms for study. Lights had to be out at eleven o'clock.

Yale neither remained wholly orthodox nor acquired true independence. With the assembly's grant of support and the extension of privileges to scholars and tutors went the assembly's determination to exercise a measure of oversight and control over a college meant to serve the whole colony and, later, outsiders as well. And with the gradual diversification of Connecticut's religious life, breaches appeared in the wall of orthodoxy designed to keep Yale pure. In 1722 after Rector Timothy Cutler and two of his tutors embraced Anglicanism, there followed a period of many years when only those of the strictest orthodoxy could secure employment at Yale. But in time a number of Anglican students graduated from Yale, some even going into the ministry. Even that most orthodox of presidents, Thomas Clap, dared not purge Anglican students for fear Yale's charter would be called in question before the home government. What Yale lacked in religious uniformity among its students, however, it made up for by its inculcation of respect for property, authority, and the status quo. The ministers and other leaders it trained became the pillars of Connecticut's Standing Order.

For this role, the college paid a price; it was too intertwined with men of substance and power to be allowed to go its own way. Always scrambling for funds, the college had to rely for many years on annual grants from the assembly, and from time to time the legislature did more: it granted a total of 1500 acres of land in the new western townships in 1732, diverted money from the impost on rum, paid for repairs, authorized a lottery, made up deficits. And not unnaturally the assembly exerted authority over the trustees, not hesitating to interfere in internal matters at the college. The rector and undertakers did not like this interference and tried to avoid it, with only slight success.

The answer of Thomas Clap was the Yale charter of 1745, which made the college into a self-perpetuating corporate body, concentrating more power in the hands of a president and leaving rule-making power to him and the fellows. Still, the legislature had oversight and could even disallow the rules laid down by the president and the fellows. Under a strong leader like Clap, however, interference became rare; indeed, not until Clap himself became obnoxious to Old Lights in the General Assembly was the annual grant cut off, allegedly because of anticipated expenses in the French and Indian War. After the war, public support was resumed. Clap had successfully fought off a legislative investigation in 1763, but rebellious students finally forced him out of office in 1766. Within a month the legislature was ordering changes: cutting back the tutors by one, demanding an annual accounting, and stipulating that parents be better informed about fines for students' misdeeds. In 1772, the assembly set up a committee to review "the state of education and learning . . . the government, laws and constitutions" of the college.

By the eve of the Revolution, Yale had strayed from the design of its founders. Only a small part of its graduates entered the ministry, and although 75 percent of its students came from Connecticut, it also drew students from New York and further away. Among colonial colleges, Yale, along with the colleges in New Jersey and Rhode Island, attracted the greatest proportion of students from outside its own borders, largely because of its relative cheapness. Those Connecticut boys who left the colony to attend college elsewhere did so largely for religious reasons, at a time when New Light ideas were anathema to President Clap. Clap became a political New Light in 1755, but the turmoil marking his last years and arising from the rigidity of his rules produced a decline in enrollments that persisted to the Revolution. Yet Yale continued to play its role of supplying the leaders for Connecticut's political and religious life.

*   *   *

The social structure of the colonies was hierarchical throughout the colonial period, but recent studies suggest that classes were neither well defined nor rigid. Contempories referred most often to the "better" sort, the "middling" sort, and the "lower orders." At the top of Connecticut society, obviously, were the well-to-do and the political elite, the latter made up of those repeatedly elected or appointed to the higher offices in the colony—assistants, superior court judges, representatives, and high-ranking military officers. Though such officials came generally from among the affluent, wealth was not the sole criterion for membership among the better sort. Office itself conferred status. Military rank seems most consistently to have been recognized, even for men whose military service was long past or for men whose rank was as low as sergeant. Also recognized were college graduates, who had pursued a liberal education, thus rising above any kind of manual labor. One such, indignant that he was expected to serve in the militia, successfully petitioned the General Assembly for exemption, remarking that he "had obtained the honor of a Diploma . . . which may be supposed to elevate the gentleman adorned with such a laurel something above the vulgar order." The clergy, of course, were universally respected, designated in the early records usually as "Mr." for "master" and later as "reverend" and often as both. Leading laymen, as well, like deacons, enjoyed the distinction of being so addressed.

The honorific "Mr.," read also as "mister," is of uncertain distinction. From the first in Connecticut, the magistrates were designated in the records as "Mr." or by their military titles. But for many years only some of the representatives enjoyed the title of "Mr.," the number increasing with the passage of time. Men from smaller or newer towns were listed without any honorific until repeated election brought them such recognition. The secretary sometimes revealed uncertainty by occasionally dropping the honorific and then restoring it.*

By October 1700, all representatives, with one exception, were listed as "Mr." or with military titles, but citizens petitioning the General Assembly were designated by first and last names only, unless they were persons of some dignity. That officials had some concern about recognizing one's proper place is suggested by this passage taken at random from early records: "This Court . . . have appointed Mr. Blackman, Goodman Beardsley, Mr. Fairchild and Joseph Judson, as a Committee." Blackman was a minister, and Beardsley had served earlier as a minor judicial officer.

For those at the top of the political structure, the word "esquire" was used—at first for governors and deputy governors, and by the late seventeenth century for some of the magistrates or assistants.† By 1701, and about the time all representatives were called "Mr.," all magistrates, unless they had a military title, were designated "esquire."

The honorific "goodman" appears only rarely in the printed records and soon passed out of fashion; it was a designation for those of the mid-

---

* For examples, see Peter Bewell of Simsbury, *Conn. Col. Records,* vol. 3, pp. 230, 237, 239; vol. 4, pp. 55, 174. Also David Brainerd of Haddum, vol. 4, pp. 138, 174, 197, 244, and Samuel Hayes of Norwalk, vol. 4, pp. 138, 158, 197, 245.

† In the seventeenth century two listings of all magistrates with "esquire" seem to be aberrations. *Ibid.,* vol. 3, p. 129; vol. 4, p. 221.

dling sort but apparently was not used with the care of military titles and "Mr." Ordinary farmers, small tradesmen, and artisans made up the bulk of the middle ranks. The line between them and the better sort, however, was not clear; one class tended to shade into the other. Moreover, within each town the distinctions may not have accorded with those of the colony at large. Thus men repeatedly elected as selectmen might form part of a local elite, but outside their towns they were part of the undifferentiated middle. Many towns in Connecticut had no particularly rich men, and the number without any land at all tended to increase in the late eighteenth century with the rise of population and the growing scarcity of land. Landless laborers without any particular skill formed the bottom fringe of the middling sort, shading over into the poor of the lowest class. In the newer towns some of these could expect to improve their economic position; some fell into the ranks of the permanently poor.

A recent study by Jackson Turner Main has made a statistical analysis of the distribution of property in the colony. Relying on probate records and the inventories they furnish and adjusting the bias in these to take account of the living population, he has concluded that "about one-third of the adult males owned very little property," but virtually all these were young and unmarried. For most of them, poverty, if it is defined as owning less than £50, was a temporary condition. Main concludes that "an overwhelming majority of men accumulated estates ranging from £100 to £500," figures that remained stable despite the large increase in the population—1,000 percent between 1690 and 1775. Although some few men accumulated estates well above these figures, Connecticut produced no extremely rich men. Estates totaling £5,000 were very rare at any given time during the colonial period. Much greater fortunes could be found in some of the other colonies. Over the years there were some changes in the concentration of wealth, but these showed neither extreme swings nor steady movement in any one direction. Between 1650 and 1684 Main estimates that the upper 10 percent owned over half the total wealth, largely because many men were without land. By 1700 the top group owned only 39 percent, and for the rest of the century the figure rose to only 45 percent.* Property, then, was relatively well dis-

---

* Jackson Turner Main, "The Distribution of Property in Colonial Connecticut," in James Kirby Martin, ed., *The Human Dimensions of Nation Making* (Madision, Wis.: The State Historical Society of Wisconsin, 1976), pp. 58, 90–91.

tributed compared with the prevailing pattern in Europe and in America in later periods.

This is not to say that no one was genuinely poor. Statistics deal in averages; individuals make appeals for help. These poor, along with bound servants, Indians who lived among whites, and slaves, were at the bottom of the social scale. Poverty is, of course, a relative term, and from one point of view may be regarded as voluntary or involuntary. Among the voluntary poor the authorities classed the vagabonds and sturdy beggars who made a living of sorts by "idling away . . . their time" practicing "unlawful games . . . common plays, interludes, or other crafty science &c." Their lot, the General Assembly decreed in 1718, was to be fifteen strokes on the naked body and expulsion from town within twenty-four hours, until they were moved town by town out of the colony. By 1727, the increase in idlers and tricksters caused the assembly to order a workhouse built at colony expense either in Hartford, New Haven, or New London, which was to accommodate also those too distracted to be allowed to go at large. By 1753, every county was ordered to consider a workhouse for thieves as well as vagabonds, and further regulations for operation of workhouses were laid down in 1769.

There was no formal definition of the involuntary poor, but everyone knew who they were—those unable to pay their taxes and for whom an abatement might be granted. This kind of poverty seems to have begun in the eighteenth century; at least there are no printed records of abatements earlier for individuals, only for whole towns pleading the costs of getting started. The published laws of 1702 provided that poll taxes could be abated for sickness and infirmity, and the assembly granted an occasional abatement for those who directly petitioned for it. In 1765, the assembly specifically empowered selectmen to abate colony taxes for those too poor to pay.

The town as a whole then became liable for the missing taxes and any costs arising from commitment of such poor people to the workhouse or jail. Naturally, it was better to head off such a situation before it occurred, and the General Assembly as early as 1719 had authorized selectmen, with the approval of the nearest civil authority, to take care of those headed for financial disaster, "disposing them to service or otherwise" and managing their estates. In official parlance, such persons were deemed likely through "idleness, mismanagement, and bad husbandry" to expend their entire estate. No sale of any part of their real estate could take place without assembly approval, but the records contain many examples of selectmen who itemized the costs of care for a man or woman or a whole family and successfully pleaded for permission to sell enough real estate to cover past expenditures. Those accused of bad management were not without recourse. Thomas Gold of Reading protested to the assembly the seizure of his estate by the selectmen, insisting that he was prudent and industrious and that "what of his estate he hath expended has been in charitable deeds, according to the dictates of his conscience." Apparently the selectmen did not recognize charity when they saw it, but the assembly agreed with Gold.

In a similar category were the infirm, the chronically ill, and the mentally deficient. Responsibility for their care belonged first to their relatives, then to their towns; or if they had significant amounts of property, the county court might name a conservator to manage their holdings. Joseph Hickcox of Durham, named by the county court, spent nearly £42 in a single year to care for Samuel Wilkinson and his family, against which he credited only £8 for his use of Wilkinson's real estate. The General Assembly allowed sale of enough property to make up the difference. The selectmen of Cornwall cared for Abiel Dudley, a distracted person, for fifteen years, spending nearly £28 in that time. To repay the selectmen the assembly permitted sale of part of Dudley's small amount of unimproved land. Since Dudley had never had any personal estate, his life during those years must have been a bare existence. Perhaps another indicator of poverty is the large number of executors or administrators of estates who petitioned the assembly for permission to sell part of the real estate of the deceased because personal property was insufficient to cover remaining debts. Most often, their total did not exceed £100, lawful money, suggesting that the deceased had been barely keeping his head above water.

By the eighteenth century the towns' responsibility in these matters had been made abundantly clear. In 1764, when Thomas Judd, grown old and unable to support himself, petitioned the General Assembly for relief, saying that he lived upon a "wedge of land not within the bounds of any township," the assembly decreed that Simsbury should provide his support until legal action determined that some other town was responsible for him. If the responsibility lay elsewhere, Simsbury could recover its costs. The New England practice of "warning out" protected a town from inadvertently acquiring responsibility for persons or whole families that might settle and become a public charge. Warning out could take place any time up to within a year of a person's arrival in a town. Admission as an inhabitant in a town, as noted earlier, depended upon clear procedures.

But what of those transients who became sick or were otherwise unable to move on as expected? The initial responsibility for providing for their care fell to the town, but its selectmen could receive reimbursement from the colony upon proof of expenditures. By the 1770s reviewing such accounts became a major part of the business of the governor and Council, and the names of some transient persons appear time after time in these records, some towns being apparently unable to shake off these dependents. The General Assembly itself was happy to speed their way out of the colony if means could be found; occasionally, for example, a person born in England might be sent back there.

For those whose troubles grew out of sudden disaster—triplets born to a mother herself sick and with a sick husband, an incurable and expensive ailment in the thigh of another mother's child, frozen toes that crippled a married man with a family to support—the General Assembly might authorize "a brief, craving the contribution and charity of the good people" in specified towns or parishes. The assembly would urge appropriate ministers to bring the plight of the afflicted to the attention of their congregations and would designate some suitable person to receive the contributions and deliver the money to the needy person. The same means was used to raise money for the victims of a Boston fire in 1760. Obviously, voluntary solicitation had to have the sanction of the government lest fraud be perpetrated and the undeserving bilk their betters.

If the poor received grudging care, the lot of others at the bottom of society could be even worse. Like the other colonies, Connecticut took in indentured servants, men and women who in return for payment of their passage to the colonies agreed to work for room and board for a period of years. Typically, they signed an indenture, which was a legally binding contract, and upon their arrival in a colony were sold to those seeking their services. Other servants in Connecticut might be debtors bound out to their creditors, or convicted criminals who were unable to make restitution and pay their court costs.

Local debtors and criminals apart, the New England colonies had proportionately fewer bound servants than colonies to the southward because Puritans were suspicious of strangers with uncertain religious be-liefs and because such servants saw fewer opportunities after freedom to make their own way. The New England method of compact settlement of new towns made it harder for the freed servant to get a start. Lists of the names of bound servants emigrating from England between 1654 and 1686 show that a bare fraction of the totals went to New England, as contrasted with Virginia; and between 1720 and 1732, the pattern was repeated, with Maryland, Virginia, and Pennsylvania receiving the great bulk of the arrivals.*

Under Connecticut's Code of 1650, the servant enjoyed far less protec-tion than his counterpart in Massachusetts Bay; indeed, the Connecticut provisions are purely punitive: runaways were to be brought back by force of arms; servants engaging in trade without their masters' permis-sion were to suffer fines or corporal punishment; and shirkers could have their time extended threefold to compensate their masters for lost time, this last being the only addition Connecticut made to the Massachusetts code of 1648. Rebellious servants, like rebellious children, could be committed to the house of correction at "hard labour and sever punishment,—so long as the Court . . . shall judge meet." Lacking in the records is any serious concern for their spiritual welfare, although heads of families undoubtedly saw to it that servants attended Scripture readings and learned the catechism. If a servant fled from a master who abused him, later law declared that he was to be protected by those in the same town to whose homes he fled, and the authorities were to be no-tified. This provision had been in the Massachusetts law from the begin-ning. By 1750, the law stated that if a magistrate could not bring about a reconciliation between such abused servant and his master, the matter could be tried before the next county court and the servant freed if the master was at fault.

Connecticut's laws affecting servants failed, most importantly, to spell out freedom dues, which normally guaranteed bonded persons at the end of their term a minimal means to start on a free life. The relatively small number of indentured servants in Connecticut probably accounts for the infrequent mention of them in the printed records after 1650. Later when

---

* Abbot E. Smith, *Colonists in Bondage: White Servitude and Convict Labor in America, 1607–1776* (Chapel Hill, N.C.: University of North Carolina Press, 1947), pp. 296, 308, 310, 316–17.

the word *servant* appears, it is usually understood to apply to Indians and Negroes, who are categorized as "servants or slaves" up until the 1720s.

In 1680, in the first of a series of replies Connecticut and other colonies were to make to English officials over the years, it was asserted that there were "but fewe servants amongst us, and less slaves, not above 30." Connecticut was then getting each year from Barbados but three or four Negroes, who sold for about twenty-two pounds apiece. But by the Revolution, Connecticut had the largest number of black slaves of the New England colonies, although they were not of central importance to Connecticut's economy and masters increasingly tended to free them. Most slaves worked as domestic servants in the homes of the well-to-do and as farm hands, when they reputedly were treated often as virtual members of the family. Because subsequent replies to English officials do not always maintain a distinction between slaves and blacks and sometimes lump Indians and blacks together, precise conclusions about growth in the number of Negro slaves cannot be made. If one assumes that practically all blacks were slaves and that the number of Indian slaves became insignificant, the real increase in Connecticut slaves came between 1749 and 1756, when the number rose from 1,000 to 3,019 or 3,587, depending on which figure one accepts. A further 52 percent increase had occurred by 1761, and only an 11 percent additional increase by the revolutionary period.

The first mention of Negroes, who were in all likelihood slaves, came in the Code of 1650, which stipulated that Indians seized for satisfaction of offenses against whites might be sent out of the colony and exchanged for Negroes if a tribe gave no satisfaction. In 1660, the General Court decreed that neither Indian nor Negro servants were to serve in the militia or as watch and ward, but despite repeated renewals of this prohibition, slaves did fight in various wars, simply because they were needed. The legislature gradually worked out a kind of slave code, which it often applied to Indian as well as Negro slaves, or servants, as they were also called.

In 1690, Negro servants away from home were required to have a pass from either the authorities or their masters, and those without such passes could be seized by any inhabitant. Even free Negroes lacking certificates might be seized and required to pay costs after proving their status. No mention is made in this statute of Indian servants. In 1703, the General Assembly decreed that no taverner "shall suffer any either mens sonnes, apprentices, servants, or negroes to set drinking in his or her house" without permission of their respective parents or masters. Obviously this enactment was aimed at a whole class, but the assumption was that Negroes had masters. The assembly in 1708 made it a crime for a free person to receive or buy goods without permission from a master, from "any Indian, molato or negro servant or slave," the presumption being, of course, that such goods belonged to the master. The same statute singled out mulattoes and Negroes as numerous in some areas and likely to be turbulent, stipulating thirty stripes for those who disturbed the peace or offered to strike a white person, the first reference to skin color rather than to status as inhabitant or free person.

Fear of Indian slaves brought from the Carolinas, where the Indians were hostile, caused Connecticut in 1715 to forbid the importation of such slaves of whatever age or sex; but Indian slavery did not die out at that time, for in 1723 a curfew was imposed on Indian and Negro servants and slaves, who could not be out after 9:00 P.M., on pain of receiving ten stripes. And in 1730, forty stripes were assigned to Negro, Indian, or mulatto slaves who uttered words that would be actionable if uttered by a free person. The reference here was to slaves, not to servants or slaves. Still, the language of the statute in limiting slander to actionable words implied that the slave would have a true hearing of the evidence before a justice.

Of these several laws forming a kind of slave code, only one concerns the responsibilities of the master: a statute of 1702 that made the owner of a Negro or mulatto servant or slave responsible for the freed man if he was later unable to support himself. The intent, of course, was to protect the community from having to bear the costs of caring for poor freedmen, since some masters allegedly foisted old and worn-out slaves upon the community. Despite the reasoning of the preamble, however, the statute does not restrict its application to old or infirm slaves, and the master's responsibility descended to his heirs. Two possible implications are concealed in the background: free blacks were likely to have trouble supporting themselves, and blacks could never become part of the community and expect the support to which the poor were entitled.

One or two other references to slaves are worth mention. As late as 1757, Indians were apparently still held in slavery, for an enactment of that year stipulated that the heirs of Indian volunteers who had died in the war were to get any wages due, provided the volunteers were "not under bondage either for term of time or for life." In 1774, Connecticut forbade the importation of either Indian or Negro slaves, such importation being declared "injurious to the poor and inconvenient." Finally, while the statutes did not offer protection to slaves any more than to servants, the courts seem to have offered some. In 1775, a native of the Cape Verde Islands named Jonah sought relief from a justice of the peace, who appealed to the General Assembly for a ruling. No record of its ruling has been found, however. Connecticut made manumission of black males capable of military service somewhat easier during the Revolution, and in the 1780s it began gradual emancipation.

Just how many free Indians lived peaceably within the colony's borders is difficult to ascertain. Periodically the government reported population, shipping, and other statistics to the Board of Trade, but it showed little consistency in its method of reporting Indian population. In 1680, Indians were said to number five hundred warriors. In 1725, Governor Talcott listed the number of Indians by tribe and location, his figures totaling 1,245, although he estimated the total in round figures at 1,600. In 1730, the governor repeated that estimate for the Board of Trade. Yet in 1749, the official total was declared to be 500. In 1756, a county-by-county census showed 617 for New London County and none for the other five counties, an obvious oversight. In 1761, the total reported was 930, and in 1774, 1,363. Customarily the Indians were referred to as "a few small tribes" centered in a half dozen towns.

Free Indians were the subjects of much legislation from the beginning of the Connecticut colony, for understandable reasons. It was hoped that a compound of restraint on Indian activity and of just treatment would prevent untoward incidents and possible reprisals. The colony very early banned the sale of arms to Indians, a prohibition that was regularly repeated. In the 1640s trade with Indians in iron and steel products was banned, and in 1656, at the suggestion of the United Colonies, the prohibition was extended to the sale of horses and boats. Extension of credit was denied in any kind of sale to Indians, and restrictions were put upon Indian movement. After the Pequot War, Indians who moved to the vicinity of an English town had to name their sachem, who was required to be fully liable for trespasses and damages to farm animals. In the 1640s magistrates ordered that no white was to permit any Indian to come into his home unless the homeowner was a magistrate or trader, and, even then, no more than four men could accompany a sachem.

(Uncas, Mohegan friend to Connecticut, was allowed twenty, however.) In 1652, a flat prohibition forbade Indians to come near English homes except to hear public preaching, and in 1660 it was decreed that no Indians could live closer than a quarter mile from English settlements.

Yet the colonial government sought to see justice extended to the Indians. No white could take it upon himself to punish Indians for wrongdoing; that was within the jurisdiction of a magistrate and only upon evident cause. The cloak of the law's protection was thrown around Indian debtors also; white creditors could not seize corn or other goods from Indians without an order from lawful authority.

These laws and orders were enactments of the seventeenth century, when the settlers seem to have been motivated by a mixture of fear and condescension, or even contempt. In Puritan eyes the Indians were, of course, heathens in the grip of Satan. Moreover, they were savage heathens; Puritans made little effort to understand their culture or their outlook on life. And when Indians became corrupted by the Englishman's strong drink, as many did, they were dismissed as filthy drunkards, and lazy to boot, because they were reluctant to adopt the work habits commanded by the Puritan ethic. The seventeenth-century colonists wanted to hold the Indians at arm's length for fear they themselves would be corrupted. Thus in 1642, noting that "divers persons" had left the settlements to live among the Indians, particular court magistrates decreed that such persons should suffer three years' imprisonment in a house of correction, as well as such fines and corporal punishment as were fitting. Five years later the General Court forbade the renting of land to Indians because the mixing of the two races would corrupt the manners of many young men. The only exceptions were to be peaceable Indians who would "subjecte themselves to be ordered by the English."

The Puritans were not entirely unmindful of the Christian injunction to spread the Word and to bring sinners to Christ, but in the seventeenth century in Connecticut, when energies were drained by the struggle for survival, the effort was certainly minimal. At the suggestion of the United Colonies, Connecticut in 1654, in order to rescue "those poore, lost, naked sonnes of Adam," offered to train a young man as interpreter who could work with the ministers so that effective religious instruction could go forward.

Not until the eighteenth century did Connecticut do much more.

Then its attitude was that of a hopeful protector. The tribes had been reduced to mere dependents, who pleaded repeatedly for government protection of their land rights, which were threatened by white encroachers. Indians in the town of Groton petitioned the General Assembly time and again over a forty-year period to prevent whites from cutting firewood and seizing planting lands that had been reserved for the Indians. In 1730, the assembly appointed guardians for the Mohegans, and two years later it authorized them to lease Indian land to whites for a limited time, the land to be returned to Indian control at the expiration of the leases. The assembly also put the Niantics under similar guardianship. But despite guardians and leases the complaints continued, and in 1752 the assembly repealed the law it had passed twenty years earlier, noting that whites continued to cut trees in areas reserved for Indians and otherwise hindered Indian improvements. As late as 1774, Indians made such complaints about the proprietors of Groton.

Guardians or overseers not only tried to protect Indian property rights but also acted as arbiters of disputes among Indians, as inspectors of their conduct, and as agents of Christianity. For Puritans, christianizing the Indians was no easy task, since Indians were expected to meet the same standards for church membership as whites. They had to be able to read the Bible, give evidence of their understanding of theological concepts (rote recitation of the catechism never satisfied Puritans), accept Puritan standards of conduct, and at the least own the covenant if not actually give evidence of their saving faith. More was involved here than just schooling. By ancient conditioning, Indian intelligence centered on the practical, on a "detailed knowledge of places and events" rather than on abstract thinking. Moreover, the Indian was traditionally taught to avoid expressing emotions and to rely heavily upon ritual in his religious ceremonies.* Thus there were many hurdles on the way to Christianity as conceived by the Congregationalists.

Nevertheless some Indians made the effort. In the 1730s, Ben Uncas, grandson of the original Uncas, declared himself a Christian, to the great pleasure of the General Assembly, which gave him a coat and a hat and a gown for his wife. In the eighteenth century it was common for Indians

---

* A. I. Hallowell, "Some Psychological Characteristics of the Northeastern Indians," in Frederick Johnson, ed., *Man in Northeastern America* (Andover, Mass.: Phillips Academy, 1946), pp. 195–225, *passim.*

to place their children in the homes of whites for instruction, but the assembly discovered that many Connecticut families neglected their training both in the principles of religion and in reading, presumably because they were satisfied to have the children's service. The assembly ordered local officials to inspect homes having Indian children and to fine those householders who were neglectful of their duties.

Formal schooling was available to Mohegans, and there is a record of the judgment made by two divines in 1728 on the progress they had made. After eighteen months of school, the scholars were "in their Psalters and some in their Primers." "They can spell very prettily, and some of them can read tolerably without spelling." They knew the Lord's Prayer, the Creed, and the Ten Commandments and were working on the catechism. Apparently the greatest effort was made among the Mohegans, but the General Assembly also appropriated small sums to support Indian children in the schools of Farmington, for the education of Niantic children and Indians living at Potatuck. Outside the colony the assembly supported with small grants schooling in Stockbridge, Massachusetts, for Indians of the Six Nations.

One of the significant private efforts at Indian education was the school conducted in Lebanon by the Reverend Eleazer Wheelock, pastor of the Second Congregational Church. Like many other ministers, Wheelock taught a few young men preparing for college, until a young Mohegan named Samson Occom appeared one day begging for instruction. He was a convert to Christianity but could barely spell a few words. Yet in four years he was deemed fit for college. Although Occom returned to his people as a preacher rather than seek higher education, his example persuaded Wheelock to accept more Indian students until by 1762 he was teaching twenty of them. His success attracted wide interest and philanthropic support. In 1765 friends of the school financed a trip to Great Britain for Occom, who, accompanied by the Reverend Nathaniel Whitaker, toured England and Scotland, managing to raise £10,000. With this capital assuring continuance and expansion, Wheelock in 1768 moved the school to New Hampshire, where his students would be less subject to the distractions of white influences. Incorporated now as Dartmouth College, the school gradually became less centrally concerned about Indian education. Wheelock's work and the token appropriations of the General Assembly were palliative; at best these efforts could benefit only a small fraction of the Indian population.

SAMSON OCCOM. Occom was the first of Eleazer Wheelock's Indian students; although he was deemed fit for college after working with Wheelock for four years, he chose to return to his own people as a preacher. In 1765, accompanied by a minister, Occom traveled to Great Britain to raise money for an Indian school. He had great success as a fund raiser and became something of a celebrity. This mezzotint engraving, done by J. Spilsbury (or J. S. Pilsbury) after a painting by Mason Chamberlain, was published in London in 1768. *Courtesy of the Boston Public Library, Print Department.*

G. III R.

At a General Affembly of the Governor and Company of the Colony of *Connecticut*, holden at *Hartford*, on the Eighth Day of *May*, A. D. 1766.

U P O N *the Memorial of the Reverend* ELEAZAR WHEELOCK, *of* Lebanon ; *reprefenting to this Affembly at their Seffions in* May, A. D. 1763, *granted faid Memorialift the Benefit of a BRIEF throughout this Colony, for the Support and Encouragement of the Indian Charity-School under his Care.*

THAT before faid Brief was generally read in the feveral Congregations to which it was directed, it was thought prudent to fufpend the further reading the fame, on Account of fome Hoftilities committed by the Indians, until a more favourable Opportunity.

THAT faid School is yet continued, and the Numbers and Expence is greatly increafed, in fupporting a Number of Miffionaries and School-Mafters among the Indians, &c. and praying that faid BRIEF may be again Revived, and properly Encouraged, as per Memorial on File.

T H I S Affembly do thereupon Grant and Order a BRIEF throughout this Colony ; recommending it to all Perfons charitably and liberally to Contribute to fuch pious and important Defign : and that the Monies fo Collected, be by the Perfons therewith intrufted in the feveral Congregations, delivered, as foon as may be, to the faid Mr. WHEELOCK, (taking his Receipt therefor) to be by him applied for the Ufe and Benefit of faid School, as prayed for.

AND it is further Refolved, That printed Copies of this Act be feafonably delivered to the feveral Minifters of the Gofpel in this Colony, who are hereby alfo directed to read the fame in their feveral Congregations ; and thereon appoint a Time for making fuch Contributions.

A true Copy of Record, examin'd by

George Wyllys, Sec'".

✻✦✢⦿✦✦⦿✦✦⦿✦✢✦✢✻✦✢✻✢✦✻✦✢(✦✢✻✦✢✻)✦✢✻✦✢✦✻✢✦

New-London : Printed by *T. Green,* Printer to the Governor and Company.

BROADSIDE IN BEHALF OF WHEELOCK'S INDIAN SCHOOL. This kind of "brief," issued by the authority of the General Assembly, was necessary if charitable funds were to be raised through the colony's ministers. The latter were "directed" to read the appeal to their congregations, and persons were appointed to collect the contributions. It will be noted that the Reverend Wheelock made his request of the Assembly in 1763, but that Indian hostilities made it prudent to defer the solicitation for three years. *Courtesy of the Boston Public Library, Rare Books Department.*

Within a century the Indians of Connecticut generally had become pathetic wards of the state, almost swallowed up by the thousands of whites who had planted fields and established towns in their country.

Two other groups in Connecticut also suffered disabilities: tenants and women. Almost nothing has been written on tenancy in New England, for the overwhelming numbers of farmers were freeholders; yet tenants existed in Connecticut from the earliest days, perhaps more than in Massachusetts Bay, for the laws of Connecticut required land rights to be occupied if they were to remain valid. John Winthrop, Jr., leased some of his lands to tenants, and Andrew Belcher in 1703 obtained from the General Assembly a patent to 470 acres of land because he had built houses and settled tenants upon it. Yale College kept tenants on farms that it owned in the towns of Norfolk and Canaan. A law of 1728 took note of the frequency with which persons living in one town had settled tenants and livestock on farms at some distance from their hometowns and stipulated that the livestock on tenant farms should go into the tenant's listing, the tax presumably paid by the owner. Tenants did not have the right to vote in colony elections, although the evidence is strong that during the last two-thirds of the eighteenth century they could vote in town affairs if they were admitted inhabitants. Tenancy remains an elusive topic meriting further exploration. If Governor Talcott is to be believed, landlords in the first part of the eighteenth century could not expect to get rich from their rents: "In this poor country, if the landlord lives, the tenant starves: few estates here will let for little more than for maintaining fences and paying taxes." But using tenants had the advantage of maintaining one's right to land until such time as it could be sold at a profit.

The position of women changed relatively little during the seventeenth and eighteenth centuries. For women even more than for men, marriage was regarded as the normal state, and Puritan doctrine taught that although the wife was a partner of her husband, she was a subordinate one. According to the Code of 1650, no marriage contract could be entered into without public announcement eight days before, and another eight days had to pass before the wedding. Originally, marriages were wholly civil affairs, the contract spelling out carefully in advance what property each set of parents was willing to settle upon the couple, but, in 1694, Connecticut allowed ministers to perform marriages for those whose consciences desired a religious ceremony. The code forbade any suit for marriage to begin without the consent of parents or masters; a father whose daughter was courted without his permission could bring suit. In a sense, then, marriages were arranged, but no young people were to be married against their will. They were to marry only those whom they could grow to love. Love in Puritan thinking came after the marriage; it was not a precondition.

Within the household, the woman played a significant economic role in preserving and preparing food, spinning, weaving, cleaning, and making soap, candles, and other household necessities. She shared with her husband the nurturing of children and the supervision of servants and apprentices, if there were any. Though the father had ultimate responsibility for directing and supervising the spiritual development of family members and for training his sons in some useful occupation, the mother's authority over children and servants was recognized, and she, of course, had the responsibility for teaching her daughters the household arts.

So far as laws go, the chief gain made by women in Connecticut in the colonial period was improved recognition of their property rights as wives, widows, and divorcees. In 1723 the General Assembly, stating that land had become more valuable than it had been when the colony began, decreed that a wife must consent to her husband's disposal of property that had come into her possession before or during marriage. Before this enactment, a husband had been able to sell or otherwise dispose of his wife's real estate even without her knowledge. Now a wife could bring suit for recovery if her husband ignored this new law. An example of its operation is William Howard's petition to the assembly for permission to sell a small piece of land belonging to his wife, who was distracted and could not legally give her consent. In the old days he would not have hesitated. In 1773, a thoughtful wife willed her husband enough of her real estate to cover the expenses of her long last illness— about half the value of her property; the record is silent on what she did with the rest. And in 1775, a husband and wife quarreled over control of the wife's real estate. In answer to her petition, the assembly ruled that the husband should have the use and improvement of twenty-five acres; the remainder was to be under the wife's control as though she were not married.

The property rights of widows and divorcees was of concern because of the perennial fear of increasing the class of those dependent upon the community if proper provision was not made for them. Traditionally a widow had a dower right to one third of her deceased husband's property for use during her lifetime, provided she did not bring to the marriage significant amounts of real estate. In 1736, the General Assembly confirmed this old law and established ways for widows or divorcees who were injured parties to claim their dowers at law; and in 1769, the assembly went further in that it made heirs liable for the support of widows if the legal dower or the provisions of the will were insufficient for support.

Divorce was available to Connecticut couples on three grounds: adultery, fraudulent contract, and willful desertion or providential absence for three or seven years, respectively. The earliest divorces were apparently granted by the General Court, but in 1677 the Court of Assistants, later the Superior Court, was given that power. In one instance, however, the General Assembly reversed the court's judgment even though the divorced woman had meanwhile remarried. Despite the limited provisions of the law, the assembly in 1753 granted a divorce to a woman on grounds that her husband severely abused her, and in another case acquiesced in separation and support payments. Divorce was possible, then, and on more grounds than some modern states until recently allowed, but it was rare.

One final note on the position of women. Petitions to the General Assembly show many instances of women who were administrators or executors of their husband's estates, sometimes with the assistance of a man, but by no means always. Such a position of trust, accepted by the courts, suggests that women were not regarded as incompetent or childlike in legal and business affairs. In fact, colonial women, as widows, often took over management of their husbands' businesses as printers, tavern-keepers, and the like. And women, of course, served as teachers; but then, as now, they were not regarded as men's equals. Norwich schools, for example, stayed open each year a term of months and days proportionate to the school district's taxable wealth, but if a woman was doing the teaching at half a man's pay, the school could stay open twice as long. By the eighteenth century, Connecticut had its ladies. In the words of Samuel Peters, "The women of Connecticut are strictly virtuous, and to be compared to the prude rather than the European polite lady. They are not permitted to read plays; cannot converse about whist, quadrille, or opera, but will freely talk upon the subject of history, geography, and mathematics. They are great casuists and polemical divines; and I have known not a few of them so well skilled in Greek and Latin as often to put to the blush learned gentlemen."

*   *   *

Another area of local responsibility was public health and policing, these, like so many things, being managed, under the direction of the colony government. The first mention of a physician in Connecticut is in the printed records of 1652, in which Thomas Lord agreed to stay for a year to set bones "and otherwise," for which the General Court promised a subsidy of fifteen pounds and fixed his rates for house calls in Hartford and nearby towns. Subsequently the records show that the legislature licensed at various times from 1684 to the mid-eighteenth century a dozen or so physicians, sometimes indicating their fitness for a license, more often not. Apparently the approval of the General Assembly was not required for practice, but the granting of a license perhaps brought a certain cachet.

For the control of contagious diseases, particularly smallpox, the assembly laid down policies for local authorities to carry out. For the most part, the burden lay on town selectmen to see that goods arriving from a distant and infected area were properly aired before they certified them for sale and that infected persons were quarantined. An outbreak of smallpox in 1721 brought various isolation measures: houses with infected persons had their windows boarded up on the street side; discarded materials had to be well buried "to prevent the dilating of any ill scent in the air"; local officials were to examine peddlers' packs to determine the place of origin of their goods; and dogs resorting to the areas of infection had to be destroyed. In a thorough-going measure passed in 1732, the assembly required the selectmen to provide nursing care for the sick at their own or their parents' or masters' expense, or at the charge of the town if none of these could pay for it. In the event persons fell sick away from home, charges would be assessed against their hometown if they could not pay, but strangers to the colony in such a case would have their charges paid by the public treasury. To provide for care, which must have been onerous, given the fear that smallpox aroused, two justices could issue a warrant for the impressment of nurses; refusal to serve without sufficient cause could bring a jail sentence. The law further required that a large white flag be flown on a ten-foot pole or from the mast of a ship to mark infected places.

Another flurry of legislation occurred in the 1760s to deal with the practice of inoculation, which, while it offered immunity through giving a mild case of smallpox to the inoculated person, made him contagious for a time to those not undergoing inoculation. The procedure could safely be practiced only with the strictest provisions for isolation. Claiming that the people were terrified by those who sought inoculation without seeking permission, the General Assembly forbade the practice without the combined approval of selectmen and the majority of the civil authorities resident in the town. Passed in March 1760, the law was continued for a year, but only with the proviso that the town meeting had to assent to the granting of certificates permitting inoculation. Then in 1761, because smallpox was spreading, inoculation was forbidden altogether, the prohibition continuing from session to session until it was passed without time limit in May 1769.

To protect the community against other hazards, able-bodied men were required to serve in the watch and ward organization. Watchmen reported to the constable at the end of daylight to receive their charge for the night, their duty ending with the break of dawn. They were charged to look out for danger and fire and cry out the necessary alarm ("fire!" or "arm! arm!"). Persons walking "unseasonably" in the streets could be challenged and made to give an account of themselves; and if their account seemed unsatisfactory, they were taken to the constable, who could require their appearance before a magistrate.

*   *   *

The Code of 1650, following the example of Massachusetts Bay, lists twelve capital crimes and adds several more for good measure. The code also defines burglary and theft, for which the punishment was branding and whipping, and on the third offense, death. Although it is not mentioned in the code, convicted thieves usually had to make restitution at double or more the value of the goods stolen. A thief who could not pay such damages and court costs could be put to service for a term of years. He would be sold, as any servant was, for a sum to cover restitution and costs, the sale not necessarily made to his victim, who, understandably, might not want him in his household. If the going price was insufficient, the victim and the government would share proportionately, for the government always sought to have someone pay for costs. After workhouses were established, thieves were sometimes sent there to earn both court costs and damages. Even if a person was found innocent of a serious charge, he could be jailed for inability to pay the costs of prosecution if bound service was not possible because of ill health. Nancy Mitchell, found innocent of manslaughter in 1774, was to be bound out to pay not only prosecution costs but also the costs of keeping her in jail for a time!

The eighteenth century brought new crimes and punishments. The government's resort to paper money afforded an opportunity that counterfeiters could not resist, and counterfeiting became one of the most frequent of serious crimes. The first laws against counterfeiting, passed in 1710 and 1711, provided six months imprisonment as well as fines and possible corporal punishment. Within a few years, such punishment being deemed insufficient and counterfeiting becoming more widespread, the General Assembly decreed branding with a "C," the cropping of the right ear, life imprisonment in a workhouse (although the assembly could alter this provision if it saw fit in particular cases), and forfeiture of the criminal's entire estate. The convicted counterfeiter was also forever barred from engaging in trade in the colony. Still, this array of punishments apparently did not prove an effective deterrent.

The assembly in 1735, complaining of wholesale counterfeiting to the injury of "many innocent people," ordered a new issue of bills of credit from new plates, but the criminals kept at their work. The sentence of life imprisonment was premature, for the assembly did not order the building of a workhouse until 1727, three years after the punishment was decreed. In fact, actual practice was to confine the convicted counterfeiter no longer than six months or more, usually until he paid his fine. In 1773, imprisonment was set at ten years of hard labor for counterfeiters as well as burglars and robbers, and at the same time the Simsbury copper mines were made ready to receive them. A second offense could bring life imprisonment.

Two other crimes received specific mention in the eighteenth century, seizing timber and lumber products being floated down rivers, and horse stealing. Floating products might wash up on land or form obstructions, so that detailed provisions were made for registering marks of ownership with a clerk and, as a way of reducing outright theft, damages were specified for those honestly reporting their finds. The penalties for horse

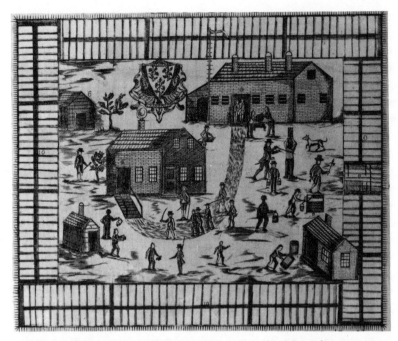

A VIEW OF OLD NEWGATE PRISON, 1800. Early in the eighteenth century, copper mining began in that part of Simsbury which is now part of East Granby, but the mine proved unprofitable within a few decades. By 1773 the colony began to use the mine as a prison, sentencing those convicted of counterfeiting, theft, and horsestealing to long terms in its dank, gloomy depths. During the Revolution, Newgate became a prison for dangerous loyalists. It is now a state park. According to the legend, trimmed off here, one descended thirty-five feet, "from thence Desending in various Serpentine Directions 75 Yards." The largest building depicted was the workshop and the one with steps, the guardhouse, through which prisoners made their descent into the mine; they remained there when not working. *Courtesy of the Massachusetts Historical Society.*

stealing at first called for triple damages, fifteen stripes, three months imprisonment, and a fine, but within two years horse stealing was lumped with other serious crimes and brought ten years in the copper mines.

These mines had long since proved unprofitable, and the willingness of the government by 1773 to sentence men to long terms there suggests a change in attitude of some significance. Heretofore men had been jailed only briefly, being returned to the community as bound servants to work out damages and court costs. Workhouses were created at first to provide a means of support for the wandering, voluntary poor, those not really part of the community; and common thieves were ordered sent there in 1753 for a term of one to three months for a first conviction, their earnings to go toward restitution and costs. If these earnings were insufficient, such thieves could be bound out to service as well. Ten years in the copper mines, life for a second offense, meant that some men were not being corrected, but punished; they were being removed from the community, which was washing its hands of them. Neither their labor nor their productivity was of any concern. Incarceration, which meant the loss of a citizen who might be made useful, was now acceptable. The colony had grown to the point at which some individuals could be dispensed with, particularly when watchful concern for one's neighbors seemed less feasible or important.

Two interesting exceptions to severe punishment are worth mention. Two young men convicted of counterfeiting, one in 1772 and the other in 1774, who had run away to escape punishment, were allowed on the plea of their fathers to return to their families on condition that bonds be posted for their future good behavior. Presumably because these young men came from solid families willing to take responsibility for them, they were viewed not as common criminals but as members of the community worthy of rehabilitation.

Serious offenses against property were not the only crimes that appear in the records, of course. Instances of fornication, adultery, bastardy, and rape dot the records, with fines and public whippings regularly meted out to the guilty. Rape brought the death penalty, but one convicted man successfully pleaded his ignorance of the law's penalty and hoped "that regard being had to the singular difficulties attending the proof of some of the facts constituting such crime in generall as well as to the certain circumstances" of his own case not brought out in the trial, his punishment would be reduced. The General Assembly ordered that he be exhibited on the gallows for an hour, that he receive thirty-nine lashes, that his right ear be nailed to a post and cut off, that he be returned to jail for a month, and that finally he be whipped again with thirty-nine strokes and sent from the colony. Exile was occasionally decreed for those deemed incorrigible. Luckily for Richard Steel, described as the "noted burglarian," the Simsbury mines opened up some months after the Fairfield sheriff transported him to the West Indies.

Seventeenth-century Connecticut had its witches, and the eighteenth, its confidence men and quacks. In 1648, a jury indicted Mary Jonson for familiarity with the devil, and apparently there was a witch scare in Saybrook in 1659. In 1692, Connecticut had its own witchcraft trials, in which four women were indicted, three being acquitted and one sentenced to death. But even the guilty one was probably pardoned, so Connecticut escaped the hysteria that broke out in Massachusetts Bay. In 1721, a persuasive man went around showing a map of buried treasure until he found a victim to help him dig it up. They found a chest of gold bars, which the victim eagerly purchased for £165, only to find later that he had mistaken brass for gold. In 1773, the General Assembly passed a law to prevent mountebanks from selling useless nostrums to the gullible, at least half the objection of the legislature being that these healers attracted a crowd by "games, tricks, plays, juggling or feats of uncommon agility of body." Such performances were as reprehensible as the useless medicine being peddled.

One thing that did not change from one century to the next was insistence that proper respect be paid one's superiors at the risk of condign punishment. For saying that he hoped to meet some of the church members in hell ere long, Peter Bussaker was put into the pillory and severely whipped in 1648, and a few years later John Dawes, for uttering "threatening malicious speeches" against a former governor for the justice he had meted out to Dawes's wife, was banished from the colony on pain of death if he returned. Criticism of the General Assembly or its members always brought swift retaliation. In 1743, for libel against two magistrates, a minister, and the government in general, Roger Bidwell of Hartford lost his voting rights for over three years; and William Leet made the mistake of saying that if he could not answer the assembly "by ballarag," he could "by small sword." He was seized, brought before the assembly, and after examination turned over to a justice of the peace for sentencing. These insults took place during the heat of the Great Awakening, but the assembly was ever watchful that its dignity and honor not be called into contempt by the low or the high.

Colonial Connecticut has a reputation for steadiness and for shunning the violence that sometimes burst out in neighboring Massachusetts Bay in the eighteenth century, but Connecticut men could get their dander up on occasion—although one has to sift the records pretty finely to turn up the evidence. In 1718, after it had been decided that Yale should be located in New Haven, the sheriff, armed with a warrant from the governor and Council, went to Saybrook to gather up the books belonging to the college. He found the house containing the volumes surrounded by people determined not to lose the school, and he and his men had to force their way inside. Even so, some of the books were stolen and never recovered.

More serious was the riot at Hartford in 1722, when a mob released from jail Jeremiah Fitch, who had been jailed for nonpayment of court costs after losing a suit to Major John Clark over land in Coventry. The land in question lay in the area that the General Assembly had temporarily conveyed to the towns of Hartford and Windsor during the Andros regime in order to forestall their seizure by the Crown. The intention was that these western lands should revert to the control of the colony at an appropriate time. The two towns nevertheless sold some of the lands. The title that Fitch claimed was viewed as illegal by the colony government; but if his title was unfounded, so were the titles of others. Fitch's rescue from jail was meant to assert the validity of such titles. Allegedly, the sheriff was unable to seize the rioters for fear of his life. The immediate response of the assembly was to pass a riot act, but ultimately the government had to reach a compromise with the two towns, giving them the eastern half of the townships in dispute.

In 1733, Governor William Cosby of New York complained that Connecticut men had pulled down and burned a house in the Oblong, an area along Connecticut's western border that had recently been ceded to New York. Cosby feared further violence in the area. The only other mention of mob action before the revolutionary era was the seizure in the Connecticut River of a ship being held for sale to satisfy an execution at law. The governor and Council dispatched the sheriff to read the riot act to the dozen or so men holding the vessel. He was empowered to raise the militia if force had to be applied. Presumably the rioters dispersed.

On the whole, Connecticut's record for crowd violence is a rather quiet one. Disputes were settled through resort to the courts or to arbitration, often under the aegis of the General Assembly. In a dozen ways the pressures to conform and to abide by authority were heavy. There were social deviants, of course, but if they could not readily be rehabilitated, their punishment was swift and severe. Men of means and ability or of deep conviction challenged the system from time to time, but until the prerevolutionary era, the challenges were absorbed; if concessions were made, they were grudging and minimal. Those in power found ways to benefit from their positions, but without qualms, for they were serving the public; and they identified their interests with the colony's own.

8

DAILY LIVING, RECREATION,
AND THE ARTS

The typical Connecticut home was a frame house that evolved from a simple structure of the mid-seventeenth century into a pleasingly proportioned and often handsomely finished building by the revolutionary period. The earliest houses were of one or two rooms with a single chimney and a room or two on a second story, with a garret above. The frame was of post and beam construction; that is, posts ten by twelve or twelve by twelve inches were placed at the corners of the house and at each side of the entrance and chimney and set into the sills on top of the masonry foundation by means of tenon and mortise joints. By the same means the posts held beams and girts that provided the support for the floor joists of the second story. Posts, beams, and girts, usually of oak, were hand-hewn and left exposed, and in the better homes the exposed supports were planed and chamfered. In this period the second story was built to overhang the first in the front, a design carried over from England.

In the two-room floor plan the chimney stood in the center of the house, its back wall in line with the rear wall of the building; access was through a door in the long side of the house into an entry, which was placed in front of the chimney, the stairs rising by the chimney wall to the second floor. Access to the first floor rooms was by doors leading off the entry to the left and right. In the one-room plan the chimney was at one end of the room with its fireplace facing the short side of the house and its entry and stairs once again by the chimney wall. When such a house was expanded, the additional room was placed on the other side of the chimney to give it the central position of the two-room house. The rooms were finished with wainscoting of wide vertical boards.

First Period

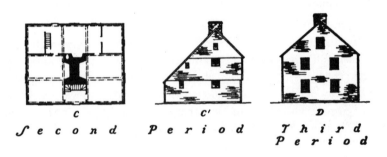

Second Period Third Period

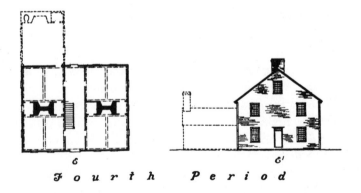

Fourth Period

DIAGRAMS OF EARLY CONNECTICUT HOUSES. Taken from Frederick Kelly's *Connecticut's Old Houses,* this figure shows the evolution of the house from a one-room structure with room and garret above, to a saltbox, and thence to a house with full second story and central hall. *Courtesy of the Antiquarian and Landmarks Society, Hartford.*

Further expansion was made by addition of a lean-to running the entire length of the house at the back. The lean-to was usually divided into three rooms, a large central room and smaller rooms at each end, with provision for storage space above the ceiling of the lean-to. Because the roof on the addition was less steep than the roof on the main part of the house, the roof line at the back was a broken one. The Whitfield house in Guilford, built in 1639, and the Thomas Lee house in East Lyme, built in 1664, are examples of houses from this first period that have been preserved.

In the last quarter of the seventeenth century the lean-to was incorporated into the design of the house from the beginning so that the back roof line was one long continuous sweep, giving the characteristic saltbox appearance. A fireplace for the lean-to section could now be provided with proper design of the chimney. Other changes were the reduction or even elimination of the second story overhang in the front and the use of plaster rather than wainscoting for finishing the rooms. In some areas brick with lime mortar began to replace stone and clay for the chimney. The first-floor plan of five rooms arranged around a central chimney remained unchanged. The Eels-Stowe house in Milford, built between 1685 and 1690, is a good example of this style.

The basic floor plan continued well into the eighteenth century, but the outside appearance changed markedly with the disappearance of the integrated lean-to and thus the long line of the saltbox. In its place was a full second story with its floor plan matching that of the first floor below. This alteration provided more of the rooms on the second floor with full headroom and a gentler slope to the roof. This period saw also the substitution of sliding windows for the casement type, which swung out. Diamond-shaped glass lights held in place by lead were replaced with rectangular ones held in place with wooden bars. Exposed beams now were usually cased. Only in those areas, like Guilford and Norwich, where easily split stone was plentiful, did that material continue in use for chimneys. The Hyland-Wildman house in Guilford, built about 1720, is a good example of the houses in this third period.

By 1750 Connecticut houses were frequently built with a central hall running from front to back and providing space for the stairs. On either side of the hall were two rooms, each pair with a chimney between them. This alteration was not so great a departure as it at first seems, for basically it had the hall joining two two-room plans of the earliest period, which had been turned ninety degrees. The two chimneys instead of a central one meant that there could be a fireplace in every room; and the hall both facilitated movement through the house and had some psychological significance as well. Since it was now possible to reach different rooms without having to go through adjoining ones, members of the household might enjoy greater privacy. Along with the change of floor plan went better finishing of the interior—higher ceilings, beams hidden behind plaster, and paneling around fireplaces, for example. Some Connecticut houses added a kitchen ell, and a few before the Revolution were built of brick. The Joseph Webb house in Wethersfield, built in 1752, is an example of the central-hall house.

In these Connecticut homes lived relatively large families during the colonial period, but not so large as some have imagined today. The family of twelve or fourteen children was not typical. One quantitative study done on eighteenth-century Guilford shows the average completed family size to be about six children.* This finding approximates results obtained by scholars who have studied Massachusetts towns. In that colony the average number of children per family born during the course of a marriage was between seven and nine, depending upon the particular period examined. If one considers only children surviving to age twenty-one, the average in these Massachusetts towns falls to between six and eight children per family. Thus infant mortality was not so severe as often stated, although periodic epidemics could raise the figures sharply and beyond anything known in the United States today. An important difference between colonial and modern families, aside from size, is the spacing of children. Most modern women end their childbearing in their late twenties or early thirties. Colonial mothers bore children over a longer time, spacing them usually about two years or a little more apart. It was more common then than now to have a fully grown child and an infant in the same household, with all age gradations in between. Large families and the arrangement and dimensions of rooms meant that individuals had little of the privacy that our smaller families enjoy today. Moreover, Puritan standards required close supervision of all family members, and all members except infants were expected to contribute to the almost endless variety of tasks that a farm required.

Life on a colonial farm was hard by any standard. The work day was

---

* John Waters, "Patrimony, Succession, and Social Stability: Guilford, Connecticut, in the Eighteenth Century," *Perspectives in American History* 10 (1976): 144–48.

from sun-up to sun-down, or approximately fourteen hours, during the growing season, six days a week. Sunday, a day of rest by Puritan rules, brought only partial relief, for the livestock had to be cared for without any of the mechanical aids enjoyed by farmers today. Attendance at church twice on that day left but little time for pleasurable pursuits even if the religious code had permitted. Harvesting and gathering the crops did not usher in a slack season, for there was grain to thresh with hand flails and to winnow by tossing, flax and hemp to hatchel, stumps to grub out, wood to chop for winter fires and to convert into lumber and other products, fences to strengthen, shoes to repair and even to make if one could not afford the services of a traveling shoemaker, harness to mend, and a hundred other jobs in addition to the daily chores. Every member of a large family could be kept busy until it was time again to prepare the fields for planting. There was work aplenty for every day of the year. And the work was made the harder because of swarms of insects—mosquitoes, flies, grasshoppers—and the diseases that blighted the crops and sickened the animals.

Yet the colonists found time for recreation. Puritans did not celebrate holidays like Christmas and Easter, which were considered to be as popish as the saints' days that crowded the Catholic and Anglican calendars, but in the New World some days were regularly made festive occasions. Guy Fawkes Day on November 5, commemorating Fawkes's attempt to blow up Parliament in the Gunpowder Plot, was celebrated in urban areas with bonfires and parades featuring effigies of Guy and the Pope, since the plot was deemed of Roman Catholic origin. Rowdyism was an unwelcome accompaniment. Contemporaries tell of celebrants accosting passers-by in the streets or knocking on doors demanding small sums for bonfires and drink, but Connecticut towns seem not to have had the gang warfare that marked Boston's annual fête. Until the revolutionary era, commemoration of the sovereign's birthday was obligatory, as was the birth of a royal heir or the succession of a new king. A sedate procession of dignitaries and an official dinner might distinguish the day, with an illumination at night and a firing of cannon in deference to the ruler three thousand miles away. Election Day, when the votes were counted and the governor and magistrates were sworn in, offered another opportunity for breaking the routine of life. In Hartford, as in Boston, the day included the "Nigger 'Lection," when blacks chose their own governor and paraded through the streets.

Less fixed and perhaps more spontaneous were several other occasions for high spirits. The arrival of shad and salmon in the rivers was an excuse for merrymaking and feasting. The shad were so plentiful in Connecticut that those who prized their dignity refused to eat them, and even servants complained if they were asked to eat salmon more than three times a week. The maiden voyage of a ship on the Connecticut River was an occasion for celebration, too. Crowds lined the banks, while pennants were hoisted, speeches made, and prayers said. Thanksgiving, which had begun as a harvest festival, was celebrated at various times of the year to offer thanks for a number of reasons. A victory or the ending of an epidemic or drought might lead the authorities to declare a day for fasting and prayer, which, intentionally or not, would be followed by a feast and revelry, particularly in the eighteenth century. In Norwich, tradition called for the burning of high piles of barrels, which were built by competing teams. The fire on a high hill attracted people from miles around. Training day was another important occasion. The turning out of militiamen to demonstrate their readiness for emergencies and their skill in performing certain military maneuvers brought out many onlookers. Often a contest for marksmanship was a highlight; in Connecticut a token prize like a silk handkerchief was awarded the best shot.

Aside from celebrating specially designated days and traditional events, men and women found other sources of amusement. Organized wolf hunts provided excitement and sometimes cruel entertainment afterwards, when wolves, captured alive, were baited with dogs. Or on moonlit nights foxes were attracted to piles of bait next to a wall where the light was brightest; then hunters in the shadows picked them off with their guns. Since these animals were predators, fun was combined with the serious purpose of protecting domestic animals. More frivolous, and frowned upon by the magistrates, were card playing, dancing at balls and weddings (although permitted at ordinations in the eighteenth century), little plays (called drolls), and puppet shows. The latter included "Taylor Riding to Brentford" and "Harlequin and Scaramouch." These, of course, would be available only in the larger towns. Drama as such was outlawed by Puritans as a great source of immorality. Traveling showings of an African lion or other exotic beasts would attract many. Such an animal was carted around in Connecticut in 1728. Other events that offered more opportunity for instruction were public whippings of miscreants and hangings of grosser criminals. The latter were prayed over and encouraged to give testimony to their wicked courses and their remorse—shiveringly too late.

Children played games whose origin is lost in antiquity, the rules and songs being passed down from child to child, generation after generation. *The Pretty Little Pocket Book,* published during the Revolution, provides the names of many and directions in verse for playing them, each description accompanied with a moral. Chuck-farthing, stool-ball, blindman's buff, leap-frog, hop-hat, hop-scotch, marbles, battledore, and shuttlecock are only a few. The directions for chuck-farthing went thus:

> As you value your Pence
> At the Hole take your Aim.
> Chuck all safely in,
> And You'll win the Game.
>
> Moral
>
> Chuck-farthing like Trade,
> Requires great Care.
> The more you observe
> The better you'll fare.*

Children also flew kites, played with dolls, rolled hoops, and in the winter went coasting and ice-skating. The earliest skates were apparently bones tied to the feet, but in 1763 in Wethersfield brass skates were offered for sale. A favorite pastime of boys and their fathers was whittling. While the sons whittled out whistles and toy windmills and waterwheels, the men made spoons, bowls, and other useful objects.

Numerous excellent craftsmen in wood plied their trade in Connecticut settlements, but very few of the cabinetmakers and joiners of the colonial period have left identities behind. Perhaps the best-known piece of furniture is the Hartford chest produced in the late seventeenth century. These chests, known for the area where most of them have been found, were undoubtedly made by more than one craftsman, but they show a similarity of design that makes them unique and identifiable as a type. The Hartford chest stands about forty inches high and includes one or two drawers as well as the chest proper. Excellently proportioned and sturdily built of white oak and yellow pine, it is ornamented with raised and incised decorations on the front and ends. The ornamentation includes stylized tulips and sunflowers, half spindles, and egg-shaped bos-

---

* Quoted by Alice Morse Earle, *Child Life in Colonial Days* (New York, 1899), p. 347.

TWO-DRAWER SUNFLOWER CHEST. An example of the so-called Hartford chest, made by local craftsmen between 1680 and 1700. Originally it may have been designed as a marriage chest for a young woman. The woods used in this example are oak, pine, and maple. Some examples of this type of chest used a tulip motif in preference to the sunflower. *Courtesy of the Wadsworth Atheneum, Hartford.*

ses. The overall effect is one of balance and pleasing lines, honest craftsmanship without clutter. In a day before closets, the chest was important for storing clothes, valuables, and other goods. In Connecticut homes the Hartford chest must have been one of the most prized pieces of furniture.

It may also have held the few books owned by early families. Bookcases were necessary only for the learned and the affluent; but most families had a Bible and perhaps one or two other works. Besides nurturing religion, reading was a source of recreation and, of course, education. Fragmentary evidence suggests that some children's books were available —stories, picturebooks, books of jokes and riddles—but relatively few before the Revolution. Children also turned to books that were favorites with adults: *Pilgrim's Progress, Robinson Crusoe,* and *Gulliver's Travels.* Connecticut was long handicapped in lacking a flourishing press such as Massachusetts had enjoyed from the early seventeenth century. One consequence was that those who wished to air local issues had either to seek a printer outside the colony or circulate in manuscript their contributions to public enlightenment.

Gershom Bulkeley, Wethersfield minister and physician, mentioned earlier as an opponent of those who resumed government under the charter after the overthrow of Sir Edmund Andros, was one of the earliest and most persistent of Connecticut pamphleteers. In 1689 he brought out *The People's Right to Election*, which he had printed in Philadelphia. In this he defended the legality of the Andros government and reminded the people that only the king could authorize reestablishment of the charter. His tone was temperate, sometimes wry, but his excessively royalist approach to the problems of government did not attract widespread support. He was answered with two manuscript rebuttals by James Fitch, and he countered with "Will and Doom" in 1692, which also lacked a printer, and which has been called "the ablest colonial writing that came out of the 'Glorious Revolution.' "* Bulkeley began with a series of assertions that all lawful government was an ordinance of God and that the king was God's minister. He then proceeded to show how the colony had violated English law and how liberty had been denied because privileges went only to freemen, a message not likely to win him a following.

---

* Samuel E. Morison, *The Intellectual Life of Colonial New England* (New York: New York University Press, 1956), p. 203.

Connecticut's first press was set up in 1709 at New London by Thomas Short, who printed sermons, religious tracts, and such official pronouncements as the government required. Short was succeeded in 1714 by Timothy Green, whom the government paid a salary of fifty pounds per year to print laws, proclamations, and election sermons. He was free to do printing on his own, but his taste ran to religious tracts, which he ran off in unsalable quantities.

By the eve of the Revolution, Connecticut had four newspapers, all of them of relatively recent origin. Two of them have continued publication into our own day. The first newspaper in the colony was the *Connecticut Gazette*, established in New Haven in 1755. With one interruption of about a year, it was published continuously until 1768. When it began to founder, its name was taken over by a New London paper, which had begun as the *Summary* and then became the *New London Gazette*. As the *Connecticut Gazette* it lasted until the mid-nineteenth century. Next in order of establishment came the *Connecticut Courant*, which began publishing at the end of 1764. At first it supported the American cause less vigorously than did the New London paper, but under Ebenezer Watson, who succeeded Thomas Green as publisher about 1767, the *Courant* became more outspokenly patriotic. It continues as the *Hartford Courant* today. The *Connecticut Journal* was begun in New Haven in 1767 and continues there today as the *Courier-Journal*. The original publishers, Samuel and Thomas Green, kept the *Journal* moderate in tone and even dared to print articles by men who were condemned as pro-British. The fourth newspaper appearing regularly during the Revolution was the *Norwich Packet*, founded in 1773 and continuing into the nineteenth century, when it was renamed the *Connecticut Centinel*. With four newspapers circulating in the larger commercial centers of the colony, the Connecticut citizen was kept reasonably well informed about developments at home and in other colonies.

Appearing weekly, usually in a four-page format, newspapers carried military news, accounts of the activities of every level of government, political and literary essays contributed by the articulate of the community, notices of extraordinary occurrences, as well as advertisements for runaways, newly received goods, and real estate for sale. Despite the small size of their papers, publishers carried articles with datelines ranging from New Hampshire to Georgia simply by copying from whatever newspapers came to hand. Before the War for Independence intensified, the London dateline was always prominently featured. There were no professional reporters; some of the most interesting items were submitted by recipients of letters sent from afar who allowed the publisher to use private communications if the names of correspondents remained unidentified. By modern standards, the news was stale, weeks or even months old, but it was fresh enough to those who had no other means of knowing what was happening. Publishers did not normally editorialize; instead they printed polemical pieces by contributors who concealed their indentities under fanciful or self-righteous pseudonyms. The figures on total circulation of colonial newspapers are seldom known, but it has been estimated that one of the most prominent Connecticut papers had five or six hundred subscribers. In any case such figures do not reveal how many people read these newspapers, since copies were available in coffee houses, taverns, and other public places, and certainly subscribers' copies passed from hand to hand.

The appearance of newspapers and printers stimulated polemical writing when such issues as the Susquehannah Company's claim began to occupy public attention. Dr. Benjamin Gale led off in 1769 with a *Letter to J. W. Esquire.* This pamphlet, which first appeared serially in the *New London Gazette,* criticized the General Assembly's election of Jonathan Trumbull as governor, complained of excessive tax abatements, ridiculed the company's claim to western lands, and attacked it for exerting pressure on the legislature. Gale was answered by Eliphalet Dyer, prominent lawyer and member of the company, whose writing also appeared first in the *New London Gazette.* Dyer's answer in *Remarks on Dr. Gale's Letter to J. W. Esq.,* addressed to the "sweet pacific Doctor," was as biting and condescending as the author could make it. Gale replied with a dissection of Dyer's defense of the legality of the western claim. By the 1770s the newspapers were ablaze with charge and countercharge. The historian Benjamin Trumbull produced a long and thoughtful pamphlet that was widely circulated, but it first ran in the *Connecticut Journal* in three installments. To *A Plea in Vindication of the Connecticut Title to the Contested Lands Lying West of the Province of New York* Connecticut owes the first suggestion that money from the sale of western lands might be used to establish a permanent fund for the support of public education. Another significant by-product of the debate over the Susquehannah Company's claim was a greater interest in the colony's origins and a determination to preserve better the early records on which so much hinged. Writers were led also to read such works of history as William Stith's on Virginia, Thomas Hutchinson's on Massachusetts Bay, William Smith's on New Jersey, and William Douglass's on the British settlements.

Of true literature before the Revolution there was very little in Connecticut, and that was strongly didactic. The only notable figure was John Trumbull, already mentioned as the author of the *Progress of Dulness*. In 1775 he completed *McFingal: A Modern Epic Poem . . . or the Town Meeting,* which was published in Philadelphia, where he had sent it for the perusal of one or two close friends. Silas Deane at the Continental Congress received strict orders not to reveal its authorship except to John Adams, also a member of the congress and Trumbull's former law teacher. Men like Deane had already recognized the young man's talent for satire and probably urged Trumbull to put it to use in behalf of the American cause. A few months earlier, in the *Connecticut Courant,* Trumbull had published a piece ridiculing Thomas Gage, royal governor of Massachusetts, for his penchant for issuing proclamations. *McFingal,* written in the style of Samuel Butler's *Hudibras*, describes the confrontation between the Tory Squire McFingal and the honest patriot Honorius, thought by some to be modeled on Adams. Trumbull himself insisted that Honorius was "anyone whose Sentiments are agreeable to his speeches."* The town meeting in the poem took place after the Battle of Lexington and Concord. The poem was so successful that its author reissued it in expanded form after the Battle of Yorktown, and the various editions of it in both America and England made Trumbull a significant literary figure for his times.

No such distinction marked the performance of music in the colony. Connecticut people had long been accustomed to the unaccompanied psalm singing favored by the Puritans. The practice of lining out—the deacon read a line of the psalm and perhaps even explained it before the congregation sang it, and so on, in alternation—did not lend itself to any sustained musical effect. Worse, the typical congregation knew only a few tunes, and too often individual members chose their own rather than the one they were supposed to sing. More than one contemporary has testified to the resulting cacophony. But the "old way" was traditional; change, when it came in the eighteenth century, was vigorously

---

* Trumbull to John Adams, November 14, 1775, Adams Papers, Massachusetts Historical Society.

resisted in some quarters. The new way, called "singing by rule," meant learning to read notes and singing in unison. Gradually those so trained were grouped together to form a sort of choir. These changes, so grudgingly made in some churches, did not do a great deal to nurture musicianship; such talent as gained even local recognition did not develop until the period after the War for Independence. Of course there was singing of a secular kind—ballads, folk tunes, and the like—in the taverns and around the hearths of those insufficiently straitlaced to protest. Music outside of the church was regarded as frivolous, hardly worth serious effort.

Painting, however, particularly of portraits, did find favor among those of solid achievement and substantial income. Scholars have even identified a Connecticut school with a discernible style and some influence that has become known to the art world only in relatively recent years. Best known among the group is Ralph Earl (1751–1801), who came from Massachusetts and opened a studio in New Haven about 1774. With his friend Amos Doolittle he toured the Lexington and Concord area after the battles to make sketches commemorating the event. Then he painted four scenes, only one of which, "A View of the Town of Concord," is extant. From these Doolittle made rather crude copper engravings, prints from which went on sale in December 1775.

Earl was one of the earliest painters of historical scenes with considerably more talent as a draftsman than Paul Revere. And despite Earl's turning to portraiture, where the money lay, he did not give up his love for landscape. One of the characteristics of his portraits is the inclusion of a bit of landscape, charmingly done even if only visible through a window by which the subject is seated. Earl did not stay in Connecticut long. Probably by 1777 he was off to England, where he remained until 1785. The portraits that he did there and upon his return to the United States are a distinguished group. But the earliest known and one of the best is his full-length study of Roger Sherman, done about 1775 or 1776. Although he had not yet achieved full command of his talent, the portrait shows a rugged strength and simplicity suitable to the subject. Most of his portraits reveal a grasp of character in no way diminished by the sophisticated skills he acquired while abroad. Ironically, Earl, a loyalist, achieved his fame as a painter of Connecticut revolutionists.

Another Connecticut portraitist was William Johnston (1732–1772), who during the 1760s worked in New London, Hartford, and New

Haven and finished his career in Barbados. A checklist has identified thirty-three paintings attributable to him, most of them done in Connecticut. Johnston was acquainted with John Singleton Copley and probably John Smibert, for in the area of Boston where he grew up these men were neighbors. Johnston's portraits have been compared to those of the young Copley, but they show other influences as well. The stiffness of some of his figures suggests traits of the limner; yet Johnston, like Earl, captures the personality of his subjects and demonstrates remarkable ability in handling drapery and the texture of fabrics.

Less well known and less studied are several others in the Connecticut School: Winthrop Chandler, Reverend Joseph Steward, and John Durand. Chandler, who lived in Windham County virtually all his life, painted an excellent portrait of Ebenezer Devotion in 1770, which has been praised for its "incisiveness of characterization" and "boldness of composition."* Steward did a huge full-length portrait of John Phillips, an early donor to Dartmouth College, which commissioned the portrait. Durand worked in the late 1760s, first in New York and then in Connecticut. Of the group he is closest to the limners. The restoring of this little school in the last two decades to its rightful place in the history of early American art has been a noteworthy achievement, dependent upon perceptive analysis of paintings and lucky discoveries of corroborating documentary evidence.

Those who sat for their portraits were unaware of any school and probably did not look beyond the personal pleasure that a good likeness afforded. Of potentially greater significance than the work of portraitists were the scientific activities, broadly defined, of two or three Connecticut men. John Winthrop, Jr., was the first American colonist to be elected to the Royal Society of London, an honor that came to him while he was seeking a charter for Connecticut. Winthrop was a practicing physician, one who adhered to a chemical approach dependent upon drugs of mineral origin. Winthrop managed to keep in touch with the best medical knowledge in Europe through book purchases, but probably his election to the society was owing as much to his knowledge of a strange New World. He could talk about its native products and urged development of its minerals. He had earlier started salt and iron works

---

* Samuel M. Green, "Uncovering the Connecticut School," *Art News* 51 (January 1953): 57.

and had opened a graphite mine. After he returned and when the press of official business permitted, he kept up a correspondence with the members, sending to England such things as dwarf oak trees, wheat samples, milkweed pods, rattlesnake skins, a humming bird's nest, and a horseshoe crab. For the uninitiated he distinguished the crab's head from its tail. With his telescope, which was over three feet in length, he claimed to have seen five moons around the planet Jupiter. Obviously there was a practical motive in many of his activities. His mining and manufacturing efforts were well advertised to attract investors, and there was some thought that the milkweed pods could be used for silk making. But he also had a curious and free-ranging mind. He was fascinated by the unusual and sought the dissemination of sound knowledge. It was typical of him that he sought confirmation of his sighting of a fifth moon around Jupiter, but that did not come till some two hundred years later.

Another physician, and teacher of physicians as well, was Jared Eliot (1685–1763) of Killingworth, who won election to the Royal Society for his essay on making iron from black sand along the coast. But his greatest contribution was to agriculture in his notable *Essays upon Field-Husbandry in New England*, collected from his newspaper articles and published in 1760. Using a gentle approach, he warned farmers about mining their soil. Citing Scripture, he suggested using goats to clear out brush and fertilize the land with droppings, employing more oxen for better plowing, and planting when the soil was moist. He wrote about sheep raising, the control of weeds, the drainage of swamps, and the planting of timothy, clover, and other cover and forage crops. Widely read, his essays had influence, but probably no ordinary farmer tried very many of his proposals. The temptation to reap as much and as quickly as possible from virgin soil was too great. When the land soured, fresh land beckoned from the distance.

One of Eliot's students was Benjamin Gale (1715–1790), who became a distinguished doctor in his own right as well as a legislator and political polemicist, and, incidentally, married Eliot's daughter and settled in Killingworth. Gale was interested in agricultural reforms being undertaken in Europe, particularly the rotation of crops and development of the possibilities of new or untried strains. Encouraged by Peter Collinson, Gale wrote an essay in 1766 on "Black Grass," which was indigenous to Connecticut, suggesting it was a plant that might be introduced elsewhere. He experimented with growing rhubarb and obtained

Smyrna wheat, which he sent to the president of the American Academy of Arts and Sciences in hope that it might prove a satisfactory strain in America, although nothing came of his effort. He invented a drill that delivered manure with the seeds that it planted in the soil. For this he received a gold medal from the Royal Society in 1770.

But, as a scientist, Gale is best known for his recommendation that prior to inoculation for smallpox mercury and antimony be rubbed into the skin. His was not an empty recommendation. He gathered figures on mortality rates in epidemics where his treatment was tried and determined that inunction reduced fatalities from 1 in 100 to 1 in 800. He communicated his findings to the English physician John Huxham, who saw that this contribution to medical science appeared in the *Philosophical Transactions* of the Royal Society. It appeared in 1766 with a characteristic eighteenth-century title: *Historical Memoirs relating to the Practice of Inoculation for the Small Pox, in the British American Provinces, Particularly New England.* Gale's careful statistical record of population and mortality was in the best scientific tradition. In 1765 the *Transactions* published his essay on treatment of rattlesnake bite. Gale even studied Indian medical practice, seeking to learn about useful drugs. His curiosity, his methodical testing, and his reports of his findings all marked the true scientist.

Gale, a firm and outspoken American patriot, was active in another way. He closely observed the work of David Bushnell (c. 1742–1824) of Saybrook, who developed the first submarine. While a student at Yale, Bushnell demonstrated that gunpowder would explode under water, and soon after graduation he was at work on a device to blow up British warships. By 1775 he had constructed the "American Turtle," a man-powered boat designed to submerge and attach a mine to the hull of an enemy ship. Built of oak and looking like two upper turtle shells put together, it was moved by vertical and horizontal screw propellers worked by hand from inside. Pumps operated by foot and by hand admitted and expelled water for lowering and raising the craft, and from the top rose a brass tube for providing air. The mine, which rested on the outside of the Turtle's hull, had a clock mechanism that could delay firing up to twelve hours, and the clock started automatically when the Turtle pulled away from its target. The Connecticut Council of Safety, impressed with what it heard, offered support, and several tests were made to check the boat's navigational abilities. Gale was able to report to

Silas Deane that Bushnell had "made every requisite experiment in proof of the machine, and it answers expectations."* One problem remained, however. The light source for the compass and the depth gauge, critical for the operator's escape after planting the mine, failed in cold weather. A substitute for phosphorescent rotten wood had to be found. Presumably this difficulty was overcome, for the forerunner of the submarine was tried out against the British in New York and Philadelphia. Ultimate failure was said to be owing to lack of a skilled operator. Bushnell's originality has recently been questioned. A convincing analysis of circumstantial evidence suggests that the Connecticut inventor very likely obtained his idea and methods for putting it to work from predecessors, particularly English scientist Robert Boyle and French inventor Denis Papin. The latter devised two submarine plans, one of which was translated and published in the *Gentleman's Magazine.* Bushnell could easily have had access to the writings of both Boyle and Papin. But these findings do not take from Bushnell the credit for making a practical working prototype of the submarine.

During subsequent decades Connecticut was to see the birth of many other inventive ideas, some growing into large-scale industry, but these were postrevolutionary developments. It is remarkable that in the colonial period, when Connecticut was overwhelmingly agricultural and lacked urban centers comparable to Boston, New York, or Philadelphia, it was able to nurture the artists and scientists that it did.

---

* Benjamin Gale to Silas Deane, December 7, 1775, Connecticut Historical Society, *Collections,* 2 (1870): 334.

9

CONNECTICUT AND THE EMPIRE

After the Glorious Revolution, some Englishmen in high places sought to extend firmer control over the colonies, particularly over those such as Connecticut that lacked royal governors and the other machinery to make the Crown's will effective. For its part Connecticut was determined to resist, however tactfully and inconsistently, any infringements upon its charter rights.

It is almost impossible to exaggerate the reverence for the guarantees of the charter shared by most men of affairs in Connecticut. In 1740 Governor Joseph Talcott expressed the feeling simply and directly: "Our Charter next to the Loyalty we bear to oure Sovraigne, and our lives, is the Dearest thing to us on earth." In granting the privileges of Englishmen, the charter seemed, in the view of Connecticut officials, only to be stating the obvious. In 1728 the House of Representatives had asserted in a private letter to its agent "that it's the Privilege of Englishmen, and the natural right of all men who have not forfeited it, to be governed by laws made by their own Consent."

Connecticut is often described as a virtually self-governing colony whose connection to the Crown was nearly a formality; yet the colony was brought to heel on occasion and went through some dangerous times when leaders feared that the charter might be drastically altered or even voided. Although the colony survived the Dominion of New England without surrendering its charter, the years after the Glorious Revolution bred confusion; and interested and greedy colonists challenged the powers that Connecticut claimed and even suggested that its legal status be refashioned. At issue usually was the relationship between English and Connecticut laws. More specifically, what was meant by the charter stipulation that the colony's laws must conform to those of England? Did the charter take precedence over acts of Parliament?

To Connecticut what was meant depended upon circumstances. It has already been noted that in boundary disputes Connecticut might or might not find it in its interest to insist that only the Crown could alter jurisdictional rights over territory, that conforming to the laws of England might or might not mean accepting the royal prerogative as traditionally understood. Boundary disputes, however, were only one issue that raised questions about Connecticut's relationship to the home government. In the first half of the eighteenth century particularly, when political forces in England tried at various times to reduce the autonomy of nonroyal colonies, Connecticut found itself under attack, sometimes through the initiatives of powerful dissidents within its own borders.

Among these were opponents of Connecticut's resumption of its charter after the fall of the Dominion of New England, notably, Gershom Bulkeley, mentioned earlier as the author of "Will and Doom," an attack upon Connecticut's excesses under its charter; Edward Palmes, brother-in-law of Fitz-John Winthrop, passionate foes as only brothers-in-law can be; and William Rosewell, who like Palmes and Bulkeley had enjoyed the favor of Sir Edmund Andros, deposed governor of the dominion. Resumption of the charter meant that these men lost their places, and, in their view, royal action was required to reinstitute the charter. Until then, the acts of the Connecticut government were illegal. They found allies in Joseph Dudley of Massachusetts Bay, John and Nicholas Hallam, James Fitch, and the heirs of Major John Mason, conqueror of the Pequots. These men were not contending only for an abstract principle. Family rivalries over money and lands were at issue, and the stakes were big enough to embroil the colony and expose it to attacks upon its autonomy from abroad.

Trouble began for Connecticut in 1701, when John and Nicholas Hallam decided to appeal to the Privy Council the ruling of a probate court and a higher one on their mother's will. The challenge came at an awkward time for Connecticut because a bill had been introduced in Parliament to reassert the Crown's power over *all* the colonies; yet in the view of a majority of the Court of Assistants in Connecticut, an appeal to the Privy Council was in violation of the charter, since that document made no mention of such a right. To assert charter rights, however, might only stir up the wrath of those who wanted to end Connecticut's special status within the empire.

The story behind the will is a complicated one. John Liveen, second husband of Alice Hallam, died in 1689, leaving two-thirds of his estate to the clergy of New Haven, although he was not a Congregationalist and was on friendly terms with his wife's sons, to whom he left only small legacies. To his wife he bequeathed the remaining third of his estate during her lifetime; at her death this portion was also to go to the clergy. When Alice Liveen died in 1698, she ignored her husband's will and left her property to her sons. Since the executors of Liveen's will were Fitz-John Winthrop and Edward Palmes, the sons, claiming that their stepfather had been mentally incompetent, brought suit against Winthrop for all of the Liveen estate, wishing thereby to set aside the original ruling of the probate court. Palmes, as co-executor, had opposed having Liveen's will probated on the ground that in 1689, when Liveen died, Connecticut as a former member of the Dominion of New England had no legal existence. Before the Court of Assistants, the Hallam brothers argued that to give Liveen's property to the clergy would violate the Statute of Mortmain, which, to preserve feudal rights to the king, forbade gifts of property to the church. The court replied that this ancient law was inapplicable because its language did not embrace the colonies!

Edward Palmes, who was married to a daughter of old Governor John Winthrop, now took occasion to demand from his brothers-in-law, Fitz-John and Wait-Still Winthrop, an inventory of the former governor's estate, only to have the court refuse to order one. Palmes and the two Hallams then joined in an appeal to the Privy Council in 1701. The highest legal authorities in England ruled that whatever Connecticut's charter might or might not say, the Crown had an inherent right to hear appeals, even though Connecticut's agent vigorously argued that these appeals violated the charter. Palmes took the occasion of his going to England to transmit to the Privy Council a list of grievances lifted from Bulkeley's "Will and Doom," which among other things accused the colony of violating the Acts of Trade and Navigation, not contributing adequately to colonial defense, refusing appeals to England in court cases, and banning religious meetings without license. James Fitch, political rival to Fitz-John Winthrop and presumably leader of a popular faction, threw in his lot with Palmes and the Hallams. He held that colony money should not be spent on these purely private contests, that the challenge to the charter did not warrant expenditure of public funds. Fitch was getting ready to move with them against the colony in another matter—the Mohegan case, to be discussed below. Despite the black look of affairs, the Privy Council in 1704 ruled against the Hallam arguments.

But Connecticut's struggle to maintain its charter privileges and the integrity of its laws had just begun. In 1705 the Crown disallowed a Connecticut law against heretics appearing in the collection of laws of 1702. Connecticut's charter made no mention of the Crown's right to review laws or of Connecticut's obligation to send laws for approval, but the Crown acted nonetheless. It was moved to do so by an appeal from English Quakers, and it acted without giving Connecticut an opportunity to reply. Connecticut's agent, Sir Henry Ashurst, saw the hand of Joseph Dudley behind it all. Actually, Connecticut had eased the position of Quakers in 1675, a fact that the compilation of laws in 1702 may have overlooked. In any case, Connecticut in May 1706 repealed the law against heretics in so far as it applied to Quakers, and in doing so, it made no acknowledgment of the queen's disallowance, perhaps thus maintaining its assumption that Connecticut's laws were not subject to the Crown's review.

Within a few years, the colony was to be disabused of this notion. Once again a legal contest provided the basis for a challenge, this time a contest over the validity of Connecticut's 1699 law affecting the division of the property of persons dying intestate. English common law required that such property go intact to the eldest son, a provision handed down from feudal times, when an estate was the support for a fighting man obligated to serve his overlord. The Puritans of Massachusetts Bay and Connecticut, however, had preferred the rule of Deuteronomy, which divided the intestate's property, after provision for the widow, among all the children, with only a double portion going to the eldest son. Making provision for all the sons and daughters made sense in a colony with abundant land and no feudal obligations. Connecticut practiced this kind of division long before it made specific provision for it by law in 1699, a law copied from a Massachusetts act of 1692. The delay perhaps came from the knowledge that the practice was contrary to common law, and avowing it might raise awkward questions. When Connecticut did act, it did so to forestall greedy first sons who sought to apply the common law principle. Since the Massachusetts law had never been disallowed (as a royal colony Massachusetts had to submit its laws for Crown review), and since Connecticut had based its law on that of its neighbor, Connecticut had no particular qualms about what it had done.

Not until 1717 was the intestacy law contested. In that year Wait-Still

Winthrop died intestate, and John Winthrop IV, as his father's administrator, claimed all the real estate as heir under English common law. In 1724 Thomas Lechmere, husband to Anna, who was John Winthrop's sister, brought suit to claim on his wife's behalf a share of the real estate. When the probate court in 1726 vacated John's letters of administration, he signified his intention to appeal to the Privy Council and to ignore the highest court in Connecticut, the General Assembly. Protesting the assembly's dismissal of his memorial, he was held in contempt and turned over to the sheriff, but he readily made his escape. When Winthrop presented his case in England, he took the opportunity to repeat old charges against Connecticut: it did not send laws to England for approval; it denied the right of appeal from its courts to the Crown; it ignored binding statutes; officials did not take an oath of allegiance to the king. In fact, it was strongly suggested that Connecticut ought to be converted to a royal colony.

In the hearing held before the Privy Council, Winthrop was represented by the solicitor and attorney generals, acting in their private capacities, but Lechmere had an incompetent lawyer who could not show that Connecticut practice had been customary or even cite one instance of how the intestacy law had operated. Although Connecticut's agent, Jeremiah Dummer, had drawn up a list of cogent reasons why the law should not be disallowed (an obvious one was the chaos that would result from calling into question the validity of hundreds of past decisions), Lechmere's lawyer made no use of these reasons. He did not even suggest the customary referral of the matter to the Board of Trade for determining the expediency of Connecticut's law. The result was disallowance in February 1728. For some time thereafter Connecticut sought to obtain an act of Parliament that would validate all past intestacy decisions and permit it to continue its practice, but the price demanded for this sort of relief was too high. Called upon for advice, the Board of Trade suggested a new charter for Connecticut "more consistent with the Honour and Interest of Great Britain." Connecticut then abandoned the appeal to Parliament. It never repealed its 1699 law nor acted as though the law had been disallowed. Its courts simply divided intestate estates according to "rules of natural equity." In practice, families of deceased persons petitioned for an equal division of estates, usually with a double portion for the eldest son, but not always. Families promised not to contest court decisions if the court acted in accordance with their wishes. When eldest sons would not cooperate in this fashion, the courts simply delayed any decision on the division of estates. So matters stood until 1745.

In that year one Samuel Clark, having appealed a case to England on the grounds that equal division among the heirs of an intestate was illegal, had his petition for reversal thrown out, even though his lawyer cited the ruling in the Winthrop-Lechmere case. This time Connecticut saw to it that money was made available to Thomas Tousey, Clark's adversary. The central point at issue was whether common law applied to the colonies automatically. Connecticut held that it did not and pointed out that the Massachusetts law on intestacy had been upheld on appeal even though it violated common law. The Clark case at long last resolved the intestacy law in Connecticut's favor.

What English laws Connecticut had to follow under its charter remained a matter of confusion, however. In 1733, Connecticut's agent, Francis Wilks, insisted that common law applied to all the colonies, and those statutes of Parliament, as well, that were in force before and at the time of settlement. Governor Talcott in reply expressed the view of Connecticut that only those statutes specifically naming the colonies were binding. If common law and existing statutes all bound the colonies, Talcott asserted, there was little sense in granting them legislative power: as a practical matter, different circumstances would require different measures. A colony acted contrary to the laws of England only when it passed laws conflicting with statutes naming the colony.

Yet Connecticut was not always consistent in its views on the applicability of English law. In the long drawn-out struggle over Connecticut's rights to Mohegan lands, the colony found it convenient to appeal to common law in seeking to protect its property rights. In this instance Connecticut argued that title to land could be determined only through a jury trial as guaranteed by the common law. England tried to settle the dispute by resorting to commissioners who sat without a jury and finally made its definitive ruling through a decision of the Privy Council, an instrument of the royal prerogative.

The Mohegan dispute involved some of Connecticut's most powerful families—the Masons and the Winthrops as well as James Fitch. The dispute arose because the heirs of Major John Mason claimed lands granted by the Mohegan sachem Uncas to Mason. Connecticut's contention was that Mason had acted merely as the colony's agent in obtaining the lands, but the heirs argued that all Mason had surrendered to the

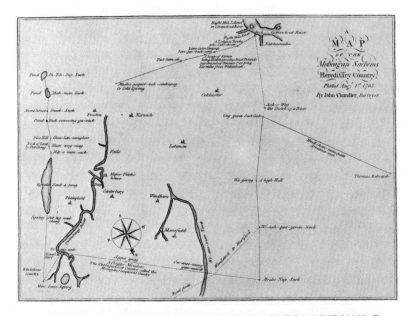

MAP OF THE HEREDITARY COUNTRY OF THE MOHEGAN INDIANS. Drawn
in 1705 by John Chandler and published in *Governor and Company of Connecticut and
Mohegan Indians, by Their Guardians. Certified Copy of Book of Proceedings before Commissioners of Review, MDCCXLIII,* London, 1769. On the whole the placement of the towns is
reasonably accurate, except that Colchester has been put south instead of somewhat north
of Norwich. (Note that the surveyor made south at the top of his map.) The We-am man
Tuck River is now the Willimantic. *Courtesy of the Houghton Library, Harvard University.*

colony in his deed of 1661 was jurisdiction, not rights to the soil. In 1659 Governor John Winthrop had obtained permission to purchase from Wysmuck sachems a tract along the Quinebaug River within the limits of modern Plainfield; yet in 1680 Oweneco, son of Uncas, sold to James Fitch a deed of trusteeship to this same tract, claiming it was personal not tribal land. And in 1684 Oweneco deeded in trust to Samuel and Daniel Mason power to dispose of all Mohegan lands, including what is now known as Colchester, but this same area was purchased by the Winthrop heirs from the Mohegans through permission of the General Assembly.

The Masons and Fitch as trustees disposed of lands to Edward Palmes, John Hallam, Joseph Dudley, and others, the very men who were to embroil the colony in law suits dangerous to its charter. During King William's War, Sheriff Fitch actually sent armed men to destroy the hay and livestock of settlers whom Winthrop had admitted to the Quinebaug tract. Obviously it was in the interest of the Masons and of Fitch to deny Connecticut's claim to any of these lands lying roughly between the Quinebaug and the Connecticut, running south to the northern boundaries of New London and Lyme, and extending north somewhat above Mansfield.

Early in 1704, about the time the Hallam appeal was failing, Nicholas Hallam petitioned the Crown for impartial persons to look into Connecticut's treatment of the Mohegan Indians, alleging that the colony was taking their lands unlawfully and so angering the Mohegans that they might join the Maine Indians, who were harassing the Massachusetts border. The specter was raised of a repetition of the Indian war of 1676. Only their ignorance kept English officials from laughing out of court this flight of fancy. At the time, the Mohegans were so few in number as to constitute little threat no matter whom they might join. But ignoring Connecticut's request for delay, the legal advisors to the Crown said the queen had a right to order the matter looked into; and upon recommendation of the Board of Trade, the Privy Council commissioned Joseph Dudley, Edward Palmes, and a number of their associates to examine whether Connecticut had violated Mohegan property rights. A less impartial commission one could hardly imagine.

Meeting at Stonington in 1705 the Dudley commission did not hold an inquiry but rather set about to determine the issue. When Connecticut representatives refused to cooperate with the commission, convinced that it was going beyond its powers, Dudley and the others found that 120 square miles of disputed land belonged to Oweneco, the Mohegan sachem. In effect, they were judges in their own cause. Not only was the commission biased, but in the view of Connecticut, title to land could be settled only in a court with a jury, not by appointees of the Crown acting alone. Sir Henry Ashurst, Connecticut's agent, managed to block any confirmation of the commission's ruling, helped considerably by the change in political climate in England by 1706, when men less hostile to the chartered colonies came to power. But the Mohegan case was far from over.

It was brought to life again through the efforts of Captain John Mason, grandson of the famous major. John had been acting as guardian and schoolteacher to the Mohegans. Going to England to challenge the lawfulness of Connecticut's claim to Mohegan lands, he took with him an Indian called Mahomet, allegedly the true sachem of the tribe. Connecticut recognized Ben Uncas II, son of Ben Uncas, who had been an illegitimate son of Uncas. Connecticut contended that Oweneco had never recognized Mahomet as his grandson and that the tribe had never accepted him as a sachem. Ben Uncas II was ready and willing to recognize Connecticut's right to the land in question and did so in a formal statement supported by other Mohegans. It should be understood that the Mohegans had not been deprived of all land. For planting purposes they had something over 4,700 acres of which only about 100 were under crops in 1736, when there were fewer than fifty males and females over twelve years old.

On the suggestion of the Board of Trade a new commission was to meet in 1738, its members made up of officials from Rhode Island and New York. When this commission heard testimony from neither the Masons nor the Indians on their side, although they were present and ready to testify, the New York commissioners withdrew in protest. Then the Rhode Island officials, swayed by deeds signed by Ben Uncas II in 1737 and 1738 giving Connecticut quitclaims to the disputed lands, overturned the judgment of the Dudley commision of 1705, neglecting to mention in their records, however, what that earlier judgment had been—a fatal but not accidental oversight. As chartered colonies, neither Rhode Island nor Connecticut wanted to acknowledge the legitimacy of the earlier commission. When the ruling of the commission arrived in England, the Privy Council, after noting the defects in its procedures, held its work invalid and appointed a new commission, which met in Norwich in 1743.

This third commission, headed by Cadwallader Colden of New York, ruled that deeds granted by Uncas to Connecticut in 1640 and 1659 were valid and that the charter of 1662 vested all lands in Connecticut. Moreover, it noted that Connecticut had "treated the said Indians with much Humanity at all Times, and have at all Times provided them with a Sufficiency at least of Lands to Plant on."* By a three-to-two vote the commission declared that the judgment of the Dudley commission ought to be declared null and void. Although the two dissenters, Daniel Horsmanden of New York and Robert Hunter Morris of New Jersey took a different interpretation of the various deeds reviewed, they signed the report along with the majority. And that ought to have settled the dispute, for no further review was held. Yet in 1766 at the instigation of the two sons of Captain John Mason, the whole matter was stirred up again. John and Samuel Mason requested the Privy Council to overturn the decision of 1743.

The challenge came at an awkward time. Connecticut's governor was William Pitkin, a member of the Sons of Liberty, and Connecticut's agent was Richard Jackson, one of the moderate members of Parliament at the time of the Stamp Act crisis and its aftermath. Both took the view that land titles should be tried in a court with a jury in accordance with common law and that any appeal should go to the Court of King's Bench. But since Connecticut had accepted the decision of 1743 made by a Crown-appointed commission, it was hardly in a favorable position to deny jurisdiction to the Privy Council. The General Assembly named William Samuel Johnson, an attorney, as special agent to assist Jackson in managing the defense before the Privy Council, which was to begin its hearings in February 1767. Johnson did not return to the colony until the fall of 1771, and even then no definitive judgment had been reached. Ostensibly delays were owing to the illness and absence of council members, but actually England procrastinated to avoid offending either the Indians or Connecticut. Although the Mohegans were now reduced to several dozen families, English officials imagined that bad treatment would provoke the Six Nations. The lingering turmoil over revenue measures, of course, made England wish to gain support among the

---

* Public Record Office, London, CO 5: 1272, p. 107.

colonies wherever it could. In December 1772, the Privy Council wrote the finale to a dispute that had dragged on for over three-quarters of a century. At the end, as at the beginning, it was not justice to Indians that was at stake but the speculative ambitions of the Mason heirs. Connecticut was given clear title to lands long since settled but not through the procedures of the common law.

Not so celebrated as the Mohegan, intestacy, and Hallam cases was Connecticut's struggle with a collector of customs, which nonetheless raised fundamental issues, for his insistence upon naming ports of clearance violated the charter right to designate such ports.* And this struggle, early in the eighteenth century, came at the time when the charter was under heaviest attack in England.

John Shackmaple, an Englishman, was the first royal official to operate in Connecticut, as collector of customs beginning in 1707. He had not been in office two years when he decreed that New London would be the only port for clearance, a decree that worked considerable hardship, particularly for coasting vessels. Connecticut had deputy collectors at a half dozen or more ports when Shackmaple ordered all ships to obtain clearance from him alone. Proceeding under an act of Parliament, he was motivated in part by his suspicions of the lax system that had been in operation. When he moved against ships that had not cleared at New London, the Connecticut Council, by issuing writs of *prohibe*, prevented him from seeking judgment in the New York Vice-Admiralty Court, holding that ships could enter and clear from any Connecticut port with a naval officer, a customs official appointed by the colonial government. When Shackmaple tested the Connecticut position before the Admiralty Court in Rhode Island, using a provisions ship that had arrived there with only a clearance from a naval officer, the judge held that Connecticut was following the spirit if not the letter of the Navigation Acts. Provision ships, he said, should not have to go far out of their way (the ship had cleared from Guilford) to seek out the royal collector. Connecticut was not wholly intransigent; it was willing to have fewer ports for the clearance of ships engaged in foreign trade if convenient ports were designated for coastal commerce.

---

* The account of this conflict is based largely on Parker Bradley Nutting, "Charter and Crown: Relations of Connecticut with the British Government, 1662–1776," (unpublished Ph.D. dissertation, University of North Carolina, 1972), pp. 143–68.

But Shackmaple was not yet interested in compromise. When he seized a ship coming to Saybrook in 1715, sought judgment before the New York Admiralty Court, and ignored the General Assembly's directive that he use the Court of Common Pleas to avoid unwarranted delay (the Admiralty Court judge had died and Shackmaple awaited his successor), the assembly passed a law declaring that customs commissioners had to register their commissions with the colony. The assembly knew what it was about, for Shackmaple's commission had been signed only by the surveyor-general, not by the commissioners of customs, as parliamentary law decreed. Because his commission was illegal, the assembly declared the office of collector vacant; ships must now clear only with naval officers, Connecticut being prepared to prosecute ships seeking clearance from an improperly commissioned royal official. Shackmaple, of course, fought back by warning collectors elsewhere that Connecticut ships might well arrive without proper papers. The assembly was prepared to bear the costs of taking cases to trial as far as the High Court of Admiralty. Yet because of technicalities the issue was never resolved in the courts. By 1718 the commissioners of customs had given Shackmaple a new commission, and over a period of time an accommodation was reached. The commissioners quietly added New Haven to New London as a port for clearances, and two or three other ports were permitted to clear vessels engaged in coastal trade.

At issue in this controversy was whether an act of Parliament superseded the charter right to name ports for clearances. Although Connecticut was unsuccessful in asserting its charter privilege, it did force the collector to modify his order designating a single port for clearances. The challenge to the charter was seen as a very real one, fraught with danger to Connecticut's autonomy, for it came at a time when charters were under attack in England. The proprietors of Carolina had submitted to the Crown, and the pressure on charters had been pretty steady for some years. Viewing its charter as the very cornerstone of its liberties, Connecticut felt compelled to resist every encroachment in whatever guise.

In subsequent years pressure from England took the form of demands for copies of colony laws, answers to queries relating to the colony's economy, and threats to move against the charter if laws remained on the books that were detrimental to the prerogative or to the trade of Great Britain. Thus in 1731, Connecticut was sharply reprimanded for failure to send copies of its laws that had been requested some years earlier. When Governor Talcott complied with the Board of Trade's demand in 1732, alleging his belief that his predecessor had long ago sent the laws, the Board of Trade testily replied that by Talcott's own admission alteration in some laws had been made. Where were copies of the alterations? the Board asked. It requested copies of all changes and of all new laws passed in the future.

In 1734, a committee of the House of Lords reported that it would be desirable to require all laws from whatever colony, charter colonies included, to be sent to England for the king's approval within twelve months of passage, such laws to have no effect until royal approbation was secured. In addition, the committee wanted the governors of Connecticut and Rhode Island to take their required oaths before royal governors named for the purpose by the king. Governor Talcott ordered the colony's agent, Francis Wilks, to spare no expense in trying to have Connecticut exempted from these requirements should Parliament enact them. Such proposed changes would in effect "take from us the whole Charter, which we are not willing to part with." Although this legislation was not passed, authorities in England did require periodic and detailed reporting on the movement of goods into and out of Connecticut; any serious delinquency was likely to provoke demands in Parliament for copies of colonial charters for review. Subsequently the Board of Trade demanded reports on currency issues and called Connecticut to account because it made acceptance of bills of credit obligatory, a violation of a law passed in the time of Queen Anne. When Parliament sought to include in currency legislation a proviso that would have given the Connecticut governor power to veto all laws passed by the General Assembly, Connecticut was quick to instruct its agent to oppose at all costs such an illegal alteration in the charter.

Although Connecticut people relied on it for their rights and their way of life, the charter obviously did not make the colony invulnerable. Since no formal approval of Connecticut laws was required, the colony could never be certain that some law might not be summarily disapproved years after its enactment, as happened with the intestacy law. In royal colonies the king's approval of laws gave a measure of security, for once approval was given, the king could not of his own motion call the law into question. Still, in its 140 years of existence as a colony, Connecticut saw its laws challenged less than a half-dozen times; the freedom that the colony enjoyed under the charter was certainly worth the risk of possible unexpected disapproval. In 1768 Connecticut felt discriminated against because it experienced difficulty in securing passes guaranteeing safe passage for its ships from pirates in the Mediterranean. But its protests through agent Richard Jackson ended the difficulty.

Having survived persistent efforts to bypass or seriously amend its charter from the time of the Dominion of New England to the revolutionary period, Connecticut, not surprisingly, entered the revolutionary crisis convinced that its charter was an inviolable bulwark of its liberties. Only practical necessity in seeking common cause with non-chartered colonies caused it to place increasing emphasis on the rights of Englishmen and, ultimately, on the even broader claim of natural rights.

* * *

Connecticut's stubborn defense of its charter against the maneuvering of some officials in England should not lead to the inference that its concerns were parochial only, that it had no concern for the welfare of the empire. The affection of ordinary Connecticut men and officials for Britain and the king seems genuine enough, even though it may have been alloyed with fear that any failure to respond adequately might jeopardize the charter. Indeed, Connecticut often did more than its fair share in the series of four wars fought against the French, wars that were imperial in scope and that were usually resolved to suit the interests of Britain rather than those of the colonies.

Soon after William and Mary ascended the throne, the king took England into an alliance against Louis XIV, and the two nations and their colonies, along with allies, fought on until 1697. In 1690, Connecticut entered into agreement with New York and other colonies to mount an invasion of Canada, managing to get Fitz-John Winthrop named commander of the expedition. For the attack on Montreal, only Connecticut sent the entire quota of 135 men that it had promised. Massachusetts Bay and Plymouth sent none despite their commitment to furnish 160 and 60, respectively. Massachusetts Bay saved its efforts for the planned attack on Quebec. Even New York, whose governor had proposed the strike against Montreal, raised fewer than half the troops it had promised. When the expedition failed for lack of men, particularly Indian allies from the Five Nations who were stricken with disease, and for lack of supplies, Winthrop was forced to return to Albany, where Jacob Leisler, rebel head of New York after Andros's downfall, had him arrested on charges of treason. Winthrop was rescued from jail and escaped to Connecticut, where he was fully exonerated after an investigation. Leisler's high-handed treatment strained relations between the two colonies, and Connecticut was pleased when Leisler fell from power. Connecticut during the war contributed to the defense of Albany and of Massachusetts towns in the Connecticut River Valley, but it played no role in the battles fought in Maine and later in New York. Trumbull estimated that Connecticut spent well over £12,000 in the war effort.

For its participation, Connecticut relied, of course, wholly upon its militia; not until the eve of King George's War did the colony authorize the building of a war vessel. Land forces continued to be its mainstay right through the Revolution. At this point a few words about militia organization may be useful. As already mentioned, all males between sixteen and sixty (later fifty) were required to serve unless they belonged to exempt classes. Exempted originally were magistrates and church officers, but over the years the General Court expanded the list to include Indians, blacks, representatives, justices of the peace, the rector, tutors, and students at Yale, schoolmasters, attorneys, licensed physicians, holders of the M.A. degree, millers, herdsmen, mariners, ferrymen, sheriffs, constables, and the disabled. Those liable for duty had to provide themselves with appropriate and usable arms and train at stated times of the year. Absence from drill or defective weapons brought fines (by 1737 as much as six shillings per diem for footsoldiers, twelve shillings for troopers). Although the men chose their company officers—captains, lieutenants, and ensigns—their choices had to be confirmed by the General Court; and on occasion it ordered new elections or even made its own choice. Senior officers were all named by the court. In 1739, the militia was organized into regiments, the train bands of each town being assigned to a particular one, thirteen in all. The office of colonel was created to take the place of the majors who had commanded in each county; moreover, a troop of horses was assigned to each regiment. By the time of the Revolution, Connecticut had established twenty-five regiments.

Obviously some men looked upon militia service as an onerous duty and sought ways to escape it. Compliant officers sometimes excused men from drill for insufficient reasons or accepted enlistment in the regimental troop of cavalry when it was already at full strength. Ultimately the General Assembly put the troopers on the same basis as foot-soldiers, changing the troop from a purely voluntary arm to one into which men could be called. In 1769, the better to train its civilians, the assembly decreed the dropping of Bland's Exercise as "prolix and incumbered with many useless motions" in favor of the Norfolk Militia Exercise; and in 1775, the exercise was changed again to conform to that used by Continental troops, that is, the manual of exercise ordered by the king in 1764.*

Except for sudden and local emergencies, only part of the militia of a district was called into active service at any one time. The usual pattern in answering a royal or other call for military support was to summon a number of men from each militia district, drafting them if insufficient volunteers stepped forward. Volunteering was encouraged by offering bounties and a carefully graded pay scale. In 1690, a private received nine shillings a week; ensigns, lieutenants, and captains received fifteen, eighteen, and twenty-five shillings, respectively. Until the mid-eighteenth century, before the onset of inflation caused by the French and Indian War, the pay scale remained roughly equivalent.

How many effectives could Connecticut count upon? In several reports to the Board of Trade the colony listed its total of males liable for service: 8,500 in 1730, organized in five regiments, 10,000 in thirteen regiments by 1749, and 26,260 in eighteen regiments by 1774. Four additional regiments were organized about the time of this final report.

Connecticut and the other English colonies gained little from King William's War when peace was signed in 1697. All boundaries were restored to prewar status, so that the capture of Port Royal, which Massachusetts Bay had engineered early in the war, proved fruitless. Port Royal, on Annapolis Basin in Nova Scotia, was strategically located to harass the fishing fleets of New England. The colonies had some experience in military cooperation, but it was neither efficient nor sustained. For most of the war, Connecticut merely acted as guardian of its own frontiers and those of western Massachusetts. The colony had little to show for its expenditures except that it had helped to stave off French

---

* The Massachusetts Council also showed dissatisfaction with the 64th Norfolk handbook, saying that it was "clogg'd with many superfluous Motions, which only serve to burden the Memory, and perplex the Learner." *Boston Gazette,* May 13, 1776.

aggression. Louis XIV had been temporarily checked; that is what the war meant for England and its American provinces.

The colonies were tested again in Queen Anne's War, fought between 1702 and 1713. In this struggle, Connecticut chose its occasions for cooperation with other colonies. It did not elect to aid Massachusetts Bay on its exposed frontiers until after the massacre at Deerfield in February 1704; and since New York was neutral in this war until 1709, Connecticut engaged in no action in that quarter, although the corrupt governor of New York, Lord Cornbury, tried unsuccessfully to exact money quotas in lieu of troops. When Governor Joseph Dudley of Massachusetts Bay in 1707 mounted an expedition against Port Royal to end its harassment of English fishermen and invited other colonies to take part, Connecticut refused, although both New Hampshire and Rhode Island contributed men. Connecticut probably held back because so few colonies were involved and because the mother country was lending no support. The 1707 attempt was a fiasco.

But Connecticut did furnish troops for a combined operation against Montreal undertaken in 1709. Troops were also furnished by New York and New Jersey. The land invasion was to be augmented by a sea attack on Quebec and Port Royal, which would employ 1,000 New England forces and to which the British were to contribute men and ships. Here was a much more ambitious attack than that of 1707; yet it, too, ended in miserable failure. Month after month the colonials waited in the woods, poised for their strike against Montreal, only to have the British ships fail to appear; they had been diverted for use in Europe, it was learned belatedly.

A more modest plan for an attack on Port Royal alone in 1710 also drew Connecticut support, again because of wide colonial commitment and the promise of several hundred royal marines. Connecticut hired five transports to send 300 men to the siege, 26 being lost when one of the ships ran aground. The taking of Port Royal was an easy victory and encouraged a second attempt against Quebec in 1711. This time the British sent over dozens of ships and 5,000 troops. Colonial forces were to take part in a land campaign against Montreal launched from Albany as well as in the sea expedition against Quebec. Bad weather and bad piloting discouraged the British naval commander from proceeding very far up the St. Lawrence, and he abandoned the effort. Just as in 1709, colonial troops were left in the lurch at their staging area at Wood's Creek.

When peace was finally signed in 1713, the British this time kept Acadia as well as Newfoundland so that raiding by Maine Indians would be more difficult in the future. The French, however, were allowed to keep Cape Breton Island off the northeastern end of Nova Scotia, a position that would allow them to continue to harass New England fishermen. Connecticut was not, of course, directly threatened, but she could expect future calls for aid against the common enemy. In the course of Queen Anne's War, Connecticut issued £33,500 in bills of credit, forcing tax rates up to 7d. and 8d. in the pound, but the bills were receivable at a 5 percent premium at the treasury, and this together with the prudent amount issued prevented serious depreciation.

In the long interim between the end of Queen Anne's War and the start of King George's in 1744, Connecticut firmly refused to subordinate its militia to the governors of either New York or Massachusetts Bay, although both called upon it for quotas. Connecticut's excuse was that it was obligated to respond only when a state of war existed or when an invasion was imminent. Massachusetts Governor Shute's problems with the Indians in Maine in the 1720s did not seem threatening enough to warrant satisfying his demands for troops. After the attack on Northfield, Massachusetts, however, Connecticut was willing to furnish garrison troops for Hampshire County and for her own frontier defenses.

As war loomed between Britain and Spain in 1739, Connecticut obtained cannons for a battery at New London, commissioned a sloop, reorganized its militia into regiments, and gave generous bounties to those who would volunteer for the ill-fated campaign Britain mounted in the Caribbean. When the conflict came closer to home in 1744 upon the outbreak of hostilities with France, Connecticut sent 200 militiamen into New York and others into western Massachusetts and ordered forts to be built at various locations, half the expense to be borne by the towns where they were located. The high point of this third war with France, of course, was the New Englanders' successful siege in 1745 of Louisbourg, on Cape Breton Island, in cooperation with British naval vessels under Commodore Peter Warren. Connecticut furnished 500 men, and its lieutenant governor, Roger Wolcott, was made second in command under William Pepperell, Massachusetts merchant and councilman. The colony sent an additional 200 men, who arrived at Cape Breton shortly after the surrender, and was prepared to raise 300 more when news of the victory was received.

Although a remarkable feat for New England forces, the capture of

Louisbourg was in one respect a disappointment, for the terms of surrender ruled out plundering for booty on which the men had counted. What remained for many of them was the tedium of temporary garrison duty and the dangers of epidemic diseases. Nearly 900 militiamen died by the spring of 1746. Meanwhile frontiers back home lay vulnerable to Indian attack, although Connecticut had little to fear on this score. It did have cause for further disappointment in that it had counted on supplying the expected permanent garrison and naval support forces with provisions in the years to come. Here would be a way to earn sterling to shore up the paper currency the colony had issued. All New England was stunned when Britain as part of the peace terms agreed to restore Louisbourg to the French, leaving the New England fisheries once again open to easy harassment and Connecticut without the market for provisions she had counted upon.

But these disappointments lay in the future. In 1746 Connecticut voted to raise 1,000 men, offering bounties of thirty pounds old tenor to each, as its allotment of the 5,300 troops expected from New England in a planned attack against Quebec, originally suggested by Governor William Shirley of Massachusetts. Connecticut was ready to impress provisions, if necessary, to make the effort successful. Once again a colonial and British joint attempt was planned, involving contributions of men from as far away as Virginia. Promises of booty and parliamentary reimbursement for the colonies' expenses in the Louisbourg campaign heightened the enthusiasm. Although colonial troops were ready to march by the summer of 1746, the British battalions never appeared; they had been put to use elsewhere without notification to the colonists. The mother country's bad faith was rewarded no better than it had been during Queen Anne's War. Connecticut neither took part in any other significant attacks nor planned campaigns in this war; in fact, in January 1747, it refused an invitation to join with Massachusetts Bay and New York in an attack on Crown Point because of the difficulties of a winter campaign and the dangers of smallpox. The attack never took place.

During King George's War, which ended officially in 1748, Connecticut issued approximately £80,000 in bills of credit, old and new tenor, to finance her efforts. As explained earlier, depreciation soon set in for even the new issue; but parliamentary reimbursement for Connecticut's contribution to the capture of Louisbourg, amounting to nearly £29,000 and given on condition that it be used to redeem the colony's paper, went a long way toward stabilizing Connecticut's currency before the colony had once again to issue large amounts in the course of the French and Indian War.

As the fourth war with France began to loom, Great Britain urged the colonies to meet together to cope with the disaffection of the Iroquois and to discuss concerted measures in opposition to the expansionist moves of the French in the Ohio River country. The Iroquois resented English encroachments on their lands, and they complained that the English were not providing them with sufficient security against the French, who were staking out claims to territory and building forts in regions that the Iroquois customarily dominated for trading purposes. Representatives from the New England colonies and from New York, Pennsylvania, and Maryland met in June 1754 at Albany. Virginia and New Jersey were also invited but failed to send delegates. As its representatives Connecticut sent William Pitkin, Roger Wolcott, Jr., and Elisha Williams, who could make no binding agreements without the consent of the General Assembly. The main message they were to convey was that Connecticut had been put to vast expense in the past and that French encroachments affected chiefly southern colonies, which had contributed very little to past wars against the French.

The men at Albany adopted a "Representation on the Present State of the Colonies," which declared as indisputably English the coast from Georgia to Nova Scotia and all the land from sea to sea between the thirty-fourth and forty-eighth parallels. It called upon the French to cease their activities in territory claimed by the Indians, and to calm Indian apprehension, it proposed regulating the sale of Indian lands and limiting existing colonies to the mountains as their western border. Territory west of the mountains would be carved into new colonies by the British Crown, a stipulation that pleased land speculators like Benjamin Franklin, who came from a colony lacking the generous bounds of a sea-to-sea charter. The other main item of business was consideration of proposals to confederate the colonies for defensive and other purposes.

The idea of confederation was in the air before the congress met, and four proposals were actually considered. Of these, the most famous was Franklin's Plan of Union, which he had worked on for several years, and which had appeared in print with the famous "Join or Die" symbol. Franklin envisioned a union called into being by act of Parliament that would provide for a President-General royally appointed and a Grand

Council, or intercolonial representative body. These instruments of confederation would be empowered to make treaties with the Indians binding on all the colonies, to purchase Indian lands outside colony boundaries, to make war, and to levy taxes, all decisions being subject to
British approval or rejection within a three-year period. The President-
General, with council approval, would commission all military officers;
the council, with the president's consent, all civil officials.

None of the colonies accepted the Albany Plan in the period after the
conference. Connecticut's particular objections were that the area to be
centrally governed was too large for proper defense and administration,
and worse, that the scheme would subvert the liberties and privileges of
the people, for the power to tax would override the guarantees of
Connecticut's charter and put a heavy burden on the people. Governor
Thomas Fitch particularly feared the control that might be exerted over
the colony's militia by officers commissioned by a distant authority.
Connecticut men might be asked to do garrison duty in neighboring
colonies, and they were always restless when under the direction of
"foreign" officers. What Connecticut would have preferred at the least
was commissioning by the President-General of general officers only on
nomination of the Grand Council, lesser officers being nominated by the
respective colonial legislatures; raising quotas by request, not by demand; and restricting the union to New York, New Jersey, and New
England. When other colonies raised similar objections about the plan's
military features and its impact on local prerogatives, British authorities
gave up any hope of effective confederation. (There is some question as to
whether Britain really wanted one.) Thus the colonies entered the French
and Indian War no better coordinated in their efforts than they had been
in past wars.

The immediate source of conflict in this fourth encounter with France
was rival claims to the Ohio River country, where Connecticut had no
direct interest. Virginia, Pennsylvania, and the Albany fur traders stood
to suffer most immediately from the claims that Captain de Bienville had
staked out in 1749. He buried lead plates at the head of the Allegheny
River and at intermediate points all the way to the mouth of the Great
Miami, claiming all the land adjacent to the Ohio and on both sides of
the rivers flowing into it, from source to mouth. The initiative for challenging these extensive claims fell to Virginia and the Ohio Company,
spurred on by Governor Robert Dinwiddie. Young George Washington's

surrender at Fort Necessity in 1754 and General Braddock's defeat in 1755 were preliminary to the formal declaration of war between England and France in the following year.

Less well known among the preliminaries is the colonial attempt to drive the French from Crown Point in 1755, in which Connecticut played a significant role. Command of the expedition was given to William Johnson, New York's Indian agent, but his second in command was Phineas Lyman of Connecticut. It was Lyman who oversaw the construction of Fort Edward on the Hudson and who, with Johnson, began a fort at the head of Lake George, which was to be called Fort William Henry. For the expedition against Crown Point, Connecticut originally committed itself to raising 1,000 troops, a proportion that seemed high to the General Assembly when Rhode Island's contribution was only 400 and New Hampshire's 600. Nonetheless Connecticut raised an additional 500 and then contributed two regiments, totaling 1,500 men, for a total for the campaign of 3,000 troops. In addition it raised 300 men for the service of New York and in its pay.

Despite the response of Connecticut and other northern colonies, the expedition accomplished little. French forces under Baron Dieskau on their way to attack Fort Edward ambushed an attacking party sent out against them from Lake George. The French attempt to take the fortified position of the English failed in the face of artillery fire. While the French were resting from two engagements fought on the same September day, they were attacked by a force coming up from Fort Edward and had to beat a retreat. Although the English had driven the French back, this French southward thrust so delayed the English that they concluded the season was too far advanced to move against Fort Frederic at Crown Point. And colonial troops had to face the prospect of winter garrison duty in Fort Edward. The Connecticut assembly voted a special gratuity for its own forces to compensate them for the hardship. But the Connecticut troops grew surly, rejecting guard duty and refusing to work in the building of Fort William Henry.

Meanwhile back in the colony, officials were preparing to receive several hundred Acadians, a part of those expelled from Nova Scotia and distributed among the various colonies. Despite British provision for religious freedom and exemption from military duty, the Acadians generally had refused the part of loyal citizens. They preferred loyalty to the French, who still controlled the northern shore of Nova Scotia even though that peninsula had been ceded to the English at the Peace of Utrecht in 1713. When a Massachusetts expedition joined with royal forces defeated the French in 1755, deportation of the Acadians followed as a military measure. Connecticut distributed its quota among the towns, with a care to keeping families together, in numbers roughly proportional to total tax listings, thirteen being assigned to Hartford, nineteen to New Haven, sixteen to Middletown, and so on. Selectmen were to "manage and support them as tho' they were inhabitants," except that no French could leave their assigned towns without permission.

The rest of Connecticut's efforts in the French and Indian War were largely confined to the same area as the campaign of 1755. Under the Earl of Loudoun in 1756 and again in 1757, Connecticut men formed over a third of the colonial armies collected to attack the French fort at Crown Point. In July 1756, when Loudoun arrived, the season was too far advanced for a campaign, and news of the French capture of Oswego only added to the gloom; but Connecticut responded to Loudoun's call for reinforcements by promising to send an additional 800 men. No serious campaigning in that sector took place in 1756, however. The following year Connecticut raised even more troops than it had promised to Loudoun. When Fort William Henry was put under siege, partly because the French sensed the weakness of the British (Loudoun had packed the regulars off to Nova Scotia for an attack on Louisbourg), Connecticut responded to pleas from the commander at Fort Edward for reinforcements by sending 1,100 more men and then committing 5,000 more to the cause. Before these fresh troops could become effective the besieged men at Fort William Henry had to surrender, but the presence in the area of the rather large colonial army of over 12,000 troops persuaded General Montcalm to return to Canada.

In 1758 and 1759 Connecticut responded to general calls for colonial troops issuing from William Pitt, who sacked Loudoun in favor first of General James Abercromby and then of General Jeffrey Amherst. In the first of these years Connecticut agreed to raise 5,000 men, who were supposed to be part of a total provincial force of 20,000, but the actual force amounted to only 9,000. These, joined with 6,000 regulars, mounted a frontal assault on Fort Ticonderoga in July only to fail miserably and to suffer 2,000 casualties. Abercromby showed himself to be wholly inept. The next year, Connecticut, feeling the strain, agreed to raise only 4,000 men, of whom at least 400 had to be volunteers—1,000 short of Pitt's expectations. Connecticut justified its retrenchment on the grounds that Connecticut men serving in the regulars and in the militia of other colonies probably totaled 1,000. When General Amherst suggested that Connecticut might fail to get compensation if it did not meet its quota, the colony agreed to raise enough volunteers to bring its force up to strength. Connecticut troops formed the bulk of the army that now took both forts Ticonderoga and Crown Point without a struggle; the French abandoned them as pressure on Canada from General Wolfe's forces began to be felt.

In 1760 Connecticut once again acted favorably upon a call for troops from Pitt, engaging to raise 5,000 volunteers for the attack on Montreal; but even though the colony increased its bounties, it managed to raise only 3,000. In the two subsequent years the totals fell to 2,300, although each time Pitt called for two-thirds of the 1760 quota of 5,000. Thus during the entire period of the war Connecticut had committed itself to raising about 28,000 men; and although the annual commitment was not in every instance fulfilled, Connecticut found itself more than once putting into the field far more than its fair share. At times fully a fourth of its entire militia was on duty beyond the colony's boundaries.

The strain of this effort was severe. The colony, of course, much preferred recruitment of volunteers to impressment, and to encourage men to come forward the General Assembly offered bounties. At the start of the French and Indian War thirty shillings lawful money went to each soldier who enlisted, besides allowances for weapons and blankets that the militiaman furnished himself. In 1757, the bounty was raised to forty-two shillings, and in 1758, 1759, and 1760 to four pounds, with greater sums going to those who had had previous service. In 1761 and 1762 the bounty went up again, to seven pounds for a soldier without previous experience. Other inducements were proffered as well—exemption from poll taxes in 1758, for example, and occasionally releases from prison for those criminals willing to serve in the campaigns. Private persons of some means also offered sums to enlistees, fearful lest too few volunteers might result in their having to go off to war themselves.

Still, the incentives were not sufficient to procure all the volunteers needed, and as the war lengthened, impressment became the chief resort. The General Assembly did not feel safe in stipulating that more than a fraction of the quota would have to be volunteers. Impressment brought resistance. Some men failed to turn out for musters, or if detached from their militia companies for war service, refused to join the troops. For such slackers, the assembly in 1758 ordered swift application of the law. In 1759, it ordered fines of ten pounds for the purpose of hiring substitutes for those who wanted to escape impressment; for those who simply failed to turn out, it ordered prosecution. Finally, the colony, noting that time after time it had raised more than its proper share of a total force, simply tried to meet demands wholly with volunteers; and when their numbers fell short, the colony protested it could do no better.

The General Assembly was meticulous about providing compensation to those soldiers who lost horses or other property in the fighting, whether the animals or equipment had been impressed or furnished voluntarily. But property was its concern. No general provision was made for compensation to widowed wives or to soldiers sustaining long-term or permanent injuries. Families could expect to collect back wages, even with interest, but disability compensation was left to individual appeals from the weakened and helpless to the mercy and generosity of the General Assembly. In numerous special acts the legislature granted lump sums, like seven pounds or ten pounds, to those unable to do ordinary labor; for loss of a hand or arm the sum might run as high as fifty pounds. Only rarely did the legislators provide for annual support payments; for those unable to do ordinary work they might grant licenses to peddle goods for a period of time. Injury and loss of life were expected as the products of war; only those in the most desperate straits could expect a legislature hard-pressed for funds to make compensation.

The cost of the French and Indian War to Connecticut was far more than a matter of bounties and the like. On orders from the Crown in the early stages of the war, the individual colonies were expected to pay, arm, and clothe the men they raised—provisions and ammunition to come from the Crown. By 1758, arms were to be furnished by the king, and promise of parliamentary reimbursement for colonial expenses was offered. Nevertheless, immediate heavy expenditures were required. Connecticut during the war issued about £340,000 in lawful money bills of credit, declared equivalent to sterling in the ratio of four to three. These bills were redeemable in specie or bills of exchange only upon maturity, when interest at 5 percent was payable. Meanwhile they circulated at less than par, and although they were not legal tender, they could be used to pay taxes. To meet redemption schedules, Connecticut legislators were required steadily to raise tax rates on property far beyond the usual pre-war amounts. Although normally the colony had raised about £4,000 annually for nonschool purposes by assessing one penny in the pound on polls and estates, in the later war years the rate reached 15d. and even 17d. The colony did expect reimbursement from Parliament, but the amounts were uncertain and the payments delayed; meanwhile property owners had to pay up. But they could pay with temporarily depreciating currency that was in plentiful supply.

Even so, tax measures were insufficient at times. In 1756, Connecticut borrowed £10,000 sterling from Governor William Shirley of Massachusetts, commander-in-chief, and it also authorized borrowing a total of £6,000 from private persons, largely because taxes were slow to come in. The General Assembly urged the rich to pay their taxes early, and through the churches it sought voluntary contributions, which it hoped would total £5,000 to £6,000. An authorized public lottery was expected to raise £8,000. In 1757, the colony sought additional revenues by levying a clearance tax on Connecticut-owned vessels of 3d. to 6d. per ton, depending upon destination, and an entry tax on vessels owned outside Connecticut of 1s. per ton. At the same time the colony imposed a 6d. tax on tea brought in by water or land and a 5 percent tax on goods imported by noninhabitants, although there were many exceptions to the latter. In 1758, despite £30,000 issued in bills of credit and a tax of 9d. in the pound, the assembly authorized the borrowing of £25,000 at 6 percent interest.

Despite astronomical increases in tax rates and currency, Connecticut came out of the war rather well financially. Although the colony declared in 1764 that it had paid out £400,000 over and above the grants from Parliament, "the large Arrears of which Sum will remain a heavy distressing Burden upon the People for many Years to come," the picture was not so bleak as the colony tried to paint it. Most of the bills of credit were retired soon after the war's end, and during the war Connecticut, as mentioned earlier, enjoyed an excellent market for its provisions. Most of the money spent by the colony was paid to its own inhabitants; as Lawrence Gipson noted some years ago, "Connecticut undoubtedly during the war years floated on the crest of a wave of prosperity."*

---

* Lawrence H. Gipson, "Connecticut Taxation and Parliamentary Aid preceding the Revolutionary War," *American Historical Review* 36 (April 1931): 726.

The staunch loyalty Connecticut displayed through four French Wars dissolved quickly in the 1760s. The colony did not furnish, as did Massachusetts and Virginia, leaders in the Revolutionary movement who won intercolonial acclaim, but Connecticut men were forthright in expression of their rights and capable of direct action to secure them. The colony's transition to complete independence was the easier because its citizens had long enjoyed so much of it under their charter.

10

THE CRISIS OF THE REVOLUTION

The first of Britain's revenue measures, the Sugar Act, followed closely by the proposal for a stamp tax, came at a time when Connecticut people complained loudly about the hard times of postwar depression. Although the colonial government had virtually managed to pay off its war debt by 1765, the years immediately after the Peace of Paris of 1763 were marked by private and public complaints about ruin and bankruptcy. Money was scarce, trade was stagnant, and land values were sinking. It is little wonder that Parliament's revenue measures were perceived as an economic threat.

Even before Parliament passed the Sugar Act, Connecticut merchants, stirred to action by those in Boston, addressed the General Assembly in January 1764; their appeal underscored the economic hardship that would ensue from enforcing the existing duties on foreign molasses embodied in the Molasses Act of 1733, now about to have its life extended. Connecticut, like other colonies, had virtually ignored the law over the years; but George Grenville, chancellor of the exchequer, was determined to make the customs service efficient and to secure additional revenues from America to help Britain meet the heavy new costs of running its empire. To the merchants' petition, presented by Jared Ingersoll, the General Assembly responded by naming a committee to muster arguments against enforcement, for dispatch to the colony's agent, Richard Jackson. But before anything could be accomplished, Grenville appeared before Parliament in March to outline new revenue proposals that within a month took form as the Sugar Act of 1764. In introducing his proposals, Grenville also mentioned the possibility of stamp taxes as additional sources of revenue. The Sugar Act levied reduced duties on foreign molasses imported into the colonies, which the rejuvenated customs service would enforce, and also included impositions on wines, sugar, luxury textiles, and a variety of other things that Connecticut imported directly and indirectly.

While several colonies raised questions about the right of Parliament to levy duties to raise a revenue rather than just to regulate the flow of trade, most saw the Sugar Act as an economic hardship. It was the proposed stamp tax that provoked all the colonies into examining Parliament's right to tax and the meaning that taxation would have for colonial liberties. Within the colonies, conservatives satisfied with the status quo, moderates, and those wanting significant change all agreed upon the danger of parliamentary taxation and warned that Americans would not submit to it without a struggle. Only when Parliament proceeded anyway and American opposition elicited both formal condemnation and mob violence did conservatives draw back and radicals press ahead, asserting their willingness to defend principle with arms; thus, Americans divided into two camps.

Grenville's speech to Parliament in March 1764 proposing stamp duties was reported to Connecticut by agent Richard Jackson in March and acted upon by the General Assembly in May. A committee of three was named to assist Governor Thomas Fitch in making an appropriate response: Ebenezer Silliman, a member of the upper house, George Wyllys, secretary of the colony, and Jared Ingersoll, former colonial agent, who had heard privately about the tax from Thomas Whately. Grenville had assigned to Whately the task of drafting the stamp tax measure; and when Whately wrote to Ingersoll to find out how Americans would react to such a measure, Ingersoll replied that colonists everywhere would resent it. Fitch and the three-man committee drafted a pamphlet approved by the assembly and entitled *Reasons Why the British Colonies in America Should Not Be Charged with Internal Taxes by Authority of Parliament* . . . . (1764). This pamphlet repeated familiar charges against the mother country for taxing subjects without the consent of their own elected representatives.

Unlike most colonial statements, Connecticut's also referred to the injustice of internal taxes and implied by the use of the term a distinction between internal and external duties; yet the pamphlet urged acceptance only of incidental taxes arising from the regulation of trade, a position that all the colonies were to support. Connecticut conceded that Parliament might through the regulation of trade "affect the Property of *American* Subjects, in a Way which, in some Sense, may be said to be independent upon or without the Will or Consent of the People." This official pamphlet was almost eager in its desire to acknowledge Parliament as the "supreme Authority of the Nation" and to assert that the colonies would be far from "pretending to prescribe Bounds or Limits to the exercise of [that "august" Assembly's] Dominion." Connecticut took the occasion to remind Great Britain of its past services in the king's wars and to question whether the small benefits the wars had brought were worth the price Connecticut had paid. If, however, revenues from America were necessary, Connecticut suggested duties on imported slaves and on the fur trade, neither of which was of much concern to the colony. Altogether the tone of the pamphlet was cautious and respectful but nonetheless steady in its insistence upon charter rights and the rights of Englishmen under the British Constitution. Months later Governor Fitch in a letter to Ingersoll pointedly called attention to Connecticut's acceptance of parliamentary power.

Despite the objections of Connecticut and other colonies, Parliament proceeded in early 1765 to pass the Stamp Act, which was to become effective on November 1, and which taxed a wide variety of legal and other documents, newspaper and newspaper advertisements, almanacs, and pamphlets, in addition to playing cards and dice. The taxes directly affected men of influence and molders of opinion—lawyers, merchants, tavern keepers, and printers. Before Parliament acted, several colonial agents met with Grenville in February 1765 in a final effort to head off the tax; Jared Ingersoll, empowered by Connecticut to act in its behalf in cooperation with Jackson, was present. This last-minute meeting did nothing to change Grenville's mind, but Ingersoll continued to play a role. He explained to Whately that the tax might raise about £3,500 in Connecticut, and he used his influence to lower some of the duties and to eliminate from the drafted bill stamp duties on marriage licenses, the commissions of justices of the peace, and promissory notes. Although Ingersoll had earlier opposed such Parliamentary taxation, he saw nothing wrong in trying to make it as palatable as possible when the ministry's determination had become certain. Nor did he see anything wrong in accepting the position of Connecticut's stamp distributor—better him than some less sympathetic person. But in thinking so, he made a serious mistake.

The colonies generally did not condemn enactment of the Stamp Act until after Patrick Henry's famous resolves were passed in May in the Virginia House of Burgesses and printed in colonial newspapers, along with two of the resolves that had not passed. In Connecticut, the summer of 1765 saw a barrage of newspaper attacks on the Stamp Act, several congregational ministers denounce it from their pulpits or in the press, and outraged citizens of the eastern towns of New London, Norwich, Lebanon, and Windham hang Jared Ingersoll in effigy. But Thomas Fitch took the position of most conservatives: although he had opposed parliamentary taxation, the supreme legislature had acted, and it was the citizen's obligation dutifully to submit. Jonathan Trumbull, member of the upper house and leader from eastern Connecticut, insisted, however, that the governor summon the legislature into special session, particularly to respond to Massachusetts's call for an October meeting of delegates from all the colonies in New York to concert relief efforts. Popular demand pressured Fitch into summoning the General Assembly.

Meeting in September 1765, the special session named as delegates to the New York congress Eliphalet Dyer of Windham, a member of the upper house, William Samuel Johnson, deputy from Stratford, and David Rowland, deputy from Fairfield. Although Dyer was a prominent member of the Susquehannah Company and associated with those who pressed hard for opposition to the Stamp Act, the other two were moderates from the less boisterous part of Connecticut. Having decided to be represented at the Stamp Act Congress, the General Assembly was careful to instruct its delegates that they could not be bound by a majority vote of the congress but must report back to the assembly, which would make its own judgment about the best course of action. The assembly took the opportunity of its special session to condemn the riotous behavior of recent weeks and to request Governor Fitch to issue a proclamation calling upon all officers to prevent and suppress "riots, tumults, and unlawful assemblies." The General Assembly had in mind, no doubt, the burning of effigies of Ingersoll and, possibly, the treatment he had received as he tried to make his way to Hartford at the time of the special session.

Despite the defense made by Ingersoll or by friends in his behalf and his promise that he would not go against the people's desires, men from a number of towns in eastern Connecticut—calling themselves Sons of Liberty—were satisfied with nothing less than his public resignation from his new office. Some five hundred men stopped Ingersoll at Wethersfield; and although he tried to argue with them and remonstrate against so relatively few determining an issue for all Connecticut, they demanded his resignation. They even required him to repeat his resignation before the meeting place of the General Assembly in Hartford. Adamant though the crowd was, it was a well-disciplined one. Ingersoll suffered no indignities other than having to give three rousing cheers after his resignation. Pauline Maier has noted the contrast between this crowd's behavior and that of the mob in Boston, where houses were torn down and lives threatened. She sees this as the "ordered resistance" that the Sons of Liberty adopted after experiencing the sobering excesses of a few weeks earlier. The Connecticut crowd was firmly under the control of its principal spokesman John Durkee, member of the Susquehannah Company and later leader of the settlers in Wyoming.

About two-and-one-half weeks after the Connecticut General Assembly held its special session, delegates from nine colonies met in New York as the Stamp Act Congress. Since no record of the proceedings has been preserved, one can gain only a limited knowledge of the role that Connecticut delegates played. One of the principal matters of debate was whether explicitly to acknowledge the authority of Parliament in areas other than taxation. A majority succeeded in inserting into the first of the congress's thirteen resolves the rather unrevealing statement that the colonies owed "all due Subordination" to Parliament. William Samuel Johnson, already a leading Connecticut lawyer, wrote a few days after the congress broke up that he wished it "had adopted the other Plan of admitting the general superintendance of Parliament and limiting their Power by the Principles and Spirit of the Constitution which sufficiently excludes all Constitutional Right to Tax us, and effectually secures the fundamental Priviledge of Trial by Jury as well as every other Right Essential to British Liberty." * Yet because Johnson thought agreement and unity were more important than his particular preference in wording, he assented to the resolves.

Having won the sanction of most delegates for its declarations, the Stamp Act Congress went on to draft petitions to the king and to each house of Parliament. It was these three petitions that the Connecticut

---

* Quoted by Edmund S. Morgan and Helen M. Morgan, *The Stamp Act Crisis: Prologue to Revolution* (Chapel Hill, N.C.: University of North Carolina Press, 1953), p. 147.

General Assembly agreed to sign and forward to Richard Jackson. The petitions were respectful, repeating that the colonies owed "all due Subordination" to Parliament, but insisted that it had no right to tax or to deny them jury trials by designating Admiralty courts as appropriate for trying offenses against the Stamp Act. The assembly then proceeded to make a statement of its own. A measure of the response that the Stamp Act provoked is the change in wording from the earlier statement of the assembly on "internal taxes," the pamphlet that was largely the work of Thomas Fitch, and the assembly's resolves of October 1765.

For one thing, the later statement makes no mention at all of the authority of Parliament, although the earlier one acknowledged Parliament as supreme and eschewed any intention to set limits on its power. Indeed, the General Assembly now declared that the "only legal Representatives of the Inhabitants of this Colony are the Persons they elect to serve as Members of the General Assembly Thereof." In this point, then, the assembly was going beyond the position that Johnson had wanted to maintain at the Stamp Act Congress, even rendering virtually meaningless the subordination to Parliament that the petitions mentioned. The whole tone of the October piece underscored the colony's special relationship to the king as its protector and was fulsome in its declared admiration for the Hanoverian line, which was obligated, of course, to honor the charter granted by Charles II. The charter stood alongside the rights of Englishmen under the British constitution as guarantor of Connecticut's rights. And there was more.

Connecticut was neither actually nor virtually represented in Parliament; thus Connecticut people profited from the cogent reasoning of Daniel Dulany, or perhaps some of his predecessors, which denied the possibility that colonists could be represented by members of Parliament. Connecticut, too, finally made clear that it saw no distinction between internal and external taxes when it stated that the king's subjects in the colony were governed by their General Assembly "in the Article of taxing and internal Police" and when it differentiated an "Act for raising Money by Duties or Taxes" from other acts of legislation.

Like the Stamp Congress resolves, the Connecticut declaration inveighed against the use of Admiralty courts to enforce the provisions of the new revenue measures for two reasons: their use would extend the jurisdiction of such courts beyond traditional bounds, and they functioned without juries and thus violated a sacred English right to trial by jury. There is irony in this last reproof, for just a little over five years earlier Connecticut had sought an Admiralty court from the Crown exclusively for the colony because it wanted to engage in the mast trade. An Admiralty court at that time would have meant more effective policing of Connecticut's lumber trade, particularly with respect to illegal exporting of lumber and the illegal seizure of floating logs. Perhaps Connecticut hoped also to free itself from the jurisdiction of Benning Wentworth of New Hampshire, surveyor-general of the king's woods. Whatever the reason, in 1760 Connecticut had not been much concerned about the Admiralty court's lack of juries.

Neither the resolutions adopted by the several colonies and the intercolonial congress nor the forced resignations of stamp distributors could prevent the Stamp Act from going into effect on November 1; and Governor Fitch, who had opposed Parliamentary taxation, but who urged obedience once Parliament had acted, felt bound to abide by the law's provisions. Specifically, as governor, he was required to take an oath to do his utmost punctually to enforce the law's clauses according to their true intent. Thus before November 1 he took the oath in the Council chamber in the presence of the four Council members who chose to stay: Ebenezer Silliman of Fairfield, John Chester of Wethersfield, Benjamin Hall of Wallingford, and Jabez Hamlin of Middletown. By that time each had been on the Council for twenty-six, eighteen, fourteen, and seven years, respectively. Politically, Fitch and his supporters had taken a fatal step. Yet their view of matters was that of all conservatives in the colony: any further resistance to Great Britain was liable to jeopardize the charter. Ranged against them were men like Jonathan Trumbull and William Williams of Lebanon, Stephen Johnson of Lyme, Hugh Ledlie and Eliphalet Dyer of Windham, Israel Putnam of Pomfret, John Durkee of Norwich, and the Huntingtons of Norwich and Windham, easterners all and most of them members of the Susquehannah Company.

November 1 was treated in Connecticut as a day of mourning replete with a mock burial of the Stamp Act and burial of an effigy of the governor. Once the Stamp Act went into effect, the question arose of whether the courts should conduct business and ships be permitted to enter and clear from ports, since writs and other legal instruments for civil (not criminal) courts, as well as ship clearances, had to be on stamped paper. Opening or closing the courts was a knotty issue, one's position depending upon a variety of considerations. If stamped paper was not available, opening the courts for business was an act of defiance, serving the cause of liberty; on the other hand, closing the courts meant debtors had nothing to fear from creditors, who could not recover money owed them if judges and lawyers were not functioning. Moreover, keeping the courts closed would make it less risky to clear from ports without the proper stamped clearance.

William Samuel Johnson, genuinely puzzled about the best course for the courts, thought that closing them would give the colony a respite from money draining away to neighboring colonies like New York and Massachusetts, through which much of Connecticut's trade was handled. Popular pressure in eastern Connecticut demanded that courts and lawyers function, but it is not clear that courts opened before the repeal of the Stamp Act. In New Haven County the courts stayed closed without harassment. The collector at the New London port, Duncan Stewart, did not open that port until December 14 because he lacked orders from his superiors, but at length he had to yield to the demands of merchants who threatened to sue. Two weeks later, ships with clearances on unstamped paper were sailing from New Haven as well.

It was the Sons of Liberty who took the initiative in organizing opposition to the Stamp Act, not only by coercing stamp distributors in the several towns but also by organizing protest meetings and drawing up strings of resolves. The Sons were crystal clear in their determination to defend their rights with their lives if necessary. As early as November 11, men from several towns meeting at Windham urged regular countywide meetings subject to a county organization. Sons in New London declared their intention "to reassume their natural Rights" if lawful methods of opposition failed; and in Pomfret and Wallingford, the Sons pledged their lives and threatened to "take to the field." Connecticut Sons have been credited with initiating such meetings, which were quickly copied in other colonies. These men were no rabble but good solid citizens of the middle class with standing in their communities.

And they looked beyond their own colony, for they were the first to take steps toward intercolonial cooperation by meeting with some of the Sons of Liberty from New York in a New London tavern December 25, 1765. Pledges of mutual aid were made, the men agreeing to take up arms and march at their own expense when properly notified. The men from the two colonies agreed to foster such mutual-aid pacts among the Sons of other colonies as well. By March 1766 Connecticut Sons from all over the colony were meeting in convention in Hartford and promising to support intercolonial associations.

One group made conspicuous by its refusal to condemn the Stamp Act and by its outspoken support of the British was Connecticut Anglicans. Their proselytizing had long made them unpopular in many towns of Connecticut, but their ranks had grown steadily, particularly in the western part of the colony. The desire of the Anglican missionaries for a bishop, for not only religious but also social control, as well as political reasons, rankled wherever Congregationalists and Presbyterians lived in large numbers, but in no colony more than in Connecticut. A pamphlet war that had broken out between Anglicans and Congregationalists in 1749, in which one of the key issues was the episcopacy, had been exacerbated by a rumor that the naming of an American bishop was imminent. Connecticut's agent played a role in helping to stop the movement for a bishop at that time.

As the leading Anglican minister and spokesman in Connecticut, Samuel Johnson, who was the father of William Samuel and had converted to Anglicanism as a young man, called steadily for an American bishop, which he and others saw as an important instrument for promoting submission and obedience to government. In Johnson's view, Connecticut was altogether too much under popular control. When he heard some time in 1764 or 1765 that Benjamin Franklin was seeking to supplant control of Pennsylvania by the Penns with royal control, Johnson fervently hoped that Franklin would urge the bringing of all colonial governments under the Crown. In the opinion of Johnson and of many other Anglican ministers in Connecticut, England would have had far less trouble administering its colonies if an American bishop had been appointed long before the crisis of the 1760s. Johnson personally thought passage of the Stamp Act was impolitic; the British might better have settled ecclesiastical affairs before attempting revenue measures.

Other Anglican ministers in their reports to the Society for the Propagation of the Gospel claimed their parishioners had submitted peaceably to the requirements of the law, setting a noble example for those dissenters who, lost to all sense of duty, riotously opposed the Stamp Act. Mixed with their admiration for their flocks (and undoubtedly a self-serving element crept into their reports home) was their fear of reprisals, particularly after the repeal of the Stamp Act, for Britain's reversal would be taken as a sign of weakness and an indication that opponents of the act had been right all along. The loyal Anglicans would be viewed as traitors to the colony, craven Englishmen unconcerned with liberty. Rogers Viets of Simsbury claimed that Anglicans there, condemned as traitors, had been forced out of the few public offices they held in reprisal for their peaceable conduct at the time of the Stamp Act troubles.

For the majority of Connecticut people, however, the repeal of the Stamp Act was a cause for jubilation and for self-congratulation. Officially, of course, a properly dignified response was called for. The General Assembly requested that the governor with the help of a committee "prepare an humble, dutiful and loyal Address to his Majesty, expressive of the filial duty, gratitude and satisfaction, of the Governor and Company of this Colony on the happy occasion of the beneficial repeal of the late American Stamp Act." Whatever contemporary Americans may have thought, modern historians are agreed that repeal was more a matter of pressure brought by English merchants and manufacturers, fearful of loss of trade from American boycotts, than of any victory for principles espoused by the colonists.

When Parliament repealed the Stamp Act in March 1766, it saw to it that the English view of Parliamentary authority over the colonies was given expression in the Declaratory Act, which asserted that Parliament could legislate for the colonies "in all cases whatsoever." As Edmund Morgan has demonstrated, colonial belief that legislation was one thing and taxation another caused the colonies to pay little attention to the Declaratory Act. But in Connecticut and elsewhere a day of thanksgiving and celebration was set aside to mark the repeal of the Stamp Act. The governor set May 23 as the official day. In Hartford, bells rang out and cannons delivered a twenty-one gun salute, but a fireworks display for the evening was spoiled when a school building temporarily storing powder blew up, killing six young men.

*   *   *

There was an explosion in politics that spring as well. Articulate and well-organized men from the eastern counties mounted a campaign to retire Governor Fitch from office along with the four magistrates who had supported his taking of the oath required by the Stamp Act. This was not the first effort to eject Fitch from the governorship. For some years Connecticut New Lights had chafed under the repressive laws, particularly the act forbidding itineracy, enacted by an assembly under the control of Old Lights. The use of political power to crush any deviance from prescribed institutional forms and to remove from office those who had supported the revival gradually turned the New Lights against traditional leaders and politicized the two religious factions. Richard Bushman has convincingly argued that an important effect of the Great Awakening was to lead men to challenge existing authority as they became more directly dependent upon God. By 1748 the New Lights were electing men to the General Assembly; in the 1750s they won control of that body; and by 1759 they sought, unsuccessfully, to oust Fitch from the governorship and the Old Lights from the upper house.

New Light strength centered in eastern Connecticut, where the Susquehannah Company, launched in 1754, had its greatest support, and where the cry for paper money was the strongest. As the New Lights gained in political strength, they sought, by using the machinery of the Saybrook Platform, to enforce orthodoxy against what they viewed as the increasing Arminianism of the Old Lights, so that in some instances the former persecutors became the persecuted. The combination of religious orthodoxy and economic issues made New Lights the strongest force in Connecticut politics by 1763 even though they did not yet dominate the government. The road to domination was opened up by Fitch's submission to the hated Stamp Act.

As governor, Fitch had gained the enmity of the Susquehannah Company because in 1762 he had issued a proclamation forbidding Connecticut people to settle on the lands in Pennsylvania that the company had purchased from the Indians. Fitch, never a believer in the claim to western lands, had acted reluctantly in response to pressure from the governor of Pennsylvania, for Fitch knew such action would hurt him in that part of Connecticut where his strength was weakest. The company's reaction to Fitch's proclamation was defiant; it doubled the number of people it planned to send as settlers. In 1766, the opportunity was at hand to use a new issue in an old cause. It is true that the Crown in June 1763 had forbidden settlement, but the company did not look at that royal order as any more permanent than the Proclamation of 1763, which was issued in October. It would be a mistake to conclude at this stage that opposition to the Stamp Act arose in some quarters because the Crown had thwarted western expansion. The issues were separate, but Fitch had been on the wrong side of both of them, as had Jared Ingersoll.

The first overt effort to organize the campaign against Fitch and the councillors came in March 1766, when a convention of the colony's Sons of Liberty met in Hartford. After resolutions had been passed expressing loyalty to both the king and the British Constitution and promising regular correspondence with Sons in other colonies, and after onlookers had left, the outspoken delegates from the eastern counties revealed their plan to secure agreement on names for governor and deputy governor. Despite some protest at the convention, electioneering, largely foreign to Connecticut tradition, won its way; and in May the voters turned out Governor Fitch in favor of his deputy, William Pitkin, and chose Jonathan Trumbull as deputy governor. All four councillors who had supported Fitch's oathtaking were turned out as well. For good measure, William Samuel Johnson, a moderate in Connecticut politics but willing to cooperate with those desiring change, won election to the Council, the first Anglican to do so.

The loss of the governorship only made Fitch and his supporters determined to recapture the office, and for some years Connecticut saw annual party strife. Supporters of the Susquehannah Company tended to identify their opponents and supporters of Fitch as the old "Stamp party," and some of Fitch's prominent backers dismissed the other side with the contemptuous label Sons of Liberty, fomenters of turmoil in 1765. Their first clash came in the election of 1767, when Pitkin won over Fitch by only thirteen hundred votes. In subsequent years Fitch remained the man around whom conservatives rallied. He was defeated for governor again in 1768 and afterwards was promoted unsuccessfully by members of the General Assembly for chief judge of the Superior Court and, in 1769, for governor and then deputy governor, when Trumbull failed to win a true majority from the voters and the choice had to be made by the assembly. When Governor Pitkin died in the fall of 1769, the assembly elected his deputy, Trumbull, to the vacancy, but only after supporters of Fitch had put up a stiff fight; and then they fought to get the deputy post for their man, also without success. A climax came in 1770, when Fitch supporters bent every effort to get him the governorship, and came so close that the election was thrown into the assembly, where Trumbull prevailed.

Connecticut had become sharply divided over men and issues. The Trumbull faction had its strength among men who were New Light in sentiment and expansionist in outlook. Their cause was the Susquehannah Company and its abundant lands to the westward; the objects of their revulsion were the revenue measures of Parliament and those in Connecticut whom they identified as insufficiently hostile to imperial enactments. The division between the two groups was sectional, Fitch drawing his heavy support from the western areas of Connecticut. Fitch and Trumbull were to clash for a final time in 1774.

Before that date, Connecticut people reacted in milder ways than they had at the time of the Stamp Act to the series of events that were leading the colonies down the road to revolution. To some degree they were distracted by the internal struggle over the Susquehannah Company's claim and the fierce factional fighting that it spawned. For example, in January 1767 Connecticut, in a special session of the legislature, dealt with a request of General Thomas Gage that the colony quarter through the winter some 188 recruits just arrived from Germany. Connecticut not only assented but appropriated public money to reimburse those with whom the soldiers lived because the official rate for the soldiers' subsistence was insufficient. The soldiers were quartered in public houses, and the General Assembly's enactment provided fines for those who refused to accept them. The only limitations were that soldiers were not to carry arms when off duty, and billeting was not to extend longer than seven days at a time in any one place. Thus Connecticut saw no threat to its liberties in having to supply billets.

Official reaction to the Townshend Acts, passed in 1767, which placed duties on glass, red and white lead, painter's colors, and tea, was rather circumspect. Petitions were sent from the General Assembly to the American secretary, Lord Hillsborough, and to the king; and although these made the familiar appeal to the charter's guarantee of the rights of Englishmen, Parliament was described as the king's "high court, the rectitude of whose intentions is never to be questioned"—a far cry from the assembly's resolve of October 1765, in which Parliament merited no mention at all. When the Connecticut legislature received the Massachusetts Circular Letter of 1768, it assured its neighbor that "no constitutional measures proper for obtaining relief ought to be neglected by any, and that it is of importance their measures for that end should harmonize with each other, as their success may in a great degree depend on their union in sentiment and practice. . . ." A proper enough response to the rather standard line laid down by Samuel Adams, author of the letter. But official Connecticut had no specific suggestions to offer.

Unofficially, opposition to the Townshend duties took the form of a demand for the nonimportation of British goods, first broached by eastern towns like Windham, New London, and Norwich. These towns began to stir about the time John Dickinson's "Letters from a Farmer" began to appear in various colonial newspapers—in the winter of 1767–1768. By the fall of 1769 Connecticut merchants were supporting the nonimportation agreement that Boston, New York, and Philadelphia had finally reached; and in 1770, Connecticut merchants met in convention in Middletown to reinforce nonimportation with plans for a society to promote the arts, commerce, agriculture, and manufacturing—all intended to lessen dependence upon Great Britain.

Violators of the nonimportation agreement might find their names printed in the newspapers or themselves condemned in town meetings, with perhaps a boycott of their business as a way of retaliating against their disaffection. When Britain repealed all the duties except that on tea and pressure mounted among merchants to ease nonimportation and re-open trade, Connecticut merchants were at first opposed to relaxation of trade restrictions. But when New York merchants abandoned nonimportation, their Connecticut counterparts could not hold out and by the summer of 1770 were replenishing their stocks of British goods.

Since Connecticut had virtually no direct trade with Great Britain, manufactured goods, now ardently desired by merchants whose profits had suffered during nonimportation, were secured in unusually large amounts on credit from New York and Boston correspondents. Many Connecticut merchants overextended themselves, having to beg the legislature for relief from debts they could not meet. And some resorted to smuggling in violation of British trade laws in the hope that illegal profits would ease their plight.

Smuggling, of course, was no new practice in Connecticut nor peculiar to that colony. In trying to cope with it, royal customs officials repeatedly asked Connecticut's Superior Court for writs of assistance, a request first made to the court in 1768. The court found various reasons to delay, raising technical queries, but in the last analysis demurred out of fear of popular reaction against a favorable ruling. This was no quiet issue, for in 1773 newspapers aired the matter fully; writs were held to be a threat to liberty. The court never did get around to a ruling.

The Tea Act of 1773, which permitted the East India Company to send its tea directly to the colonies without having to land it first in England

and to distribute it in America through favored agents instead of through colonial merchants, caused little stir in Connecticut, although colonial leaders elsewhere saw a real threat in this latest parliamentary enactment. Tea shipped directly to America could be sold cheaply despite the Townshend duty that had to be paid on it; some said it would even undersell smuggled tea. Moreover, if the East India Company enjoyed this privilege, what was to prevent Parliament from permitting it to sell other goods directly to the colonies and thereby undermining the very livelihood of merchants? But Connecticut people were too embroiled in internal issues to bother much about this new imperial threat. The Susquehannah Company and its activities in Pennsylvania were on virtually everyone's mind.

Kept out of its claimed western lands by royal proclamation in June 1763, the company had chosen to regard the treaty of Fort Stanwix in 1768 as marking the end of exclusion of Americans from western areas. In 1769 it had sent out a settling party, which was driven out a few months later by Pennsylvanians; the same fate befell a second party in 1770. But by 1771, the Connecticut settlers had managed to establish themselves so firmly that Pennsylvanians could not dislodge them. Living in a frontier area without benefit of formal government, the settlers, and the company as well, wanted Connecticut not only to acknowledge its right to western lands by virtue of its sea-to-sea charter but also to assert governing rights over those settled on these remote lands and to integrate the new settlements with the rest of the colony. In May 1771, Connecticut formally claimed western lands beyond the province of New York that lay within Connecticut's northern and southern boundaries— in short, the northern one-third of Pennsylvania and beyond. But for two and one-half years that was as far as the General Assembly would go. Settlers were left to their own devices or those of the company. Their tradition of self-government stood them in good stead. Votes in settlers' meetings and actions by an executive committee kept good order for a time, but the desire for better regulation led to "articles of agreement," which set up a system of local government. But if the claim was to be maintained against Pennsylvania, more was needed—political integration into Connecticut.

In January 1774, the General Assembly at last created the town of Westmoreland with bounds generous enough to take in all the settlements in Pennsylvania in the vicinity of the Wyoming Valley, and the town was made part of Litchfield County, although it was a long way from it. The assembly's move was made possible by a legal opinion secured by Connecticut's agent in England: four prominent attorneys held that Connecticut's boundary settlement with New York did not necessarily preclude a claim to lands west of that colony. The decision to assert governmental rights sharply divided Connecticut people.

Those who opposed any encouragement of the western claim saw heavy expenses in a cause foredoomed to failure. Connecticut had made its claim so belatedly that it seemed naive to think it could be defended before the Privy Council. A claim to lands so distant from the colony appeared absurd; meanwhile, self-deluded settlers heading west would drain the colony of people and lower land values in Connecticut. Supporters of the Susquehannah Company, delighted that the colony had assumed its responsibilities, saw the opportunity for acquiring good rich lands. Connecticut was crowded and productive farm land hard to come by; the Wyoming Valley held out hope for those dreaming of homes and speculative profit. The deep division between opponents and supporters of the western claim was to affect the spring elections of 1774 as few issues had affected any in Connecticut.

An anonymous contributor to the newspapers calling himself "Many" urged a meeting in convention of delegates from towns opposed to the western claim. On March 30 delegates from twenty-three towns assembled at Middletown, most of them from the southwestern part of the colony. The public result of their deliberations was a broadside charging that continued support of the claim would jeopardize the Connecticut charter and lead to violence in Pennsylvania. The towns accused many members of the legislature of casting a self-interested vote in creating the town of Westmoreland, for they were stockholders in the Susquehannah Company. When the convention ended, some of the delegates lingered behind to draw up a list of nominees for public office who were committed to blocking the western claim. This maneuver violated Connecticut practice in its blatant electioneering, but the Middletown convention-goers had some precedent, for it was just such tactics that had been used to remove former governor Thomas Fitch from office and keep him out. Now Fitch was put forward again, as well as Ebenezer Silliman, the defeated member of the Council who had supported Fitch when he took the oath to enforce the Stamp Act. This was Fitch's last run, and he and like-minded candidates and supporters went down to a bad defeat. Three months later Fitch was dead and his party with him. The anti-British radicals were left in the dominant position as the revolutionary crisis deepened.

*   *   *

Hard on the heels of Connecticut's spring elections came the news of punishment meted out to Boston and Massachusetts by Parliament for the Tea Party of the past December—the Coercive Acts. Although Connecticut was not directly affected, the colony could not help feeling uneasy over the high-handed way in which Parliament had so drastically altered the Massachusetts charter and closed Boston's port without regard for the effect upon innocent people. Connecticut's own charter now seemed terribly vulnerable. Yet Connecticut like most of the colonies was unwilling to adopt the extreme resistance that Massachusetts proposed—a complete trade rupture with Great Britain, Ireland, and Britain's West Indian colonies. Although individual Connecticut towns expressed support for Boston, the colony officially went no further than a set of resolves passed by the lower house in late May or early June 1774 but not accepted by the upper house until October.

These resolves, while dutifully acknowledging the sovereignty of the king, insisted once again upon Connecticut's charter rights, particularly those of self-taxation and trial by a jury of peers in the vicinity. The house insisted further that only a local government could close a port. Parliament's actions regarding Boston were subversive of liberty. Continued dependence upon Great Britain was desirable from every point of view, but a higher obligation was to transmit rights intact to posterity. By early June, then, official Connecticut was still dutiful, but it was not budging from a position it had taken several years earlier.

On June 3 the house also empowered the Committee of Correspondence, which had been created by the General Assembly about a year earlier, to meet with other such committees in a congress to reach common decisions in response to the new threat presented by Parliament's treatment of Massachusetts. This was perhaps the earliest "official" call for a continental congress, but the house was acting alone. It further empowered the Committee of Correspondence to choose delegates for the congress. On the strength of this resolution, Silas Deane, secretary for the committee, sent letters to committees up and down the coast proposing a meeting for the last week of July or the first one in August, leaving the choice of the meeting place to those agreeing to come, although he mentioned New York, Norwalk, or Fairfield as possibilities.* Within a month the committee had chosen five men, of whom three were intended actually to attend the congress: Eliphalet Dyer, Silas Deane, William Samuel Johnson, Erastus Wolcott, and Richard Law. The last three named declined their appointment, and in their place were chosen Roger Sherman and Joseph Trumbull, either of whom could attend with Dyer and Deane.

In the minds of American colonists the Quebec Act, which was passed about the time of the Coercive Acts, was part of the pattern of subversion of American rights, although Great Britain saw the measure as a humane and effective way of dealing with the French Catholic population. What Britain viewed as humane, the colonists interpreted as a bold move to undermine their religion by the extension of privileges to Catholics, who in the popular mind were historically the enemies of British liberties. In Stamford the town meeting excoriated the Quebec Act as an open indication that religious liberties were to be abolished. Curiously almost no Connecticut people seemed to recognize that the act's extension of the boundaries of Quebec to the Ohio River challenged the Connecticut claim to western lands, as well as the overlapping claims of other colonies such as New York and Virginia. William Samuel Johnson noted the meaning of this provision of the act, but he was almost alone in Connecticut in seeing the threat, judging by extant records. Connecticut's failure to protest would be held against the colony some years later when Connecticut's right to land in Pennsylvania went to trial.

The Continental Congress gathered in the fall in Philadelphia and drafted petitions to Parliament and to the king, but it also called into being the Continental Association for ending consumption and importation of British goods and the exportation of American goods (except rice) to Britain, Ireland, and the West Indies. These measures were to be enforced locally. Connecticut towns accepted the association and established committees to enforce its provisions. But in the fall of 1774 Connecticut was doing more—looking to its defenses.

In September there had been an alarm. Rumor had it that General

---

* On the effort to call a continental congress, see Merrill Jensen, *The Founding of a Nation* (New York: Oxford University Press, 1968), pp. 466–67.

Gage's troops in a move to seize gunpowder stored in Charlestown had killed six Americans. The rumor stirred hundreds of militiamen to march toward Boston. Although the alarm was false, the Connecticut General Assembly decided to put the colony's defenses in better order. A general muster of all militia companies was called for the fourth Monday in November, at which arms were to undergo inspection to determine their battle readiness. And before May 10, 1775, all companies were to meet for military exercises. (This second order was canceled in April at the time of the Lexington emergency.) In addition, the towns were to see to it that they had double the quantity of powder, flints, and bullets required by law to supply each company of sixty soldiers, and the cannon at New London were to be put in fighting condition.

Connecticut, however, was not all belligerence. In answer to a circular letter from Lord Dartmouth written in December 1774, Governor Trumbull was conciliatory and mild, but not meek. Connecticut, he said, did not wish to "weaken or impair" the authority of Parliament "in any matters essential to the welfare and happiness of the whole Empire." British supremacy and American liberty were "not incompatible with each other." That word *essential*, of course, was open to the widest interpretation. After referring to "our fellow subjects in Great Britain," who enjoyed the right of taxation in the form of a free gift to the sovereign, Trumbull closed with a plea on Boston's behalf.

It took the news of Lexington and Concord really to put Connecticut on a war footing. Spontaneously men picked up their arms and set out in the direction of Boston. Not everywhere in the colony, of course, was there agreement that the time had come to take more than a verbal stand. It is said that in New Haven, Benedict Arnold had to threaten force to get access to the powderhouse, and there were pockets of conservatives elsewhere fearful of irrevocable decisions. But officially Connecticut demonstrated that it meant business. In April of 1775, Connecticut called up one-fourth of its militia, organized into six regiments, each company containing 100 men. Major-General David Wooster was placed in command, assisted by two brigadiers, Joseph Spencer and Israel Putnam. The General Assembly ordered 100 stands of arms and offered bounties to those who enlisted. Ministers were urged to preach unity to their congregations and to invoke Providence to preserve the colony's liberties and guide its leaders. Within a month the colony was offering bounties for rifles, gun-locks, sulfur, and saltpeter locally manufactured.

A VIEW OF THE TOWN OF CONCORD, 1775. Of the four scenes painted by Ralph Earl after a tour with Amos Doolittle of the battle sites of Lexington and Concord, only this one is known to be extant. Some have called Earl's effort the earliest painting in America of a historical scene. The two British officers pictured are Major Pitcairn and Colonel Smith, who are looking at the American militia. *Courtesy of the Frick Art Reference Library* and *Concord Antiquarian Society.*

Of the six newly organized regiments, four were put on orders to be ready to march to Boston.

Defense was not all arms and ammunition. Declaring that in the existing situation it would be "prejudicial to the Colony" to jail debtors, the General Assembly temporarily suspended imprisonment for debt and applied its enactment to those already in jail, too. It also provided better internal communication by establishing courier service between the southwestern and northeastern corners of the colony, couriers arriving in Hartford and New London every Saturday. The lower house appointed two men to obtain intelligence from the provincial congresses of New York and New Jersey, and in June the assembly authorized the governor to engage a post-rider for service to Albany and points north. The assembly also established a Committee of Safety of nine or ten men, five constituting a quorum, to act with the governor in the assembly's absence. All but one of these men were members of the lower or upper house.

Meanwhile Governor Trumbull at the request of the General Assembly had written to General Gage for an explanation of events at Lexington and Concord. Connecticut's people were not certain that the news received was correct, but it appeared that "outrages have been committed as would disgrace even barbarians, and much more Britons, so highly famed for humanity as well as bravery." Trumbull warned the general that Connecticut stood ready to defend its rights "to the last extremity" and suggested that Gage suspend military operations to "quiet the minds" of Connecticut's people. Trumbull's letter was carried to Boston by two prominent men, neither identified with those pressing Britain hard in behalf of their rights: William Samuel Johnson and Colonel Erastus Wolcott. That such a mission was sent at all when Connecticut men had already hurried off to support Boston suggests that an effort was being made to allay the fears of moderates in Connecticut's assembly. Radicals were unhappy at the mission and thought that the Massachusetts version of events should have been sent at once to England without seeking explanations from the perpetrator of the disgraceful deeds of that day. Massachusetts leaders were astounded at Connecticut's action. Gage returned a self-justifying answer, but the assembly did not remain in session to receive it. Massachusetts leaders need not have worried.

At the end of April, Benedict Arnold arrived in Cambridge and in conference with Massachusetts leaders was commissioned to proceed against Fort Ticonderoga, adding to his forces by recruiting several hundred men in western Massachusetts. Meanwhile, in Connecticut, Samuel Holden Parsons had initiated, with money from the Connecticut treasury, a scheme to send agents to Ethan Allen to urge an attack on Fort Ticonderoga. This fort was a symbol of power, strategically located to check invasion from Canada or to mount a northern attack, but it also contained a number of brass cannons that could be used to fortify the high ground around Boston and thus to threaten the British occupation. Despite differences between Allen and Arnold over who was properly in command, the two leaders and their followers managed to cooperate in taking Ticonderoga without a shot being fired.

The cannons that were captured were not seized in time for use on Bunker Hill, however. At least 200 Connecticut men, led by Captain Thomas Knowlton, Jr., fought in that battle. The leading Connecticut soldier was General Israel Putnam, fifth ranking general in the continental chain of command, promoted to that position over two of his superiors in Connecticut, generals David Wooster and Joseph Spencer. Putnam's flamboyance angered some and endeared him to others. Action was what he sought above all else. He has been charged with having chosen to fortify Breed's Hill and then trying to redeem his mistake by fortifying Bunker Hill, a much more defensible position.*

In June 1775, Connecticut voted to have its troops in Massachusetts placed under the command of that colony's commander-in-chief, Artemas Ward, and urged Rhode Island and New Hampshire to follow its example. The next month Connecticut raised 1,400 additional men organized into two regiments of ten companies each; and in August, because of the threat posed by British ships off New London, the Council of War ordered one-fourth of the men of five regiments to be in readiness as minutemen, able to march on the shortest notice to meet any attack, whether by land or sea. Like other New England colonies, Connecticut recruited Negroes and Indians into its forces. By the end of the year the colony had made provision for artillery defense of four shore points: Groton, Stonington, New Haven, and Milford.

In the summer of 1775 Connecticut had begun, somewhat reluctantly, to develop a navy of sorts. In response to a vote of the General Assembly the Council of War chartered the brig *Minerva*, about 108 tons, and

---

* On General Putnam at Bunker Hill, see Allen French, *The First Year of the American Revolution* (Boston: Houghton Mifflin, 1931), pp. 149–50.

purchased a small schooner for spying purposes, appropriately named *The Spy*. At the request of the Continental Congress the brig was ordered northward late in the year to intercept two vessels carrying arms from England to Quebec, but most of the crew and marines on board refused the order, and the mission had to be aborted. By the end of the year, Connecticut had added to its fleet another brig, *Defence,* a ship, *Oliver Cromwell,* and four row galleys. The *Defence* in an engagement in June 1776 gave a good account of itself by capturing, with the help of other vessels, two transport ships and a brig. Besides these ships, something over two hundred private vessels were authorized to engage in privateering, bringing prizes into such ports as New London, Middletown, Wethersfield, and Hartford.

As in earlier wars, Connecticut was prompt in contributing to the common cause. In September 1775, the colony asked the Continental Congress for reimbursement, since the cost of defense was to be borne by "the United Colonies in just proportion," and Connecticut had been "very greatly in advance both of men and money for and in support of the grand cause of American Liberty." And the congress did vote funds for Connecticut—£15,000 for sums dispersed and £48,000 for supplies issued. Washington requested that the additional men Connecticut had raised in July be sent to Boston in September; and even though they were then busy building needed shore fortifications—Stonington had already been cannonaded—Connecticut complied with the general's request for fear of being thought uncooperative. In March 1776, the colony readily decided to accept continental currency at face value for the payment of taxes in order to encourage circulation of this paper money. Connecticut's enlisted soldiers in continental service were exempted from poll taxes in 1775 and 1776.

Connecticut clearly had something at stake; its fears for its charter were not imaginary. The Howe brothers carried with them a commission to make a last-minute effort at reconciliation with the colonies (at the same time that they were ordered to use all expedient force to bring the Americans into submission) but also "additional instructions" covering the special situation of the two self-governing colonies of Connecticut and Rhode Island. These were to be converted into royal colonies with their governors appointed by the Crown, or if that could not be obtained, new charters "explanatory" in nature were to make elected governors subject to royal approval before they entered upon their duties.

Moreover, all future laws would be subject to the Crown's veto. These were not iron-clad conditions for reconciliation, but there could be no doubt that if the king secured the upper hand, royal status was in store for Connecticut and its sister colony.*

By May 1776, Connecticut had taken a number of steps in the direction of independence. It had appointed naval officers for several ports, given jurisdiction over prizes to county courts (in accordance with the urging of the Continental Congress), and changed the wording in writs, in the Riot Act, and in the act against high treason to make it apparent that officials acted in the name of the Governor and Company of Connecticut rather than of His Majesty, and that high treason was an offense against the colony, not the king. In June, Connecticut was impressing pork and supplies of lead, with citizens having to sell at market prices any surplus beyond their own needs. The colony had set a course from which there was no turning back. On June 15 the upper house accepted a lower house resolution instructing the colony's delegates in Congress to vote for independence. The language chosen was pretty much that of the Virginia Resolves of May 15, but Connecticut did call for a general government whose form was to be approved by the several states.

Connecticut's Council of Safety received its copy of the Declaration of Independence on July 12, accompanied by a request from the Continental Congress for its publication. The matter was "largely discoursed, and many things given out relative to the matter &c. &c., and [the Council] concluded to lay it by for the present." Six days later the declaration again came up for consideration. After long discussion, particularly about "the manner of choosing Delegates &c.," the Council decided it was best "to let the matter of publishing the Independency remain for the determination of the General Assembly at their next stated session." The colony had lost none of its innate cautiousness despite the actions it had taken over the past year or so. The assembly did not meet until October, when it registered its approval at long last of the Declaration of Independence.

There were those, of course, who never did approve Connecticut's abrogation of its allegiance to Great Britain. Oscar Zeichner has estimated the colony's Loyalists at between 2,000 and 2,500, perhaps 6 percent of the adult male population. Although there were scattered

---

* Additional Instructions, Public Record Office, London, CO 5: 253, p. 5.

loyalists in the various sections of Connecticut, they were most numerous in the southwest, in towns like Ridgefield, Newtown, Fairfield, and Stamford in Fairfield County. There were pockets of loyalism in New Haven and Litchfield counties as well. Shocked by disaffection in militia companies of several regiments, the General Assembly began to take legal steps to protect the colony from internal subversion. In December 1775, those who aided "the ministerial army or navy"—Connecticut like other colonies could not yet bring itself to the realization that *royal* forces were shedding American blood—in any way, whether by furnishing food or intelligence, by procuring enlistments, or by piloting ships, would upon conviction in court forfeit their estates and face up to three years in prison. Those unable to satisfy local authorities that they were friendly to the American cause were to be disarmed. And those who defamed the resolves of the Continental Congress or the enactments of the General Assembly were to be barred from office and subject to fines and imprisonment. By June of 1776 the assembly had ordered the confiscation of weapons from all loyalists for use by Connecticut troops and had instituted a pass system, so that only those known to be patriots could travel from place to place. The final indignity was to make debts owed to loyalists payable to the colony. Connecticut's people, however, did not wait for their legislature. Angry patriots disarmed loyalist neighbors and tarred and feathered a few, but more often they demanded public confession of disloyalty to the colony and violation of the Continental Association.

Among those who suffered most were the Anglicans. Always regarded as intruders in the land of Congregationalism, and hated for their refusal to take a stand against the Stamp Act, Anglicans and their churches now came in for special attention. Soldiers returning from Boston conducted drumhead court martials to force Anglicans to post bonds guaranteeing they would not take up arms against the government or denigrate the Continental Congress. In some communities churches were vandalized, and outspoken ministers were forced to flee to the British for protection. During the course of the Revolution many Anglican churches closed. A few pastors remained to visit the sick and fulfill other pastoral duties, but they conducted no services because the prayers for the king, part of the required ritual, were anathema to patriots. Some pastors omitted objectionable phrasing and conducted services as usual, only to suffer withdrawal of support when their compromise became known to church authorities in England. Life was not easy for Connecticut Anglicans.

Loyalism was never the threat in Connecticut that it was in New York or the Carolinas, probably because the colony had always been virtually self-governing. Before the 1760s Connecticut had been loyal to the king, but the royal presence was felt much less here than in a colony where the king appointed the governor and royal patronage operated. Indeed, Connecticut had a higher loyalty, although it would never have used such words before the revolutionary crisis developed—loyalty to its charter and the self-governing rights it conveyed. To protect it Connecticut acted circumspectly, raising troops when called upon and framing loyal addresses. The revenue acts of the 1760s and 1770s were viewed as a real threat to the integrity of that charter, which had early become an ark of the covenant to be protected at all costs. One of the most serious charges brought against the Susquehannah Company was that its wild claims to western lands would put the charter in jeopardy. Fear for its survival caused the Connecticut government to proceed gingerly in challenging the Crown's disavowal of the intestacy act and in the Mohegan lands dispute. The jewel in the charter was Connecticut's right to make its own laws. The lower house in a letter to agent Jonathan Belcher in 1728 summed up well the principle that Connecticut men stood by: "That it's the Privilege of Englishmen, and the natural Right of all men who have not forfeited it, to be governed by laws made by their own Consent." Connecticut did not rush into armed conflict or into separation; but finally this appeared the only way to preserve its ancient rights.

Thus it is not surprising that in May 1775, justifying its reasons for raising troops, Connecticut in the dozen or more pronouncements stressed most the rights secured by an inviolable charter—the right to consent to revenue-raising measures, the right to jury trial within the colony before judges free of Crown influence, the right to have petitions heard. Connecticut also expressed its concern about the establishment of the Roman Catholic religion in Quebec; the Restraining Act, which closed the fisheries to New England and forbade trade except to Great Britain, Ireland, and British West Indies; and the killing of people at Lexington and Concord. Despite these complaints, the colony at this late date was still willing to leave regulation of trade to Parliament even if that meant all the advantages would be secured to the mother country, a position already abandoned by many American leaders. This was the official voice of the colony expressed through the General Assembly, but individual Connecticut men were more radical. For example, Samuel Holden Parsons, in a letter to Samuel Adams written in 1773, rejected the idea of "unalienable Allegiance to any Prince or State" and asserted that the only lawful authority the king enjoyed over the colony was that granted to him by the settlers.

Whether economic considerations played a greater role in pushing Connecticut into separation than the ideological principles set forth in public documents is more difficult to determine. Merchants, of course, supported nonimportation at the time of the Townshend Acts and apparently abandoned it with some reluctance when others resumed importing. It has been suggested that the Susquehannah Company supported independence because it hoped to gain from Connecticut what it had not secured from the Crown—recognition of its claim to lands west of the colony. It is true the members of the company and its supporters became leading patriots—Jonathan Trumbull, Eliphalet Dyer, Silas Deane, and others. But it is difficult to believe that their concern for the company loomed large in their support for independence. For one thing, the colony had already made it plain that the company would not receive carte blanche. The General Assembly retained authority to determine what rights members of the company should enjoy in the western lands now claimed by the colony. For another, English lawyers had already given the company some encouragement. To be sure, the company's claims against those of the Penns were moving very slowly through the judicial process in England, but the English government was not responsible for the delays. Almost certainly the company would have made some gain in a contest before the Privy Council. Thus independence did not of itself promise much for the company.

In short, it was the charter and the rights it conferred that concerned Connecticut's people. Rather than see those rights infringed, the colony chose to leave the empire.

11

EPILOGUE

So satisfied was Connecticut with its form of government and liberties that there was no great groundswell of opinion, once independence had been asserted, to reshape institutions or to revamp tradition. The Revolution had remarkably little effect on the tenor of political life or prevailing social arrangements. While other colonies drew up new constitutions during the revolutionary years, Connecticut, as well as Rhode Island, the two colonies most free of royal control, kept its charter and its laws with hardly a whisper of discontent. A simple statute, passed in October 1776, was sufficient to continue the charter.

In 1782, Benjamin Gale protested Connecticut's lack of a proper constitution in a pamphlet entitled *Brief, Decent but Free Remarks . . . on Laws Passed by the Legislature since 1775*. But his was virtually a lone voice calling for a convention to draft an organic law for the state. Then in 1786, two legislators disagreed over whether the charter had standing as a constitution in the sense that it was superior to mere legislative enactments. Taking the position that the charter was beyond the reach of the legislature, Joseph Hopkins of Waterbury argued that the General Assembly could not change the number of delegates to which the towns were entitled, that such an alteration could be made only by the people. James Davenport of Stamford rejected this metamorphosis of charter into constitution, holding that the Revolution had destroyed the charter and that only an act of the legislature had reinstated it. Thus, he held, Connecticut had no constitution.* But one has to search to find such ques-

---

* The positions of Hopkins and Davenport are described in Philip Jordan, "Connecticut Politics during the Revolution and Confederation, 1776–1789" (unpublished Ph.D. dissertation, Yale University, 1962), pp. 26–28.

tions raised. One need only compare the feeling in Connecticut with that in Massachusetts to gauge the relative depth of content in the two states. In the Bay State objection to continuing with the old charter brought closing of courts and armed resistance until Massachusetts adopted a constitution on its second attempt.

Perhaps some of this same spirit, when the charter itself was not at issue, explains the agitation in Connecticut for popular choice of the delegates to the Confederation Congress. To provide guidance for the General Assembly, the Articles of Confederation had been sent to the towns for their consideration. In the winter of 1777–1778 the discussions went on in better than half of the towns. Not one for which records are extant rejected the articles and at least a dozen expressed a desire for voter selection of the congressional delegates. After some delay, the assembly offered an electoral system in keeping with Connecticut tradition. Nomination of twelve men was to be made by the freemen in the fall, seven of these to be elected in the spring. From the seven the assembly would select from two to four to sit in the congress. The list of nominees given to the voters was arranged so that those who received the most votes in the fall were placed first. This arrangement was a modification of the old practice of listing first those who had held political office longest. The Articles of Confederation necessitated this change, for they provided for rotation in office.*

Although the Revolution had relatively little political impact in Connecticut, its economic repercussions were felt widely. The state suffered from inflation and the burden of taxation that wars always bring. The British blockade and state-imposed embargoes designed to conserve food and other goods created temporary hardship and resulted in some shifting of capital from trade to manufacturing. Assembly subsidies encouraged the manufacture of guns, powder, and salt. The government itself supervised lead mines in Middletown and iron works in Salisbury and Colebrook. Once the center of the fighting shifted to the southward, trade by water revived somewhat through shippers' resorting to illegal means. Small boats went to New York for much sought-after British and West Indian goods. The Connecticut government took strong measures to prevent a drain of provisions to the enemy but with only modest success. Far larger in bulk than this illegal trade, however, was the provisions trade with the Continental Army. The first commissary gen-

---

* Ibid., pp. 63–64, 67, 74–75.

eral was Joseph Trumbull, son of the governor, who had learned the trading business in his father's firm. Jeremiah Wadsworth, another Connecticut man, succeeded to the post in 1778. Both men naturally turned to the merchants whom they knew for supplies.

The profits these merchants enjoyed brought some discontent with the tax structure in Connecticut. An earlier chapter noted the relatively heavy proportion of total taxes paid by the polls. When the rate of taxes on the pound rose to very high levels (nearly three shillings compared to a penny or two in the prewar period), demands arose for steeper taxes on profits and personal estates. In 1779, the General Assembly reduced poll taxes on males under twenty-one years of age and raised taxes on savings, personal property, merchants' inventories, and the like.

But altogether these bits and pieces of change do not add up to a great deal. Even the Susquehannah Company attracted little hostile attention. All during the war, Connecticut settlers in the Wyoming Valley held fast to their land titles. They furnished troops to the Continental Army and in every way played the role of a Connecticut county despite their distance from the capital. Westmoreland had been made a county in 1776. The Wyoming Massacre of 1778, when Colonel John Butler and his Indian allies virtually destroyed the settlements, proved only a temporary setback. In fact, the hardship the Connecticut people endured in a common cause seemed to many observers to give them a moral right to the lands they claimed in Pennsylvania. Settlement of their dispute had to await the peace, and many years passed before an amicable agreement could be reached between Wyoming settlers and the Pennsylvania government.

Significant change in Connecticut's institutions lay well in the future, too. The state did not adopt a constitution until 1818, and then only after emerging political parties had broken the power of the Standing Order, which had so long given stability to Connecticut life.

BIBLIOGRAPHY

GENERAL

Students of Connecticut history have an important bibliographic aid in the periodic surveys of research completed and in progress issued by the Association for the Study of Connecticut History. These are obtainable from the Center for Connecticut Studies at Eastern Connecticut State College, Willimantic, Connecticut, 06226. The last comprehensive listing of work completed appeared in the *Connecticut History Newsletter* for June 1973 and has been supplemented in subsequent biannual issues. The association is presently compiling a comprehensive bibliography that will gather into several listings all the significant work done on the colony and state for its entire history.

Manuscript sources within the state for the colonial period are rich and well arranged. At the State Library in Hartford are bound volumes known as the Connecticut Archives, which contain papers relating to the business of the General Assembly. Included are resolutions, reports, petitions, correspondence, and the like, arranged in approximate chronological order and gathered into series of volumes under general headings such as Towns and Lands, Susquehannah Settlers, Ecclesiastical Affairs, Revolutionary War, Trade and Maritime Affairs. These massive collections are made usable through painstaking, detailed indexes. The State Library contains also the papers of Governor Jonathan Trumbull and local records of various kinds, both original and on film.

Outside the State Library the most important manuscript collections are at the Connecticut Historical Society, also in Hartford. The William Samuel Johnson Papers, the Susquehannah Company Papers, and the Silas Deane Papers are perhaps the largest for the period covered in this book. The society maintains an excellent catalogue of its manuscript holdings.

Particularly useful for part of this study were the manuscript records of the Society for the Propagation of the Gospel, Letter Series B and C, now available on microfilm. A handful of documents from the British Museum and the Public Record Office in London added significant information here and there.

The main sources for this study, however, have been printed documents and secondary material, including books, articles, and unpublished studies. Of greatest importance is J. Hammond Trumbull and Charles J. Hoadly, eds., *Public Records of the Colony of Connecticut, 1636–1776*, 15 vols. (Hartford, 1850–1890, hereafter cited as *Conn. Col. Records*), which contain laws, resolutions, appointments, petitions, some official correspondence, and other materials that yield information not only about official actions but also about poverty, religious and boundary quarrels, crime, education, social attitudes, and a host of other matters. Complementary to these volumes are the records of neighboring colonies: Nathaniel B. Shurtleff, ed., *Records of the Governor and Company of the Massachusetts Bay in New England*, 5 vols. (Boston, 1853–1854); David Pulsifer, ed., *Records of the Colony of New Plymouth in New England*, 12 vols. (Boston, 1855–1861), of which volumes 9 and 10 contain *Acts of the Commissioners of the United Colonies of New England;* Charles J. Hoadly, ed., *Records of the Colony and Plantations of New Haven, from 1638 to 1649* (Hartford, 1857); John R. Bartlett, ed., *Records of the Colony of Rhode Island and Providence Plantations in New England*, 10 vols. (Providence, 1856–1865); and *Acts and Resolves, Public and Private, of the Province of Massachusetts Bay* (1692–1786), 21 vols. (Boston, 1869–1922).

For the laws of Connecticut, some not found in *Conn. Col. Records*, one must turn to several compilations: *The Book of the General Laws for the People within the Jurisdiction of Connecticut: Collected out of the Records of the General Court* (Cambridge, Mass., 1673); and *Acts and Laws of His Majestie's Colony of Connecticut* (Boston, 1702, and New London, 1715, 1750).

These records are usefully supplemented by the correspondence of eighteenth-century governors, 1724–1769, published at Hartford in the *Collections* of the Connecticut Historical Society: *Talcott Papers, 1724–1741*, vols. 4 and 5, 1892, 1896, which were found most useful; *Law Papers, 1741–1750*, vols. 11, 13, and 15, 1907, 1911, 1914; *Wolcott Papers, 1750–1754*, vol. 16, 1916; *Fitch Papers, 1754–1766*, vols. 17 and 18, 1918, 1929; and *Pitkin Papers, 1766–1769*, vol. 19, 1921. Also useful are Royal R. Hinman, ed., *Letters from the English Kings and Queens . . . to the Governors of the Colony of Connecticut* (Hartford, 1836); *Winthrop Papers*, Massachusetts Historical Society, *Collections*, 4th ser., vols. 6 and 7 (1863, 1865); 5th ser., vols. 1, 4, and 8 (1871, 1878, 1882); and 6th ser., vols. 3 and 5 (1889, 1892).

Other collections of documents that were drawn upon for the topics of several chapters were Connecticut Historical Society *Collections*, vols. 1 and 3 (Hartford, 1860 and 1895), which bring together a variety of materials—correspondence between Hooker and Winthrop, Gershom Bulkeley's "Will and Doom," Governor Walcott's *Memoir for the History of Connecticut*, and other materials. Also useful in more than one chapter was Julian P. Boyd and Robert J. Taylor, eds., *The Susquehannah Company Papers* 11 vols. (Ithaca, N.Y.: Cornell University

Press, 1962–1971), which through letters, newspaper articles, petitions, minutes of meetings, and the like, provide insight into political strife at the mid-eighteenth century and attitudes toward landholding and governmental responsibilities. Each volume has a lengthy introduction.

General histories, written by men who lived through some of the events they describe, give a sense of immediacy that compensates to some degree for the bias and lack of perspective expected in such works. For the earliest period John Winthrop's *The History of New England from 1630 to 1649*, ed. James Savage, 2 vols. (Boston, 1853) was especially useful for a Massachusetts view on the founding of the new colony of Connecticut and the early attempts to establish a confederation of the New England colonies. The Rev. Benjamin Trumbull's *A Complete History of Connecticut, Civil and Ecclesiastical . . . to the Year 1764*, 2 vols. (New Haven, 1797, 1818, New London, 1898), is the best narrative account for the period that it covers. As one would expect, it is rich in detail on ministers and churches, but it also covers Indian relations, wars, government, and other topics. Much less reliable, but lively and useful for its point of view, is Samuel A. Peters, *A General History of Connecticut, from Its First Settlement under George Fenwick, Esq. to Its Latest Period of Amity with Great Britain* (London, 1781). Peters, an Anglican minister and loyalist, poked fun at his former compatriots, but there is affection in what he wrote, too, and a number of shrewd judgments.

More modern histories of Connecticut also vary in quality. Most recent is Albert E. Van Dusen, *Connecticut* (New York: Random House, 1961), a general survey strengthened by the author's knowledge of the economy during the revolutionary period. Older surveys tend to be uncritical narratives, rarely helpful to the modern student: Gideon H. Hollister, *The History of Connecticut, from the First Settlement of the Colony to the Adoption of the Present Constitution*, 2 vols. (Hartford, 1855); W. H. Carpenter, and T. S. Arthur, *The History of Connecticut*, (Philadelphia, 1872); and G. L. Clark, *A History of Connecticut* (New York: G. P. Putnam, 1914).

Among local studies, of which there are many of varying quality, the most helpful to the present writer was F. M. Caulkins, *History of Norwich* (Norwich, Conn., 1845) and Ellen Larned, *History of Windham County*, 2 vols. (Worcester, Mass., 1874). These and other local histories are in the antiquarian tradition, but such works contain nuggets of information useful to the researcher in various ways.

In celebration of the three-hundredth anniversary of the founding of the first towns, the state of Connecticut issued some sixty pamphlets, a Tercentenary Series, treating in popular fashion a wide range of topics in Connecticut history. Since these were done by recognized scholars, many of them are still worth consulting as comprehensive surveys on special themes. Specific titles will be noted in appropriate places. Currently the state is issuing a new such series in honor of the Bicentennial of the nation. It is being published by the Pequot Press, Chester, Connecticut, for The American Revolution Bicentennial Commission of Connecticut.

Early maps of Connecticut are carefully described, their errors noted, and their locations indicated in Edmund B. Thompson, *Maps of Connecticut before the Year 1800, a Descriptive List* (Windham, Conn.: Hawthorne House, 1940).

THE BEGINNINGS

The most recent work treating early Connecticut is Mary Jeanne Anderson Jones, *Congregational Commonwealth: Connecticut, 1636–1662* (Middletown, Conn.: Wesleyan University Press, 1968), the first two chapters of which deal with the beginnings. Her thesis is that the Fundamental Orders were designed to provide a civil environment in which the spirit of Puritanism could flourish. Her emphasis is on the independence of Connecticut and its refusal to recognize any sovereignty but the sovereignty of God. The book is most helpful in explicating the genesis of the orders and their provisions, but it is not entirely successful in handling Puritanism. Indispensable, of course, for any study of Connecticut's beginnings is Charles M. Andrews's work on Connecticut in volume 2 of *The Colonial Period of American History*, 4 vols. (New Haven: Yale University Press, 1934–1938).

For Puritan theological distinctions, most serviceable are Edmund S. Morgan, *Visible Saints: The History of a Puritan Idea* (New York: New York University Press, 1963) and *The Puritan Dilemma: The Story of John Winthrop* (Boston: Little, Brown, 1958). Both discuss subtle concepts of Puritanism with clarity and succinctness. Perry Miller, *Errand into the Wilderness* (Cambridge, Mass.: Harvard University Press, 1956), includes his essay on Thomas Hooker and democracy in Connecticut, which challenges the notion that the absence of a requirement of church membership for citizenship somehow made the colony more democratic than Massachusetts. A recent work, James W. Jones, *The Shattered Synthesis: New England Puritanism before the Great Awakening* (New Haven: Yale University Press, 1973), is useful for the distinctions between John Cotton and Thomas Hooker.

On the diplomacy between Massachusetts and the Connecticut settlements, see Samuel Eliot Morison's chapter on William Pynchon in *Builders of the Bay Colony*, rev. ed. (Boston: Houghton Mifflin, 1958), as well as John Winthrop's *History of New England* and the *Records of Massachusetts Bay*. Also used were R. V. Coleman, *The Old Patent of Connecticut* (Westport, Conn., 1936), a detailed account of the granting of patents by the New England Council, which so complicated Connecticut's claim to legitimacy, and Deborah W. Skauen,

"Connecticut-Massachusetts Political Relations, 1635–1662" (unpublished M.A. thesis, Tufts University, 1969).

On Connecticut Indians see Trumbull's *History of Connecticut*, volume 1; John W. DeForest, *History of the Indians of Connecticut* (Hartford, Conn., 1851; reprinted, Hamden, Conn.: Archon Books, 1964); and Alden T. Vaughan, *New England Frontier: Puritans and Indians, 1620–1675* (Boston: Little, Brown, 1965). The last has the best brief account of the Pequot War, on which this chapter is heavily dependent. Still worth perusing is Mathias Spiess, *The Indians of Connecticut* (New Haven: Yale University Press, 1933, Tercentenary Series).

THE EVOLUTION OF GOVERNMENT

Besides Jones, *Congregational Commonwealth* and *Conn. Col. Records*, both already mentioned, several sources were helpful in explaining the changes that took place in franchise requirements and the method of voting, the development of governmental offices and institutions, and the emergence of a court system. Daniel H. Fowler, "Connecticut's Freemen: The First Forty Years," *William and Mary Quarterly* 15 (July 1958): 312–33, is carefully researched, concluding that the franchise was not difficult to come by in the early years of the colony, a result not unlike that which scholars have found for other colonies. Albert E. McKinley's older study, *The Suffrage Franchise in the Thirteen English Colonies in America* (Philadelphia: University of Pennsylvania, 1905), is not entirely superseded because it still offers much detail, but Chilton Williamson, *American Suffrage from Property to Democracy, 1760–1860* (Princeton: Princeton University Press, 1960), is the most recent overall survey of voting qualifications that covers Connecticut. Also Charles S. Grant, *Democracy in the Connecticut Frontier Town of Kent* (New York: Columbia University Press, 1961), not only demonstrates the application of the franchise laws in this one town but also describes the method of voting that tended to perpetuate men in high office. This work can still be usefully supplemented by the much older one of Simeon E. Baldwin, "The Early History of the Ballot in Connecticut," *Papers of the American Historical Association* 4 (October 1890):407–22. Yet a recent brief study by Robert J. Dinkin, "The Nomination of Governors and Assistants in Colonial Connecticut," Connecticut Historical Society, *Bulletin* 36 (July 1971):92–96, shows that although rotation for the highest officials was infrequent, voters did nominate far more names than one would suspect.

The only modern and thorough study of how deputies from Connecticut towns to the General Assembly were perpetuated in office is Bruce C. Daniels, "Democracy and Oligarchy in Connecticut Towns: General Assembly Officeholding, 1701–1790," *Social Science Quarterly* 56 (December 1975):460–75, which not only reveals a pattern of family dominance, but finds that contrary to expectations there was least turnover during times of political conflict. That is, the percentage of representatives elected who had not served in the preceding session was lowest during the crisis leading to the Revolution and highest during wartime. In a related article, "Family Dynasties in Connecticut's Largest Towns, 1700–1760," *Canadian Journal of History* 8 (September 1973):99–110, Daniels examines in three towns length of tenure not only in the General Assembly but also in four important local offices. Only among selectmen, of whom six were elected in each town, did he find significant turnover; in other offices one family achieved a virtual monopoly in each town, Huntingtons in Norwich, Pitkins in Hartford, and Burrs in Fairfield.

An important contribution to the question of rotation in and access to office on the local level is Edward M. Cook, Jr., *The Fathers of the Towns: Leadership and Community Structure in Eighteenth-Century New England* (Baltimore: The Johns Hopkins University Press, 1976). This analysis of officeholding in seventy-four towns, which are categorized into five types, finds significant differences among these towns in ease of access to office and length of tenure. Cook's carefully defined categories should put an end to easy generalizations about "the New England Town." For the political reaction against Roger Wolcott, see Roland Mather Hooker, *The Spanish Ship Case* (New Haven: Yale University Press, 1934, Tercentenary Series), and the *Wolcott Papers*.

An excellent corrective to the notion that town government can be summed up with reference to town meetings is furnished in yet another article by Bruce Daniels: "Connecticut Villages Become Mature Towns: The Complexity of Local Institutions, 1676 to 1776," *William and Mary Quarterly*, 34 (January 1977):83–103. Daniels describes the functioning of groups like proprietors and the emergence of a variety of local offices, as well as the enlarged responsibilities of selectmen and the increase in the number of officeholders. He errs, however, in assuming that an early practice of giving selectmen the powers of justices of the peace continued throughout the colonial period. The clearest brief account of Connecticut's system of courts is in the introduction to John T. Farrell, ed., *The Superior Court Diary of William Samuel Johnson, 1772–1773* (Washington, D.C.: American Historical Association, 1942), which gives far more detail than was practicable for the overview here given.

Finally, the relationship between towns and the colonial government has been examined by Thomas Jodziewicz, "Dual Localism in Seventeenth-Century Connecticut: Relations between the General Court and the Towns, 1636–1691" (unpublished Ph.D. dissertation, College of William and Mary, 1974). Using nine towns for which satisfactory records were available, Jodziewicz concludes that although the General Court exercised a general supervisory role, its hand was not heavy, largely because the interests of town and legislature usually coincided.

EXPANSION

Robert C. Black's *The Younger John Winthrop* (New York: Columbia University Press, 1966), is a sprightly and engaging portrait of Connecticut's most successful seventeenth-century governor. Black's analysis of Winthrop's character is perceptive and not always flattering; and his recounting of Winthrop's services to the colony, particularly in securing the charter at the expense of New Haven's interests, nicely unravels a complicated story. A study of Massachusetts and Connecticut Winthrops from 1630 to 1717 that is scholarly and well written is Richard S. Dunn, *Puritans and Yankees: The Winthrop Dynasty of New England* (Princeton: Princeton University Press, 1962), which includes lesser Winthrops like Fitz-John and Wait-Still Winthrop. For the Narragansett speculation of John Winthrop, Jr., see Dunn, "John Winthrop, Jr., and the Narragansett Country," *William and Mary Quarterly* 13 (January 1956):68–86. Dunn's work is thorough and balanced in its judgments.

Still the standard work on New Haven is Isabel MacBeath Calder, *The New Haven Colony* (New Haven: Yale University Press, 1934), which understandably sees from New Haven's point of view the dispute between that colony and Connecticut at the time of the granting of the charter and should be consulted in conjunction with the analyses given by Black and Dunn.

On boundary disputes, besides *The Susquehannah Company Papers,* some of use were Rising Lake Morrow, *Connecticut Influences in Western Massachusetts and Vermont* (New Haven: Yale University Press, 1936), and Roland Mather Hooker, *Boundaries of Connecticut* (New Haven: Yale University Press, 1933), both in the Tercentenary Series. More important is Parker Bradley Nutting, "Charter and Crown: Relations of Connecticut with the British Government, 1662–1776" (unpublished Ph.D. dissertation, University of North Carolina, 1972). This study is particularly insightful for its comments on Connecticut's resort to Britain in resolving intercolonial disputes, but it covers the whole range of the colony's relations with the mother country and will be mentioned for its contribution to several other topics.

Although *Conn. Col. Records* contain much information about land grants and their conditions, one must turn to interpretive works to place the facts in perspective. On conveying land to private ownership and laying out towns, Charles M. Andrews's old study *The River Towns of Connecticut (Johns Hopkins University Studies in Historical and Political Science,* 7th ser., vols. 7–9, Baltimore, 1889), is still sound and important and includes a diagram of the division of lands. But more comprehensive and particularly valuable for its tracing of settlement patterns from the earliest to the latest towns laid out is Anthony N. B. Garvan, *Architecture and Town Planning in Colonial Connecticut* (New Haven: Yale University Press, 1951). Local analyses, offering contrasts in the methods used by two towns to dispose of common lands, are two unpublished master's theses recently

completed at the University of Bridgeport: Joan Ballen, "Fairfield, Connecticut, 1661–1691: A Demographic Study of the Economic, Political, and Social
Life of a New England Community," (1970), and Erna F. Green, "The Public
Land System of Norwalk, Connecticut, 1654–1704: A Structural Analysis of
Economic and Political Relationships" (1972). Charles Grant's study of Kent,
already mentioned, provides data on land disposal for a frontier town settled in
the mid-eighteenth century. Grant's intensive study of a single town offers a
corrective to some of the generalizations that have been made about land
speculation and absentee landholding, but one should not fall into the opposite
error of utilizing conditions in a western Connecticut town to generalize about
conditions in all New England, as Grant is tempted to do.

One of the most perceptive analyses of colonial Connecticut before the revolutionary period is Richard L. Bushman's *From Puritan to Yankee: Character and
the Social Order in Connecticut, 1690–1765* (Cambridge, Mass.: Harvard University Press, 1967), an analysis of how increasing materialism transformed what
Bushman believes was a stable society before 1690 into one rife with conflict over
economic, religious, and political issues. The outcome was the emergence of the
Yankee and a concept of liberty based on self-interest, which meant men were
ready, if necessary, to resist authority. As part of the background of these profound changes, Bushman sketches patterns of land acquisition. His interpretation of community disruption through settlers' leaving town centers should be
compared with the analysis made by Kenneth Lockridge, *A New England Town:
The First Hundred Years, Dedham, Massachusetts, 1636–1736* (New York: Norton,
1970).

CONNECTICUT AND NEW ENGLAND

The most detailed modern study of the New England Confederation is Harry M.
Ward's *The United Colonies of New England* (New York: Vantage Press, 1961), but
this is not definitive, and it is wise to supplement it with reference to the records
themselves in volumes 9 and 10 of the *Records of New Plymouth* and biographical
works about the Winthrops mentioned earlier, as well as with the records of
Massachusetts Bay and New Haven. The Indian war that virtually destroyed the
confederation has found excellent modern treatment in Douglas Edward Leach,
Flintlock and Tomahawk: New England in King Philip's War (New York: Macmillan, 1958), which not only describes events and analyzes causes and results, but
provides useful background on the Indians. Leach manages to avoid being either
condescending or sentimental. Although the account of the war in this chapter
centers on the strains within the United Colonies arising out of self-interest,
Francis Jennings's discussion in *The Invasion of America: Indians, Colonialism, and*

the Cant of Conquest (Chapel Hill, N.C.: University of North Carolina Press, 1975), deserves examination. He sees the conflict largely as a greedy struggle between Connecticut and Massachusetts for control of the Narragansett country at the expense of Rhode Island. He emphasizes the cruelty of the English, their willingness to force treaties on the Indians and to massacre them when it suited their expansionist designs.

On the period of the Dominion of New England, the only modern full-length study is David S. Lovejoy's *The Glorious Revolution in America* (New York: Harper and Row, 1972), which has relatively few pages devoted to Connecticut, understandably enough, for the uprisings occurred elsewhere. But his thorough coverage of causes and consequences in those colonies in which conflict was more than just political maneuvering gives the student a gauge by which to measure the political climate in Connecticut. Viola F. Barnes's much older work, *The Dominion of New England* (New Haven: Yale University Press, 1923), is more institutional in approach and still useful for that reason. A detailed account of Connecticut's reception of Governor Andros is found in Albert C. Bates, "Expedition of Sir Edmund Andros to Connecticut in 1687," American Antiquarian Society, *Proceedings* 48 (1938):276–99.

THE ECONOMY

The only intensive accounts of the Connecticut economy have been two unpublished doctoral studies devoted to the late eighteenth century: Albert E. Van Dusen, "The Trade of Revolutionary Connecticut" (University of Pennsylvania, 1948) and Gaspare J. Saladino, "The Economic Revolution in Late Eighteenth-Century Connecticut" (University of Wisconsin, 1962). The chief sources for this chapter have been more general works, supplemented by several special studies. Stuart Bruchey, *The Roots of American Economic Growth, 1607– 1861* (New York: Harper and Row, 1965), although a sweeping survey, does help to put Connecticut in perspective, for its generalizations about the growth of the colonial economy apply to that colony. Also worth consulting is Douglas C. North, *Growth and Welfare in the American Past* (Englewood Cliffs, N.J.: Prentice-Hall, 1966).

For Connecticut's agriculture in the first century, the reader must glean what he can from the records and from general accounts. P. W. Bidwell and J. I. Falconer, *History of Agriculture in the Northern United States, 1620–1860* (Washington, D.C.: Carnegie Institution, 1925), has sections that touch on Connecticut, as does that old but usefully detailed work by William B. Weeden, *Economic and Social History of New England, 1620–1789*, 2 vols. (Boston, 1890). For the second century the most convenient but brief summary is Albert L.

Olson's *Agricultural Economy and the Population in Eighteenth-Century Connecticut* (New Haven: Yale University Press, 1935, Tercentenary Series). Olson is critical of the methods of husbandry and perhaps too severe on farmers who had to struggle to survive. For example, there was more use of fertilizer—dung, peat, and humus from the sea—than he acknowledges. A fascinating and thorough survey of every aspect of farming is Howard S. Russell's *A Long, Deep Furrow: Three Centuries of Farming in New England* (Hanover, N.H.: The University Press of New England, 1976), of which about one-third is devoted to the period prior to 1775. This work is spotted with references to practices in Connecticut. Against the background of major historical events, Russell discusses crops, livestock, tools, and markets. One can also gather some observations on agriculture from the histories of Samuel Peters and Benjamin Trumbull, both cited in the general section of the bibliography.

Both men also supply some information on early manufacturing and trade. Robert C. Black's biography of John Winthrop, Jr., mentioned earlier, describes his early ventures and his search for profitable minerals. J. Leander Bishop, *A History of American Manufactures from 1608 to 1860*, 3d rev. ed., 2 vols. (Philadelphia, 1868), offers some factual details about Connecticut but little interpretation. W. Storrs Lee, *The Yankees of Connecticut* (New York: Henry Holt, 1957), lively and often anecdotal, includes material on manufacturing, as well as trade, farming, and other topics, drawn from a variety of secondary sources. Clockmaking is covered in Penrose R. Hooper, *Early Clockmaking in Connecticut* (New Haven: Yale University Press, 1934, Tercentenary Series). A general survey of trade is Roland Mather Hooker, *The Colonial Trade of Connecticut* (New Haven: Yale University Press, 1936, Tercentenary Series). Comparative figures on Connecticut's exports were taken from James F. Shepherd and Gary M. Walton, "Trade, Distribution, and Economic Growth in Colonial America," *Journal of Economic History* 32 (March 1972):128–45. A book by the same authors, *Shipping, Maritime Trade, and the Economic Development of Colonial North America* (Cambridge: Cambridge University Press, 1972), contains little dealing directly with Connecticut, probably because New London's port records were destroyed during the Revolution.

A good understanding of Connecticut's intercolonial trade and attempts to establish overseas connections can be obtained from the account of one family's efforts as set forth in Glenn Weaver's *Jonathan Trumbull: Connecticut's Merchant Magistrate, 1710–1785* (Hartford: Connecticut Historical Society, 1956). Trumbull managed badly and had poor luck, but his business career illustrates the methods of merchants, and Weaver's handling of detail is clear and interesting. The internal rivalries between businessmen in the eastern and western sections of the colony and what they meant for government policies with respect to paper money form an important part of Bushman's *From Puritan to Yankee*.

Connecticut's handling of paper currency issues is the subject of Lawrence H.

Gipson's "Connecticut Taxation and Parliamentary Aid preceding the Revo-
lutionary War," *American Historical Review* 36 (April 1931):721–39, and forms
the basis of his *Connecticut Taxation, 1750–1775* (New Haven: Yale University
Press, 1933, Tercentenary Series). Leslie V. Brock, *The Currency of the American
Colonies, 1700–1764: A Study in Colonial Finance and Imperial Relations* (New
York: Arno Press, 1975), discusses currency and monetary policies by regions,
taking particular note of English reactions. Joseph Albert Ernst, *Money and
Politics in America, 1755–1775* (Chapel Hill, N.C.: University of North
Carolina Press, 1973), finds little to say about Connecticut, although its exami-
nation of currency questions provides good background.

Obviously much more needs to be done on the colony's economy before anyone can write on this subject comprehensively and with assurance.

RELIGION AND THE CHURCHES

For facts about particular ministers and church quarrels Trumbull's *History* is
still useful, and Williston Walker, *The Creeds and Platforms of Congregationalism*
(1893; reprinted, Boston: Pilgrim Press, 1960), is the most convenient source of
statements of doctrine having formal acceptance. Walker did more than just
collect them, for his analytical introductions make discriminating comparisons
and provide some historical background. The most recent study on one important concept in early Congregationalism is Robert G. Pope's *The Half-Way Covenant: Church Membership in Puritan New England* (Princeton: Princeton University Press, 1969), which contains two chapters on Connecticut as well as one on
John Davenport of New Haven. Pope sees the covenant in Connecticut as only a
symbol of deeper divisions over polity—presbyterial versus congregational.
Pope's excellent monograph helps one to understand some of the church quarrels
in the seventeenth century. Paul R. Lucas, *Valley of Discord: Church and Society
along the Connecticut River, 1636–1725* (Hanover, N.H.: The University Press of
New England, 1976), makes dissension among the valley churches his central
concern to demonstrate that New England Congregationalism did not create the
harmonious society often imagined. The present chapter, although giving instances of discord, stresses the effort of the colonial government to exert control
in the interest of order and some measure of conformity.

On careful reading, *Conn. Col. Records* yield considerable information about
relations between congregations and pastors, church finance, and governmental
supervision over the churches and religious life. Edmund S. Morgan, *The Puritan Family,* rev. ed. (New York: Harper and Row, 1966), explains the role religion played within the family, and Bushman, *From Puritan to Yankee,* has a good
chapter on clerical authority, especially as it operated in Connecticut.

But Bushman's main interest is the religious revival affecting New England in the 1740s and after. His interpretation of the psychological meaning of the Great Awakening is original and helps to explain much that occurred in Connecticut's political life. A more general account of this upsurge in religious feeling is Edwin S. Gaustad, *The Great Awakening in New England* (New York: Harper and Row, 1957). C. C. Goen, *Revivalism and Separatism in New England, 1740–1800* (New Haven: Yale University Press, 1962), has examined in some depth one of the consequences of the awakening and traced its impact beyond the awakening period itself.

William G. McLoughlin's massive study, *New England Dissent, 1630–1833,* 2 vols. (Cambridge, Mass.: Harvard University Press, 1971), which contains much material on Connecticut, is indispensable for following the course of dissent in the colony, and this chapter has drawn heavily upon it. Particularly illuminating is his examination of the relationship between dissent and the emergence of genuine religious freedom. A much older work, M. Louise Greene, *The Development of Religious Liberty in Connecticut* (Boston: Houghton Mifflin, 1905), is still worth consulting because its coverage is broader than its title implies.

For two small sects, the following were found useful: John R. Bolles and Anna B. Williams, *The Rogerenes* (Boston: Stanhope Press, 1904), and Williston Walker, "The Sandemanians of New England," American Historical Association, *Annual Report for 1901* (Washington, 1902), vol. 1, 131–62. The Anglicans have received much more attention. Hector G. Kinloch, "Anglican Clergy in Connecticut, 1701–1785" (unpublished Ph.D. dissertation, Yale University, 1959), gives biographical data about the Anglican clergy and offers chapters on Anglicans during the Great Awakening and revolutionary periods. Bruce E. Steiner has corrected the old idea that Anglicans received little recognition after they were exempted from taxes to support the Congregational churches. In "Anglican Officeholding in Pre-Revolutionary Connecticut: The Parameters of New England Community," *William and Mary Quarterly* 31 (July 1974):369–406, he shows conclusively that many held office right up to 1775, and his explanations for the reasons they could and for the kind of political and military offices they held are balanced and thoughtful. The Papers of the Society for the Propagation of the Gospel, already mentioned, and William Manross, ed., *The Fulham Papers in the Lambeth Palace Library* (Oxford: Oxford University Press, 1965), are major primary sources, which can be supplemented with Francis L. Hawks and Bishop Perry, *Documentary History of the Protestant Episcopal Church in the United States of America Containing Numerous hitherto Unpublished Documents concerning the Church in Connecticut,* 2 vols. (New York, 1863–1864).

For some of the political implications of religious controversy, Louis Leonard Tucker's *Puritan Protagonist: President Thomas Clap of Yale College* (Chapel Hill, N.C.: University of North Carolina Press, 1962), is revealing for its account of how an Old Light turned New Light as political power shifted in the colony. Clap dropped his earlier views in order to fend off the General Assembly's efforts to challenge his tight control over the college.

SOCIAL SERVICES AND GOOD ORDER

On education, a scholarly and thorough study is Robert Middlekauff's *Ancients and Axioms: Secondary Education in Eighteenth-Century New England* (New Haven: Yale University Press, 1963), which has been drawn upon heavily for the first section of this chapter. Broader in its scope is Lawrence A. Cremin, *American Education: The Colonial Experience, 1607–1783* (New York: Harper and Row, 1970), which is particularly good for English sources used by Americans to shape ideas and practice and for its conception of education as something not confined to formal schools. Edmund Morgan's *The Puritan Family,* cited earlier, explores education in the home, although it looks outside as well. Tucker's biography of Thomas Clap, also already mentioned, is good on relations between Yale College and the government; and Beverly McAnear, "The Selection of an Alma Mater by Pre-Revolutionary Students," *Pennsylvania Magazine of History and Biography* 73 (October 1949): 429–40, makes some interesting comparisons among colonial colleges that help to characterize Yale. One of the best studies of Yale for its formative period is Richard Warch, *School of The Prophets: Yale College, 1701–1740* (New Haven: Yale University Press, 1973), which assays the intellectual quality of the institution and the suitability of its curriculum and teachers for the purposes for which it was founded.

A good deal of the information on social structure and welfare was taken from *Conn. Col. Records,* but Charles Grant's study of Kent has chapters on debt and poverty that are illuminating. Jackson Turner Main's recent study, "The Distribution of Property in Colonial Connecticut," in James Kirby Martin, ed., *The Human Dimensions of Nation Making* (Madison, Wis.: The State Historical Society of Wisconsin, 1976), pp. 54–104, supersedes so far as that colony is concerned Alice Hanson Jones, "Wealth Estimates for the New England Colonies about 1770," *Journal of Economic History* 32 (March 1972): 98–127. Main's earlier work, *The Social Structure of Revolutionary America* (Princeton: Princeton University Press, 1965), a pioneering attempt to define incomes, classes, patterns of consumption, and regional differences, can help the student of Connecticut construct an analytical framework. Also consulted were Gary B. Nash, *Class and Society in Early America* (Englewood Cliffs, N.J.: Prentice-Hall, 1970), which combines interpretive essays with documents, and Norman H. Dawes, "Titles as Symbols of Prestige in Seventeenth-Century New England," *William and Mary Quarterly* 6 (January 1949): 69–83, which is reprinted in Nash. A convenient summary is Edward Warren Capen's *The Historical Development of the Poor Law in Connecticut* (New York: Columbia University Press, 1905).

For the lowest orders in society, Abbot Smith's *Colonists in Bondage: White Servitude and Convict Labor in America, 1607–1776* (Chapel Hill, N.C.: University of North Carolina Press, 1947), is an important study. Although little of it applies directly to Connecticut, its analysis of indentured servitude, by contrast if in no other way, throws light on Connecticut society. The standard study of slavery in the colony is an old one: Bernard C. Steiner, *History of Slavery in Connecticut (Johns Hopkins University Studies in Historical and Political Science,* 11th ser., vols. 9, 10, Baltimore, 1893). This should be supplemented by Gwendolyn Evans Logan, "The Slave in Connecticut during the American Revolution," Connecticut Historical Society, *Bulletin* 30 (July 1965):73–80. A more general treatment, Lorenzo Johnston Greene, *The Negro in Colonial New England* (New York: Columbia University Press, 1942), covers the laws affecting both slaves and free blacks, their status as workers, and their numbers and distribution. He also supplies tables of slave ownership by towns and by persons. In addition to works on Indians cited earlier, A. I. Hallowell, "Some Psychological Characteristics of the Northeastern Indians," in Frederick Johnson, ed., *Man in Northeastern America* (Andover, Mass.: Phillips Academy, 1946), pp. 195–225, offers some unusual insights for explaining relations between the races. Francis Jennings, *The Invasion of America,* already mentioned, is an angry indictment of Englishmen for their contemptuous attitudes toward Indian "savagery," for inhumanity, and for greedy seizure of Indians' lands. Using anthropological as well as historical sources, Jennings writes appreciatively of the Indians' knowledge and practice of agriculture and medicine and of their religion and government.

DAILY LIVING, RECREATION, AND
THE ARTS

On the architecture of homes in Connecticut, see J. Frederick Kelly, *Early Domestic Architecture of Connecticut* (New Haven: Yale University Press, 1933, Tercentenary Series), and *Connecticut's Old Houses: A Handbook and Guide* (reprinted., Stoughton, Conn., 1963, Conn. Booklet No. 4). H. F. Randolph Mason, *Historic Houses of Connecticut* (Stoughton, Conn., 1963, Conn. Booklet No. 5), includes photographs of many of the houses that Kelly distinguished by period of construction. Also useful, particularly for details of framing, is a work mentioned earlier: Anthony N. B. Garvan, *Architecture and Town Planning in Colonial Connecticut.*

Some idea of family size in Connecticut can be obtained from John Waters's quantitative work on one town, "Patrimony, Succession, and Social Stability: Guilford, Connecticut, in the Eighteenth Century," *Perspectives in American History* 10 (1976): 131–60. Family size, however, is only a part of Waters's concern. He also examines male and female longevity, property distribution, and migration from the town. Work done on Massachusetts families probably has some validity for Connecticut as well. John Demos, *A Little Commonwealth: Family Life in Plymouth* (New York: Oxford University Press, 1970), is an excellent monograph, which not only analyzes family size but also explores the implications of living arrangements, family relationships, and individual development. Philip J. Greven, Jr., *Four Generations: Population, Land, and Family in Colonial Andover, Massachusetts* (Ithaca, N.Y.: Cornell University Press, 1970), covers a longer time and particularly examines conflict between the generations over control of property. David H. Flaherty's *Privacy in Colonial New England* (Charlottesville, Va.: University Press of Virginia, 1972), discusses the nature and extent of privacy within the family and the community and with respect to institutions like government, the courts, and the churches.

Alice Morse Earle published in the 1890s several books that are still helpful for information about daily life and culture despite the increasing sophistication that modern scholars are bringing to the study of social history. Much of Mrs. Earle's material is anecdotal, but she also had sources more difficult for historians to retrieve now because of the passage of time. Two of her books, *Child Life in Colonial Days* (New York, 1899) and *Customs and Fashions in Old New England* (New York, 1893), provide details about reading for pleasure, games and sports, toys, festivals, and music.

Connecticut's colonial newspapers are described in Jarvis Means Morse, *Connecticut Newspapers in the Eighteenth Century* (New Haven: Yale University Press, 1935, Tercentenary Series), but the best way to sample their flavor is to read through a few issues. Samuel Eliot Morison's *The Intellectual Life of Colonial New England* (New York: New York University Press, 1956), has a section on Gershom Bulkeley that places him among the significant polemicists of the seventeenth century. Polemical writing in the prerevolutionary period provoked by the land claims of the Susquehannah Company is printed in *The Susquehannah Company Papers,* vols. 3–4. George C. Groce, Jr., has written the only detailed account of Benjamin Gale's political activities and writings, but his "Benjamin Gale," *New England Quarterly* 10 (December 1937): 697–716, also surveys the other accomplishments of this versatile genius. Gale deserves treatment at even greater length, however. His intimate knowledge of David Bushnell's "American Turtle" is apparent in several letters written to Silas Deane in 1775 and 1776: those of November 9 and 22, December 7, and February 1 (Connecticut Historical Society, *Collections* 2 (1870): 315–18, 322–23, 333–35, 358–59). Bushnell himself has been the subject of a full-length study: Frederick Wagner, *Submarine*

Fighter of the American Revolution (New York: Dodd, Mead, 1963); but the recent article by Alex Roland, "Bushnell's Submarine: American Original or European Import?" *Technology and Culture* 18 (April 1977): 157–74, makes Bushnell appear much less of an innovator.

McFingal and the other works of John Trumbull are ably discussed by Alexander Cowie, *John Trumbull, Connecticut Wit* (Chapel Hill, N.C.: University of North Carolina Press, 1936), but also used were two letters exchanged between Trumbull and John Adams (Adams to Trumbull, November 5, 1775, [reproduction] and Trumbull to Adams, November 14, 1775, Adams Papers, Massachusetts Historical Society). Laurence B. Goodrich has written an interesting account of the work of the portraitist Ralph Earl in *Ralph Earl, Recorder for an Era* (Yellow Springs, Ohio: The Antioch Press, 1967), which contains photographs of all his important paintings and establishes dates, the identity of subjects, and the places where Earl worked. See also, William Benton Museum of Art, *The American Earls: Ralph Earl, James Earl, R. E. W. Earl* (Storrs: University of Connecticut, 1972). Some years ago Samuel M. Green brought the early Connecticut artists to the attention of critics and the general public with "Uncovering the Connecticut School," *Art News* 51 (January 1953): 38–41, 57–58. William Sawitsky did much of the work of identifying these almost unknown Connecticut painters, and after his death, his wife, Susan Sawitsky, published "The Portraits of William Johnston: A Preliminary Checklist," *New-York Historical Society Quarterly* 39 (January 1955): 79–89, which accompanied Lila Parrish Lyman's "William Johnston (1732–1772), a Forgotten Portrait Painter of New England," ibid., pp. 63–78. Trumbull, Earl, and Johnston receive mention in Kenneth Silverman, *A Cultural History of the American Revolution* (New York: Thomas Y. Crowell Co., 1976), but compared to the cultural feast enjoyed in Charleston, Williamsburg, Philadelphia, and New York, Connecticut's towns had poor fare indeed.

CONNECTICUT AND THE EMPIRE

Relations between Great Britain and Connecticut are admirably set forth in a detailed and long analysis by Nutting, "Charter and Crown," fully cited under Expansion. Besides Nutting, Roland Mather Hooker's account of Connecticut's conflict with Collector John Shackmaple in *The Colonial Trade of Connecticut* and material on the intestacy law and the Mohegan Indian case drawn from documents in the *Talcott Papers* were used. Also helpful were Charles M. Andrews, *The Connecticut Intestacy Law* (New Haven: Yale University Press, 1933, Tercentenary Series), and *Governor and Company of Connecticut and Mohegan Indians, by Their Guardians: Certified Copy of Book of Proceedings before Commissioners of Review* (London, 1769).

Nutting has a good section on the wars with the French, but Howard H. Peckham, *The Colonial Wars, 1689–1762* (Chicago: University of Chicago Press, 1964), is more readily available. Lawrence H. Gipson's massively definitive study, *The British Empire before the American Revolution,* 15 vols. (Caldwell, Idaho: Caxton, and New York: Alfred A. Knopf, 1936–1970), has scattered through it a good deal on Connecticut. Volume 14, a bibliography, has a section on the colony. Gipson's essay on Connecticut taxation, already mentoned under The Economy, relates his subject to the French wars. *Conn. Col. Records* contain a wealth of material relating to these wars: numbers of troops raised, wartime conservation measures, pay of soldiers, pensions and land grants, and other matters.

THE CRISIS OF THE
REVOLUTION

The only book-length study of Connecticut in the revolutionary era is Oscar Zeichner's *Connecticut's Years of Controversy, 1750–1776* (Chapel Hill, N.C.: University of North Carolina Press, 1949), which is detailed, often lively, and especially useful for its thorough sifting of the Connecticut press during the period, both newspapers and pamphlets. The *Connecticut Courant* is now indexed on cards for 1764 to 1820, the index being available at the Connecticut Historical Society through special permission. Zeichner's account of prerevolutionary strife in the colony now needs to be supplemented with Bushman's *From Puritan to Yankee.*

Edmund S. and Helen M. Morgan, *The Stamp Act Crisis: Prologue to Revolution* (Chapel Hill, N.C.: University of North Carolina Press, 1953), an excellently written and persuasive analysis, gives ample attention to Connecticut with a chapter on its stampmaster, Jared Ingersoll. Lawrence H. Gipson's biography, *American Loyalist: Jared Ingersoll* (New Haven: Yale University Press, 1921), should also be consulted, for it is a careful study which delves into internal politics as it affected one of the colony's prominent men. A more general but brief work on loyalism is Epaphroditus Peck, *The Loyalists of Connecticut* (New Haven: Yale University Press, 1934, Tercentenary Series). Again, the correspondence of SPG missionaries throws light on the problems of Anglican loyalists. Local violence has been examined in a recent work by Pauline Maier, *From Resistance to Revolution* (New York: Alfred A. Knopf, 1972), which traces the evolution of mob action from violence to disciplined resistance.

Biographical works that carry their stories well beyond 1776 are worth mentioning nonetheless, for they cover the preindependence period from the perspective of their subjects and thus enrich the student's understanding. George C. Groce, Jr., is the author of "Eliphalet Dyer: Connecticut Revolutionist," in Richard B. Morris, ed., *The Era of the American Revolution* (New York: Columbia University Press, 1939) and *William Samuel Johnson: A Maker of the Constitution* (New York: Columbia University Press, 1937). A modern biography of Silas Deane is badly needed, for too much has been done on Deane's associates in the Revolution for us to remain satisfied with George L. Clark's *Silas Deane, a Connecticut Leader in the American Revolution* (New York: G. P. Putnam, 1913). Coy Hilton James, *Silas Deane—Patriot or Traitor?* (East Lansing, Mich.: Michigan State University Press, 1975) is no full-scale life. In 150 pages it carries Deane from birth to death, never probing deeply any topic. James virtually ignores all secondary work done on Deane's contemporaries, diplomacy, and the period generally. Roger Sherman has been more fortunate. Older biographies by Lewis H. Boutell (*The Life of Roger Sherman* [Chicago, 1896]) and Roger S. Boardman (*Roger Sherman* [Philadelphia: University of Pennsylvania Press, 1938]) are now supplemented, if not replaced, by Christopher Collier, *Roger Sherman's Connecticut: Yankee Politics and the American Revolution* (Middletown, Conn.: Wesleyan University Press, 1971). Collier keeps his eye on issues as well as on the man and thus provides far more than a straightforward biography.

EPILOGUE

Since this account of colonial Connecticut is intended to take the reader only as far as the colony's acceptance of the Declaration of Independence, the author has merely listed the three or four works that he relied upon for his brief interpretation of the Revolution's meaning in Connecticut. For the period from independence to the adoption of the United States Constitution the only extensive study is Philip H. Jordan, Jr., "Connecticut Politics during the Revolution and Confederation" (unpublished Ph.D. dissertation, Yale University, 1962). An old work that centers attention on Connecticut's struggle to break the hold of the Standing Order and to give the state a true constitution is Richard J. Purcell, *Connecticut in Transition, 1775–1818* (Washington, D.C.: American Historical Association, 1918; reprinted, Middletown, Conn.: Wesleyan University Press, 1963). For the period that he covers, Purcell discusses religion, the economy, and the rise of political parties. James R. Beasley's "Emerging Republicanism and the Standing Order: The Appropriation Act Controversy in Connecticut, 1793 to 1795," *William and Mary Quarterly* 29 (October 1972): 587–610, illustrates the persistence in the state, long after the Revolution, of the belief that the Congregational churches should enjoy support from public funds. Genuine separation of church and state did not come, of course, until the Constitution of 1818.

INDEX

Abercromby, General James, 216
Absentee proprietors, complaints about, 71–72
Acadians, deported to Connecticut, 215–16
Acts of Trade and Navigation, violation of, 95–96, 204–5, 234
Adams, John, and *McFingal*, 188
Admitted inhabitants
under charter, 30
under Fundamental Orders, 22–24
Agawam (Springfield), Mass.
contested jurisdiction over, 17–18
founded by Pynchon, 8
and Pequot War, 17
Agents, for Connecticut, 88, 197–99, 202–3, 206, 246
Agriculture
character of farm life, 181
crops grown, 92–93
methods of, 92–94
open field system, 67
planting fields, 68
subsistence level of, 90
tools for, 93
Albany Convention, 213–14
Plan of Union, 214
Allen, Ethan, 242
Allen, Reverend Timothy, 121
Allyn, John, 39, 86
American Revolution, 239–47, 249–50

"American Turtle" (submarine), 192–93
Amherst, Jeffrey, 216
Andros, Sir Edmund
claims Connecticut land for Duke of York, 80
supports Rhode Island's boundary claim, 58
takes Connecticut into Dominion of New England, 86
Anglicans
numbers of, 127
and officeholding, 129n, 232
and schools, 147
seek bishop for America, 126, 229
and Stamp Act, 229–30
suffer as Loyalists, 245–46
and taxation, 124–25
and Yale, 128, 150
Appleton, Major Samuel, 81–82
Architecture, domestic, 177–80
Arnold, Benedict
attacks Fort Ticonderoga, 241–42
and Battle of Lexington and Concord, 239
Articles of Confederation
accepted by towns, 249
election of delegates under, 249
Ashurst, Sir Henry, as Connecticut agent, 197, 202
Assistants. *See* Magistrates.
Atherton Company, acquires Nar-

and Dominion of New England, 86
and Hallam case, 195–97
Winthrop, John
compared with Thomas Hooker, 19
and jurisdiction over Agawam, 18
and powers of magistrates, 6
Winthrop, John, Jr.
and absorption of New Haven Colony, 52
agent to lay out lands, 7–8
and charter negotiations, 57–58
as commissioner to United Colonies of New England, 82
as diplomat, 27, 29
as governor, 26–27, 37
lands granted to, 65
mining rights and iron furnace of, 98
and New London, 49
partner in Atherton Company, 56
as scientist, 190–91
Winthrop, John IV, as heir appeals to Privy Council, 125, 198
Winthrop, Wait-Still
dies intestate, 197–98
law suit against, 196
Witches, 174
Wolcott, Erastus, 238, 241
Wolcott, Governor Roger
and siege of Louisbourg, 211
voted out of office, 37

Wolcott, Roger, Jr., delegate to Albany Convention, 213
Women
position of, 167
and property rights, 167–68
and Puritan doctrine, 166–67
Woodbury
ecclesiastical society in, 112
rules for church membership in, 119
Woodstock
chooses Cambridge Platform, 120
and Connecticut's northern boundary, 54
size of home lots in, 69
Woodward, Nathaniel, runs boundary line with Massachusetts, 53
Wooster, David, 239, 242
Workhouses, 154, 173
Wyllys, George, 222
Wyoming Massacre, 250
Wyoming Valley, Pa., Connecticut settlements in, 60

Yale College
charter for, 150
concessions to Anglicanism at, 126
on eve of Revolution, 151
origins, purpose, and character of, 148–49
students' day at, 149–50